DIVINE DISCONTENT

Divine Discontent

The Prophetic Voice of Thomas Merton

John Moses

Foreword by Rowan Williams

BLOOMSBURY
LONDON • NEW DELHI • NEW YORK • SYDNEY

First published in Great Britain 2014

Copyright © John Moses, 2014

The moral right of the author has been asserted

No part of this book may be used or reproduced in any manner whatsoever without written permission from the Publisher except in the case of brief quotations embodied in critical articles or reviews. Every reasonable effort has been made to trace copyright holders of material reproduced in this book, but if any have been inadvertently overlooked the Publishers would be glad to hear from them.

A Continuum book

Bloomsbury Publishing Plc
50 Bedford Square
London WC1B 3DP

www.bloomsbury.com

Bloomsbury Publishing, London, New Delhi, New York and Sydney

A CIP record for this book is available from the British Library.

ISBN 978-1-4411-8062-9

10 9 8 7 6 5 4 3 2 1

Typeset by Fakenham Prepress Solutions, Fakenham, Norfolk NR21 8NN

Printed and bound in Great Britain by CPI Group (UK) Ltd, Croydon CR0 4YY

MIX
Paper from
responsible sources
FSC
www.fsc.org   FSC® C013604

In piam memoriam

H.W. and A.E.M.

Copyright Permissions

Contents

Acknowledgements

I am glad to acknowledge at the outset my indebtedness to Bishop Rowan Williams for the Foreword he has so generously provided; to Dr Paul M. Pearson, the Director and Archivist of the Thomas Merton Center at Bellarmine University, for his invaluable assistance during my visit to the Center in September 2011 and for his continuing help; to Brother Patrick Hart OCSO for the brief conversations I was able to have with him in the course of private visits to the Abbey of Our Lady of Gethsemani in March 2006 and September 2011; and to Caroline Chartres, the Senior Commissioning Editor, and Joel Simons, the Assistant Editor, at Bloomsbury Continuum for their encouragement and critical advice as my manuscript has made its way to publication.

I am glad to acknowledge the permission that has been granted to quote directly from many published works. Every attempt has been made to secure permission to use copyright material, and all such material is acknowledged in the Notes at the back of the book. The photographs that have been used throughout the book have been made available by the Thomas Merton Center and I am grateful yet again for the assistance that has been given.

But my chief word of appreciation must be to Susan, my wife, for whom the beloved monk – and more colourful descriptions have been used at times – has represented a serious incursion into the rhythm of so many days over the last five years. Thank you.

List of Illustrations

1) pp. xvi, 56, 88: Thomas Merton in his hermitage at the Abbey of Gethsemani photographed by John Howard Griffin, circa 1963. John Howard Griffin, the author of *Black Like Me*, first visited Merton in the early 1960's because of their shared interest in civil rights. Griffin helped foster a love of photography in Merton providing him with film, developing his photographs and, in January 1968, loaning Merton a Canon Camera. Griffin was initially appointed as Merton's official biographer, but was unable to finish his planned biography due to health troubles.

2) p. xxv: Thomas Merton by John Lyons. John Lyons was a brother in the Salvatorian Order who arranged a Merton exhibit at Mt. St. Paul's College, Wisconsin in 1966. He visited Merton in late 1967 at the Abbey of Gethsemani, where this photograph was taken.

3) p. 22: the Abbey Church at our Lady of Gethsemani. Photograph by Harry Hinkle.

4) p. 110: Photograph of Merton's Mount Olivet Hermitage taken in the early 1960s soon after its completion. Photography by Thomas Merton.

5) p. 136: Thomas Merton and His Holiness the Dalai Lama. During his travels in Asia in late 1968 Merton had a series of meetings in early November with the Dalai Lama in Dharamsala. Writing of those meetings in his autobiography the Dalai Lama would say that it was 'Merton who introduced me to the real meaning of the word "Christian".'

6) p. 160: Thomas Merton by Sibylle Akers. In late September of 1959, Sibylle Akers, described by Merton as 'a very gifted photographer', visited Merton at Gethsemani and took a number of photographs of Merton.

7) p. 182: Thomas Merton, Daniel Berrigan, S.J., Philip Berrigan and Anthony Walsh [back to camera] meeting with Thomas Merton in the grounds of the Abbey of Gethsemani in August 1962.

Foreword

by Rowan Williams

Thomas Merton, like C. S. Lewis and Simone Weil, has not always been best served by his most ardent admirers. It is a welcome thing that – in all these cases – we have so much 'informal' material to help us see them actually developing their ideas, testing out thoughts without feeling they have to take full responsibility for them. The trouble comes when those admirers, rather overwhelmed by the sheer volume of material, feel obliged to defend everything their heroes wrote, formal and informal, so that the fallible and multi-coloured humanity of the writer becomes a bit fixed and frozen.

John Moses makes no such mistake, but takes Merton's fallible humanity very much as his starting point. He sketches with great skill and vividness the diverse cultural hinterland out of which Merton always spoke and wrote, even in his most self-consciously 'monastic' moments, and he directs us to what is perhaps the great focal point Merton makes – that the restoration of God's image in us is the heart of what Christian theology, liturgy and contemplation all aim at. This is, indeed, as John Moses says, a Christian humanism, reminding us that the good news we so often seem to forget is that we are not only saved but enlarged by grace – made more, not less, ourselves, more aware of the mystery at the centre of who we are, more sceptical of all the various cultural disorders that seek so obsessively to make us less than we are.

As we approach the centenary of Merton's birth, this book provides a coherent and comprehensive reminder of why Merton has mattered and still matters so much to so many diverse readers. He remains hard to categorize, a dangerous ally for anyone looking for support for any kind of party. At his best – and there is so much that is his best – he diagnoses as no one else both the spiritual and the political dis-eases of the post-war world, and we can still recognize the problems. But equally he displays wonderfully the richness and resourcefulness of the renewed world of the gospel. He gives 'a summons to life', in a phrase used by John Moses at the end of this fine study. I hope there will be many to hear it.

Preface

The centenary of the birth of Thomas Merton provides an opportunity to reconsider the international reputation and the continuing relevance in today's world of a man who continues to enthral, to perplex and to challenge. There are few people in recent times whose lives have been the subject of so much study. Books, dissertations, monographs, conference addresses and informal discussion have long since explored the man and his story. His warm, vital humanity continues to delight; his questioning, searching, prophetic voice still resonates. He was in so many ways a bundle of contradictions, and yet he represents a type of discipleship – open, engaged, compassionate, critical – in which the search for God was paramount.

A conventional biography, which moves purposefully from one period of a person's life to another, will not necessarily identify with sufficient clarity the several vocations that Merton pursued, often in parallel with one another, throughout his adult years. The Chronology, which follows immediately after this Preface, provides the basic biographical information that readers might find helpful. I want those who are discovering Merton for the first time to see something of his story in its entirety, but I have judged it right to let his several vocations as a Trappist monk, as a writer, as a contemplative, as a social critic, and (in the context of world faiths) as an ecumenist, stand alongside each other.

The religious life was his primary vocation and the desert tradition, which speaks of the absolute priority of God, was the bedrock of Merton's understanding of monasticism. But the desert experience – which tells of withdrawal, solitude and encounter – runs like a golden thread through every area of his life. The vocations do not, therefore, represent self-contained areas of activity. They are clearly identifiable; they competed for space, for mental energy, for recognition; and yet they informed and enlarged each another, giving the man a range of reference points, a perspective, a depth – even, perhaps, a universal appeal – that no one vocation could have provided. They fall like a series of spotlights upon the central character, overlapping one another, but enabling a fuller, richer portrait of the man to emerge.

It remains the case, however, that this immensely fascinating man displayed throughout his adult life discontents that continue to intrigue. These discontents, which undoubtedly owed something to the contradictions with which he lived, made themselves known as he pursued his vocations. He was not a man who could easily conform; he pushed at the boundaries; he asked inconvenient questions. Could it be that the discontents, set within the austere framework of his monastic calling, served as the crucible in which his prophetic consciousness took shape, taking to itself something of the divine pathos and the divine passion?

There are, therefore, several important questions that have given me the parameters within which any study of Merton might properly be set.

First, why is this man so fascinating? How does it come about – two generations after his death – that he continues to intrigue? What is his secret?

Second, what meaning should be given to the contradictions and the discontents with which he wrestled during his years as a religious? Is it appropriate to speak of divine discontent?

Third, to what extent – and in what areas of contemporary concern – does Merton speak with a prophetic voice?

No comprehensive study of Merton that excludes these questions can begin to do justice to the man. I have wanted Merton to speak for himself and I have, therefore, quoted extensively from his writings, taking full account of the developments in his thinking over the years, but allowing his voice to be heard. It follows, however, that certain unavoidable differences are to be found when comparisons are made between the main body of the text and the quotations from his writings, both in the spelling of certain words, and far more importantly – because Merton was writing at a time when words such as man and mankind had a universal currency – in the use of inclusive language. Readers will understand the need to keep faith with the words that Merton has actually used.

But Merton's voice is heard most clearly in his prophetic awareness, his prophetic consciousness, as he moves beyond the limitations of any one of his vocations, straddling the divide between contemplation and action. Engaging with God and engaging with the world, he continues to speak, asking that we might look again at our preconceived ideas in the light of all that he has to say about the natural world, the prevailing culture, the experience of alienation, institutions and the freedom of the individual, the relation of men and women, the priority of conscience, the abuses of power, questions of war and peace, the global dimension, the task of the church in a post-Christian age – and the priority of God.

John Moses

Thomas Merton: A Chronology

1915   Born (31 January) at Prades, a small French town near Spanish border, where parents Owen and Ruth had settled, having met as art students in Paris.

1918   Birth of John Paul, his younger brother.

1921   Death of Ruth, diagnosed with stomach cancer in previous year.

1922   Tom accompanies father to Bermuda, returning to maternal grandparents and younger brother in following year, before settling with father (but without John Paul) at St Antonin, in southern France.

1926   Schooling for Tom in France and England.

1929   Learns of father's illness – a malignant tumour on brain – prior to commencing at Oakham School.

1931   Death of Owen Merton, with responsibility of guardianship passing to Thomas Izod Bennett, a successful physician in London.

1933   Leaves Oakham, having secured scholarship place to read Modern Languages at Clare College, Cambridge.

           Visits Rome (his second visit), discovering the churches, the frescoes and prayer, before staying with his grandparents in summer.

1934   Completes first year at Cambridge, but fails to return to pursue his studies. Examination results had been disappointing and his wayward lifestyle, which included the fathering of an illegitimate child, leads to a break with his guardian and the decision to remain in the United States.

1935   Enrols at Columbia University, taking courses over next three years in English Literature, Spanish, German, Geology, Constitutional Law and French Renaissance Literature.

1936   Death of Merton's maternal grandfather followed in 1937 by death of grandmother.

1938   Graduates from Columbia and enrols in Graduate School for a Master's degree in English Literature.

            Conditional baptism on being received in the Catholic Church and subsequently confirmed, taking Thomas James Merton as a confirmation name.

1939   Receives Master's degree for work which included his dissertation, 'Nature and Art in William Blake'.

            Considers doctoral research, perseveres with writing, and begins to explore possibility of a vocation to religious life.

1940   Teaches at the Columbia Extension School in spring term and subsequently accepts teaching appointment at St. Bonaventure College.

            Visits Cuba – part holiday, part pilgrimage to shrine of Our Lady of Cobre.

1941   Spends Holy Week and Easter at Abbey of Our Lady of Gethsemani, a Cistercian foundation of the Strict Observance, near Bardstown, Kentucky.

            Works briefly as volunteer at Friendship House, a small lay

community in Harlem, established by Baroness Catherine de Hueck Doherty and engaged in Christian social action.

Presents himself for admission at Gethsemani (10 December).

1942   Received into novitiate and given name of Louis in religious life.

1943   John Paul, flying with the Royal Canadian Air Force, is lost in action over the English Channel.

1944   Merton takes Simple Vows (19 March).

Thirty Poems published, and other early volumes of poetry – *A Man In the Divided Sea* (1946), *Figures for an Apocalypse* (1947) and *The Tears of the Blind Lions* (1949) – appear over the following years.

1945   Commences studies for priesthood.

1947   Solemn Vows (19 March).

1948   Death of Abbot Frederic Dunne, Merton's first abbot, who had encouraged Merton to write; election of Abbot James Fox.

Publication of *The Seven Storey Mountain* and *What Is Contemplation?*

1949   Ordination as Deacon (19 March) and Priest (26 May).

Publication of *Seeds of Contemplation, Gethsemani Magnificat, The Waters of Siloe* and *Elected Silence*, Evelyn Waugh's abridged and amended version of *The Seven Storey Mountain*.

1951   Appointed Master of the Scholastics.

Granted American citizenship.

Publication of *The Ascent to Truth*.

1952   Explores possibility of moving to Carthusians or Camaldolese.

1953   Publication of *The Sign of Jonas* and *Bread in the Wilderness*.

1955   Appointed Master of the Novices.

            Publication of *No Man Is an Island*.

1956   Merton's encounter with Dr. Gregory Zilboorg, the psychiatrist.

            Publication of *The Living Bread* and *Praying the Psalms*.

1957   Publication of *Basic Principles of Monastic Spirituality, The Silent Life* and a volume of poetry, *The Strange Islands*.

1958   Publication of *Monastic Peace* and *Thoughts in Solitude*.

1960   Commences visits to Dr. James Wygal, a psychiatrist in Louisville.

1961   Addresses political and social issues with new urgency. Circulation of *Cold War Letters* commences.

1962   Continuing struggles with the Superiors of Order over censorship.

            Joins the Fellowship of Reconciliation.

            Publication of *New Seeds of Contemplation*, the prose poems *Original Bomb Child* and *Hagia Sophia*, and *A Thomas Merton Reader*.

1963   Thomas Merton Room established at Bellarmine College, now Merton Center at Bellarmine University.

            Publication of *Life of Holiness* and volume of poetry, *Emblems of a Season of Fury*.

1964   Merton, who has developed his links with scholars of several world faith communities from mid-1950s, visits Daisetz T. Suzuki, a Zen scholar, in New York.

Meeting of leaders in Peace Movement at Gethsemani.

Publication of *Seeds of Destruction*.

1965   Merton gives up his work as Master of the Novices and begins to live full time at the hermitage.

Publication of *Gandhi on Non-Violence*, *The Way of Chuang Tzu* and *Seasons of Celebration*.

1966   Merton's relationship with 'M', the young student nurse who had cared for him in hospital when he was recovering from back surgery, dominates spring and summer.

Merton signs an agreement, having spent a year in the hermitage, that he will spend rest of his life in solitude.

Publication of *Raids on the Unspeakable*, *Conjectures of a Guilty Bystander* and *Redeeming the Time*.

1967   Merton Legacy Trust established with responsibility for Merton's literary estate and for publication of his writings at any time in future.

Merton holds first of two conferences at Gethsemani with Superiors of women's contemplative communities.

Publication of *Mystics and Zen Masters*.

1968   Abbot Flavian Burns elected to succeed Abbot James Fox.

Merton visits California, New Mexico and Alaska, in part to look for a site for a hermitage.

Merton leaves the United States (15 October) for his Asian journey to Calcutta, New Delhi, the Himalayas, Ceylon, Singapore and Bangkok.

Merton's meetings with Dalai Lama (4, 6 and 8 November).

Death of Merton at Bangkok (10 December).

Merton's Funeral Mass and Interment at Gethsemani (17 December).

Publication of *Faith and Violence, Zen and the Birds of Appetite* and prose poem *Cables to the Ace.*

* * * *

1969   Publication of *My Argument with the Gestapo, Contemplative Prayer* and final book of poetry, *The Geography of Lograire.*

1970   Publication of *Opening the Bible.*

1971   Publication of *Contemplation in a World of Action, On Peace.*

1973   Publication of *The Asian Journal.*

1974   Publication of *A Thomas Merton Reader* (revised edition).

1977   Publication of *The Collected Poems of Thomas Merton.*

1979   Publication of *Love and Living.*

1980   Publication of *The Non-Violent Alternative.*

1981   Publication of *The Literary Essays of Thomas Merton, Day of a Stranger, Introductions East and West, The Foreign Prefaces of Thomas Merton* (published in an enlarged edition as *Reflections on My Work* in 1989).

1982   Publication of *Woods, Shore, Desert.*

1984   Publication of Michael Mott's official biography *The Seven Mountains of Thomas Merton.*

1985   Publication of *Eighteen Poems.*

The Letters of Thomas Merton (Volume 1). The four subsequent volumes are published in 1989, 1990, 1993 and 1994.

1987   Formation of International Thomas Merton Society.

1988   Publication of *The Alaskan Journal of Thomas Merton.*

1989   Publication of *Preview of the Asian Journal.*

1992   Publication of *The Springs of Contemplation.*

1995   Publication of *Passion for Peace.*

         The Journals of Thomas Merton (Volume 1). The six subsequent volumes are published in 1996, 1997 and 1998.

1999   Publication of *The Intimate Merton.*

2003   Publication of *The Inner Experience.*

2004   Publication of *Peace in the Post-Christian Era.*

1

The Fascination of the Man

We are all created in the image of God, but Thomas Merton seemed to be just a little bit more so.[1]

Contrary to some concepts of holiness, my idea of the raw material of sanctity is not a thick river of molasses oozing sluggishly towards Heaven. It is fire and passion and pain and frustration and failure and renewed effort. For [Merton] the struggle is over.[2]

If fascination is the power to intrigue, to attract, it is a quality that Thomas Merton possessed *and continues to possess*. His early years gave little indication of the international profile he would enjoy and the influence he would exercise in his adult life as a Trappist monk, a writer, a contemplative, a social critic and an ecumenist. He is none the less a man with whom it is notoriously difficult to come to terms. He embodied so many contradictions; he cut across so many boundaries. It was undoubtedly the case that he was a man who was marvellously alive, but he does not lend himself to easy classification. Naomi Burton Stone, his literary agent and a close friend over many years, admitted that everyone knows a different Thomas Merton,[3] while Merton acknowledged towards the end of his life that most people didn't know what to make of him.

It is one of Merton's many paradoxes that such a man, known and yet unknown, should have been so fascinating to his contemporaries and to increasingly large numbers of people throughout the world in the years since his death. But over and above the personal circumstances that inevitably shaped the man, there are the very different vocations that enabled people to see him in a different light.

From childhood and adolescence, Merton carried forward an experience of the fragility of family life and of close personal relationships; of the erratic and conflicting demands of freedom and discipline; of the traumas of rejection; of a growing self-awareness. From his student years at Columbia in the late 1930s,

he found in the midst of frenzied activity the compulsion to write; the importance of friends; an early engagement with questions of peace and justice; and
the public and the private personae, the man whom people saw and the man
who remained hidden from view. But it was also during those years that he
discovered God and faith and vocation and prayer and the search – above all
the search – for ground on which he could stand and engage with God, with
himself, with life. From the Trappist abbey at Gethsemani, near Bardstown
in the state of Kentucky, where he chose to realize his monastic vocation, he
received during the years of formation a focus and a discipline which, in spite
of many discontents and protestations to the contrary, ensured over the years a
degree of rootedness and a freedom to grow.

What emerged from these years was a beguiling combination of great
natural ability, an independence of mind and spirit, a refreshing if somewhat
mischievous good humour, deep-seated neuroses, contradictions which
continue to perplex, and an abiding, absorbing passion for God and for people
and for the questions with which he wrestled. Merton spelt out in his one work
of autobiographical fiction, *My Argument with the Gestapo*, the all-important
questions: What do I think I am living for? What is holding me back from living
completely for those things? It was only in the space between the two questions
that the identity of a person could be found, and Merton, recognizing that this
might well be the work of a lifetime and more, was quick to add: 'I am all the
time trying to make out the answer, as I go on living.'[4]

The search for Thomas Merton is in part an exploration of these two
questions and of the answers he provided as he pursued his vocations. He was
well aware of the ambiguities with which he lived and made no apology for a
life in which 'mystery [is] inscaped with paradox and contradiction';[5] but he has
been for many people more persuasive and not less persuasive because of these
things. And yet the questions remain: Where does the fascination reside? Can
it be identified? Why has it proved to be so enduring? There is no consensus,
but something of the truth may be found in five broad areas: his humanity; his
delight in the natural world; his several vocations; his prophetic awareness; and
his extraordinary capacity to make people feel that his story, his questions, his
struggles are also theirs.

A deeply human man

The fascination that Merton had for those who encountered him was undoubtedly to be found, at least initially, in his warm, vital humanity. Friends, colleagues and acquaintances tell of someone who was down to earth, direct and spontaneous in his dealings with people. He could enter into a situation and be entirely open, attentive, ready to receive and to respond; his enthusiasms spoke of an energy that he carried with him into everything he did. He was a man for whom 'it was all or nothing, now or never ... and no-thing or no-body would or could steer him away from his life-long pilgrimage',[6] yet he retained an essential simplicity, great personal charm, an inner freedom and a disarming friendliness.

And this deeply human man could be enormous fun. He was well able to laugh at himself and to laugh with others. He could be playful, delighting in the absurd with a robust, good humour. Abbot Flavian Burns, who gave the homily at Merton's funeral mass, spoke of him as 'a younger Brother, even a boyish Brother, one who could have lived to a hundred without growing old.'[7] Ebullient, dynamic, impetuous, exuberant: these are all words that have been used by those who knew him, and they could sometimes be found most conspicuously in what one of his brothers at Gethsemani called 'a certain ill-defined, latent air of daring about him'.[8]

Merton, reflecting on the role of the poet in society, observed in one of his *Literary Essays* that 'For the poet ... there is only life in all its unpredictability and all its freedom.'[9] It may be that his capacity to change and to grow in all the areas of his life owed something to this spirit of unpredictability and freedom that he embodied and articulated. He wrote of his 'need for constant self-revision, growth, leaving behind, renunciation of yesterday, yet continuity with all yesterdays'.[10] His openness to life, his intellectual curiosity, his honesty, his restless spirit could not be held in check. He needed to question, to push at the boundaries, to move on. He was 'everyone's friend [but] no one's possession'.[11]

But the ambiguities remained. He could be a deeply private person, vulnerable, tormented by self-doubt. His *Journals*, which served in part as a safety valve, tell of the occasions when his feelings got the better of his judgement, when the petty frustrations of community life became intolerable. The raw edges were at times all too apparent; Merton, writing to one of his many correspondents six months before his death, identified the two persons within himself who both demanded to be heard: 'one ascetic, conservative, traditional, monastic. The other radical, independent, and somewhat akin to beats and hippies and poets in general.'[12] It was as though a clash of temperaments, a clash of personalities, had been built into the man. He needed solitude and he needed people. He pleaded for the freedom to pursue his monastic vocation in his way, but he was held and nurtured by the community. His commitment to the religious life never wavered, and yet he needed contacts outside the monastery – from all parts of the world, from all traditions of faith. At different times and in different ways, the monk and the writer and the contemplative and the social critic and the ecumenist were at war with one another, or at the very least wrestled with one another for space and time and energy.

The editor of the most sensitive of Merton's *Journals* sees him as a man who was 'capable of profundity and pettiness, sensitivity and self-absorption, insight and illusion, focus and distraction'.[13] But what is never in doubt is his religious sensibility, his developing understanding of the meaning of faith, his passionate engagement with God and with life, his prophetic consciousness. It may well be that some part of Merton's fascination lies in the fact that he was so obviously a man who, while he could speak about God and present the claims of faith and prayer, was nevertheless a man who was wounded, compromised. And yet he is for many more impressive and more enduring because of his vibrant but flawed humanity.

Few things speak more cogently of Merton's rich humanity than his enjoyment of people. Friendships that had been formed during his student years survived and were supplemented over the years by important additions. His writing secured for him some relaxation in the Trappist discipline – a relaxation he was happy to exploit to the full – and friends became his eyes and his ears, as letters and visits kept him in touch with a wider world. He delighted in people, in the company of women and young children, in times of relaxation, in conversation, in ideas. In later years, as he became increasingly detached from the life of the community, there are references to picnics by the lakes, lunches in the woods, photography, calligraphy, conversations and the playing of Bob Dylan records in the hermitage, visits to the homes of friends in Louisville, including occasional excursions to hear jazz in one club or another. Merton was entirely disciplined in keeping the monastic rule, in saying the offices, in finding ample time for meditation, but he also exhibited an expansiveness, and there was a daredevil element with hints – and more than hints – of self-indulgence, of compensation. The boundaries of the monastic life were crossed and crossed again, and Merton, who delighted as much as anyone in the social round, admitted in the pages of his *Journal* that 'I have not always been temperate, and if I go to town and someone pours me a drink, I don't resist another or even a third. And I have sometimes gone beyond the *trivium perfectum* (the perfect third). A monk?'[14]

Those who knew Merton best had no hesitation in describing him as a wonderful friend, a man who loved people, and enjoyed drawing them out. Few encounters are more telling than Merton's chance meeting with three French students whom he found in the bookstore in the University of Louisville. They had arrived early for an exchange and no arrangements were in hand to meet them. Merton records how they went and drank coffee and talked; but then, by way of reflection, he added: 'whether or not they got anything out of it, it was a revelation of Christ to *me* – just because they were human, open, frank, sincere, interested in ideas, and in a situation where they were fully exposed to risk and possibility'.[15] Here is a pen portrait – 'human, open … fully exposed to risk and possibility' – which could stand as a commentary on what many people found in Merton himself.

By contrast with an unforeseen meeting with young adults, there is his delight in children and young people, and – in particular – the sheer simplicity of his regular dealings with the children of the O'Callaghan family in Louisville, to whom he was simply known as Uncle Tom or Uncle Louie.[16] It became something of a habit for him to visit the family after his trips to the doctor, when he would share peanut-butter-and-jelly sandwiches, help the children with their homework, play the guitar, draw pictures or doodles and provide a human swing as the younger children clambered all over him. They were rare moments of innocence and intimacy, when he could simply be himself with children who knew him, loved him, and responded to his enthusiasm for them and for their world.

What his friends recall is the gaiety, the infectious humour, the belly laughter. He was a man who could introduce himself to his newly elected abbot as 'Chop Suey Louie the mad Chinese poet';[17] who could reduce the brothers to laughter by the raising of his eyebrows, or by an expression of horror on his face, or by facetious comments in Trappist sign language during readings in the refectory or discussions in chapter; and who could be found by a friend visiting Gethsemani lying on the floor of a room in the Guest House, 'laughing half to death', as his laughter – described as 'a kind of monsoon of joy' – penetrated the silence of the Abbey Church.[18] But he was also a man who, by contrast with the restless energy that he displayed, could be in chapel 'sitting for the whole half-hour without moving a muscle or doing anything'.[19]

Merton could laugh at himself, and his *Journals* are punctuated by flashes of a wry, self-mocking humour. He could see the funny side of life and his alert and penetrating mind was never slow to respond. The vagaries of community life presented him with ample scope for a humour that could be playful, provocative or perverse. Chapel and the liturgical round gave Merton cause for concern at different times, and the discovery that an organ voluntary, which reminded him of 'the stuff you used to hear in movie theaters at the time of the silent movies', was the tune of the hymn sung by the faithful at Fatima led him to explode: 'Mother of God, why do you let these things happen?'[20] And in the last weeks of his life, as he pursued his travels in Asia, he could not forego a throwaway sentence on being asked about the renewal of monasticism and what *aggiornamento* (the spirit of renewal) meant in practice at Gethsemani, as he quipped, 'Oh sure, they're doing great. They now have cornflakes for breakfast.'[21] It was just the sort of flippant, off-the-cuff remark that amused many but caused pain to others.

Delighting in the natural world

Alongside the sheer vitality of the man and his spirited response to those whom he encountered, it is also necessary to set as another aspect of Merton's continuing fascination the overwhelming delight he found in the world of nature. The physical location of the Abbey of Gethsemani – surrounded by the fields where the Trappists worked, by extensive woods, by lakes and rivers and streams – ensured that as a writer he was able to draw upon a rich palette of colours. Certainly his writing is never more evocative than when he describes the seasons of the year, the vast array of birds and insects and small animals to be found in the woods, the sights and sounds with which he lived, and his attempts to draw out something of their meaning.

He captured the changing scene: the steel grey dawn with the hard frozen hills; a din of birds ringing through the air and the wet woods; the red flames of sunrise glowing through the cedars like a forest fire; the limpid clarity of a May morning; a tanager, like a drop of blood, singing in the tall thin pines; the sweetness of honeysuckle heavy on the air; a titmouse playing in the dry woods by the woodshed; leaves, like flashes of copper, tinkling as the breeze passes over them; meadow larks singing in the snow; the silence of the woods at midnight.[22]

He was especially good in depicting the colours of the natural world, but beyond the awareness of the senses, there was an intuitive grasp of the majesty, the miracle, of life – pulsating, free, content *to be*. He listened to the quails whistling in the fields and the woods. He had not heard them for some time and spoke of what they represented: 'Signs of life, of gentleness, of helplessness, of providence, of love. They just keep on existing and loving and making more quails and whistling in the bushes.'[23]

The satisfaction that Merton found in his natural surroundings was underscored by a profoundly prayerful sense of wonder. It led him to break into his own *Benedicite*.

> Today, Father, this blue sky lauds you. The delicate green and orange flowers of the tulip poplar tree praise you. The distant blue hills praise you, together with the sweet-smelling air that is full of brilliant light. The bickering flycatchers praise you with the lowing cattle and the quails that whistle over there. I too, Father, praise you, with all these my brothers, and they give voice to my own heart and to my own silence.[24]

Merton had stumbled upon a deeper truth: he understood the oneness, the interdependence, of all life and therefore the part that all must play in offering, consciously or unconsciously, their tribute of praise. 'Praise Christ, all you living creatures. For Him you and I were created. With every breath we love Him. My psalms fulfil your dim, unconscious song, O brothers in this wood.'[25]

Merton had a great reverence for the holiness of all created things. They were for him mirrors of God's beauty. He had known from his earliest years at Gethsemani that landscape was important for contemplation; and he could justly claim at a much later stage that as he had lived and prayed so he had also listened to the silence of the woods. His numerous complaints about the life of the community, quite apart from the long-running tug of war with his Superiors concerning his commitment to Gethsemani, never encroached upon a spontaneous delight in his physical surroundings. Indeed, there is an intense physicality about his relationship with the natural environment. He craved the solitude of the woods, but also direct contact with the sun, the grass, the dirt and the leaves.

The limited permission he had been given in the summer of 1949 to go outside the monastic enclosure and walk in the woods assumed an immense significance for Merton. It represented a modest release from the physical and mental constraints of life in a community that was highly regimented at that time. But there was something more. Merton was aware of his need for solitude if he was to engage with God in silence and in contemplative prayer. It was as though the woods enlarged his understanding of what was happening to his vocations as a religious and a priest. Could it be, he asked himself, that he might become 'something of a hermit-priest, of a priest of the woods or the deserts or the hills?'[26]

The competing interests that dominated Merton's life, together with the many and varied contradictions that he carried forward, ensured that the simplicity of such a vocation would not be realized, but his appeal as an expositor of the natural world and his recognition of its importance for any theological understanding of life are both immense. He came to see not merely the mutual interdependence of the human race with nature, but – even more – a deep sense of solidarity, of oneness. 'How absolutely central is the truth that we are first of all *part of nature*, though we are a very special part, that which is conscious of God.'[27] Humankind's unique capacity to give voice to the prayer and praise of the whole creation was for Merton an important part of the Christian vocation; but that distinctive contribution was complemented by all forms of life, and his *Prayer to God the Father* concluded with the acknowledgement that 'We are all one silence, and a diversity of voices.'[28]

Together with the priority that Merton gave to prayer and meditation, there was also for him the *'preeminence of compassion* for every living thing'.[29] But his insights as a poet, a priest, a mystic, took him beyond the constraints of systematic theology. He might observe, for example, small myrtle warblers at play on the low branches of the pines, awed by their loveliness, their quick flight, their hissings and chirpings; then he would go on to talk of a 'sense of total kinship with them as if they and I were of the same nature, and as if that nature were nothing but love. And what else but love keeps us all together in being?'[30]

But love – certainly in Merton's understanding of the word – must be related to truth, and increasingly for Merton, as his work as a social critic gathered pace, no interpretation of the truth of the contemporary scene would be adequate if it did not contain a prophetic word of judgement. He understood the delicate balance of nature. He took very seriously the myriad ways in which the human race could so easily damage the natural world. He bemoaned the fact that men and women, while being in the world and part of the whole creation, are actually 'destroying everything because we are destroying ourselves, spiritually, morally and in every way'.[31]

The intellectual and moral arguments of a later generation of environment-alists were foreshadowed by Merton in the 1960s. It was for him the fear of a nuclear holocaust that informed so much of his social criticism, but he was no less concerned about the impact of technology upon nature as he unravelled the consequences of what he termed non-ecology. He feared that the balance of creation, the ecological balance, would be seriously disturbed by arrogance, by greed, by indifference.

Merton's reflections on all that he found around him encouraged him to speak at an early stage of humankind's distinctive role in bringing to consciousness and articulating all that could be seen and heard in praise of the Creator God. It was for him a natural development that he should therefore speak at a somewhat later time of what he came to see as the primary responsibility of the Christian in a technological society to the whole creation. He pleaded for an awareness of the power of the human race to frustrate God's purposes – both for the natural world and for humankind – by misuse, by exploitation, by waste.

A man of many parts

Few insights in Merton's writing demonstrate more clearly the ways in which his several vocations informed each other. Monasticism gave him his primary focus, but the monk, the writer, the contemplative, the social critic and the ecumenist were one and the same man. The Trappist vocation is one that the world can scarcely begin to understand; yet Gethsemani gave him the rootedness that he had never known in his earliest years, enabling him to engage with life.

The monastic calling required, however, a high degree of openness to new possibilities. Merton had recognized something of this at the outset: 'I say I want to give up everything for God. With His grace, perhaps my whole life will be devoted to nothing more than finding out what those words mean.'[32] One of the transitions he was required to make was a rediscovery of the world. Merton's humanity, his sociability, his good humour, his need for friends, went hand in hand at the outset with a degree of detachment from the world – even, perhaps, a degree of denial – that went far beyond the detachment that is necessarily inseparable from the monastic life. His stance in relation to the world, and therefore, to humanity in general, at the time of his admission to Gethsemani was one that he subsequently identified as a psychological withdrawal.

Merton came to see that the vocation to the religious life was for him the right kind of withdrawal because it gave a proper perspective; but it was no less necessary for him to distance himself from any illusion that his vocation had imposed upon him a separateness, a difference in kind, from everyone else. Jean Leclercq, the Benedictine scholar with whom Merton corresponded for nearly 20 years, judged that Merton's vocation as a hermit in his later years, compromised in so many ways, nevertheless enabled him to become 'not only more a monk, but also more human: closer to men, to all men, more universal'.[33] Merton made much in his later years of the place of the monk in society as a stranger, an alien, and it was from such a position that he engaged with the world and addressed through his writings many of the political and social questions of his day.

Merton was a monk and a writer, and although he had been encouraged by his superiors to pursue his writing it was inevitable that the monk and the writer should be in conflict with each other, especially as he sought the necessary space for contemplative prayer in a community where the prevailing ethos was profoundly penitential. Merton, who has probably done more than any other spiritual writer in the twentieth century to plead for a contemplative dimension in the life of the church, recognized that contemplation – properly understood – has a prophetic dimension. Writing was the means whereby he took forward in public and in private his search for God and his search for himself; but he knew that at the heart of contemplative prayer lay a discovery of the true self in God and, even more, a discovery of all humankind in God. Contemplation, like monasticism, is not an evasion, an escape. It requires an openness to God and to the world.

Merton spoke with increasing frequency over the years about the primacy of love; but love has a cutting edge, and whatever compassion Merton had discovered for humanity in general led him on to address issues as diverse as the American dream, racial justice, nuclear weapons, the Vietnam War, and to do so with searching questions and a trenchant criticism. He had ceased to be a man who could stand aside. What is seen increasingly with the passing of the years is Merton's humanity in all areas of his life. Openness and inclusivity – yes; a willingness to take great risks – yes; but above all there was a love which was profoundly human, vulnerable, passionate.

Merton came to rejoice in his humanity, but his theological convictions regarding the mystery of God in Christ required him to go one step further and recognize the presence of Christ in all humankind. It became for him an all-embracing vision: the interdependence of all life in God; the responsibility of humankind for each other and for the whole creation. Merton's use of the hermitage in the early 1960s and his far closer proximity day by day to the physical environment that surrounded him enabled him to see that 'the universe is my home and I am nothing if not part of it'.[34] And so, writing as a poet and a mystic, Merton could say that 'the whole world and all the incidents of life tend to be sacraments – signs of God, signs of His love working in the world'.[35] It is a holistic vision of life shot through with God – and with love.

It is as a contemplative that Merton is chiefly remembered. It was no small part of his achievement that he made it possible for large numbers of people to discover the priority that might be given to interior solitude. He wrote of 'the seriousness of *solitude*', which was for him nothing less than a challenge, a vocation, that Christians might pursue.[36] He saw himself as one who had been found by solitude[37] and he compared his situation with that of 'a stranger and a wanderer on the face of the earth, who has been called out of what was familiar to him in order to seek strangely and painfully after he knows not what'.[38]

Merton's understanding of solitude had far-reaching resonances. It was a necessary building block in his search for personal freedom and responsibility; but solitude was not merely something that was appropriate for hermits. For Merton, it touched directly upon the whole future of the world. Everything was brought back to his primary vocation – the search for God – and solitude was, therefore, nothing less than 'the climate in which I can simply be what I am meant to be, and live in the presence of the living God'.[39] But beyond solitude lay contemplative prayer and, while Merton was mindful of its limitations, it was for him the means whereby Christians might come to an understanding of the world and of the part that they are called to play.

Merton struggled with his monastic life at Gethsemani, but he carried his responsibilities within the community with great diligence, and any thought that he confined himself to the role of nonconformist, of rebel, is far too simplistic. He rejected what he considered to be the trivialities of the religious life, but he was feeling after an older tradition of monasticism – less institutionalized, more committed to silence, poverty, manual labour, contemplative prayer. He reflected on the struggles within monasticism in earlier ages, but his eyes remained firmly fixed upon his world. He understood the problems posed by living in a time of great change – 'too preoccupied with what is ending or too obsessed with what seems to be beginning' – but he knew the absolute necessity of staying in touch with the present and with all its uncertain but potentially dynamic possibilities.[40]

It is precisely here that it is possible to see the underlying attitude that determined his work as a social critic and an ecumenist. The transformation that took place in Merton over the years owed much to his experience of solitude and his exploration of contemplative prayer, but he was adamant that for the religious there could be no evasion from the hard realities of life. His personal journey was illuminated by a capacious appetite for new insights, a wide-ranging imagination, a restless and impulsive spirit, a comprehensive compassion; but in solitude, in contemplation, in the dark night of the soul, Merton found that his search for God and for himself, his compassion for humankind and for the whole creation, came together.

Merton's vocations, apparently so distinctive and dissimilar, complemented each other. Jean Leclercq saw Merton not as a specialist but as 'an enlightened amateur ... a meddler-in-everything of genius'.[41] It was none the less a remarkable combination of gifts that enabled him to absorb and to assimilate, to speak out of his own experience, to bring to his varied activities a strong sense of the urgency of the present moment, and to press the questions to which he did not necessarily have an answer but which he believed to be important. He liked to think of himself as a 'solitary explorer ... [searching] ... the existential depths of faith in its silences, its ambiguities'.[42] For Merton, the experiential theologian, there were connections to be made between faith and prayer and social justice, and the authority of his writings, quite apart from the continuing appeal of the man, owes much to his emphasis that 'What is valuable is what is real, here and now'.[43]

It was a broad vision that Merton brought to his work. The global dimension was increasingly important, and whether he intervened as social critic or ecumenist he looked for a global consciousness, a global vision. He sought a world that was 'better, more free, more just, more livable, more human',[44] but he was mindful of an inheritance of contemplative wisdom that was common to all the great world religions, and he pleaded for a humanism which, because it had its roots deep in the soil of religious faith, might be able to engage with the world in a spirit of passionate and critical encounter. He understood well enough the dynamics of a changing world order – between nations, ethnic groups, faith communities – to realize that predictable responses were no longer sufficient. He feared the consequences that would follow upon nuclear warfare and, although he held back from a thoroughgoing pacifism, he identified himself increasingly with those who urged upon the world a policy of non-violent resistance. Power and the abuses of power were a constant target, and he exposed as far as he could the false promises with which men and women consoled themselves. He knew that he could be too sweeping in his social criticism, but he remained unshaken in the conviction of his later years that 'To choose the world ... is first of all an acceptance of a task and a vocation in the world, in history, and in time.'[45]

A prophetic awareness

It was no small part of Merton's vocation to bring a prophetic awareness into the concerns of his later years, and it is here also that something of his fascination for subsequent generations is to be found. The *Message* he sent to the meeting of young Latin American poets in Mexico City in February 1964 spoke of the prophetic task of the poet: 'To prophesy is not to predict but to seize upon reality in its moment of highest expectation and tension toward the new.'[46] It is in this sense that Merton, who possessed a poet's instinct and a poet's imagination, might be judged to have possessed a prophetic consciousness and to have spoken with a prophetic voice. His observations – and, even more, his strictures – might often fail to take account of the complexities of political life, but what is so telling is the degree to which his vision and his voice continue to be seen and heard.

It was a global awareness that Merton brought to contemporary debates. He had a strong sense of the interdependence of all peoples and recognized the ties – economic, cultural, sociological – which required a high degree of mutual responsibility. Alongside his undoubted emphasis upon the freedom of the individual – freedom to think, freedom to speak, freedom to live without the constraints of the collective in its various forms – there was a profound understanding of the solidarity of humankind. The boundaries of nationality and race were no longer sufficient. It was necessary to think in terms of 'one human family, one world'.[47]

Implicit in such an approach was Merton's commitment to the obligations of conscience, and this was something to be worked out in men's and women's relationship not only to each other but to the whole created order. It was not sufficient to delight in the world of nature. Something more was required. The tradition of non-violence for which he pleaded in exploring questions of war and peace could not be ignored in any discussion of the relationship with the physical environment. Before the day when environmental concerns claimed the serious attention of scientists, politicians and the general public, Merton – with his strong sense of solidarity with the whole creation – had seen that 'Our attitude toward nature is simply an extension of our attitude toward ourselves, and toward one another. We are free to be at peace with ourselves and others, and also with nature.'[48]

There is an apocalyptic dimension to be found in some of Merton's writings and it would be easy to see this as little more than an instance of his propensity to dramatize. But his instinct, informed by reading, correspondence and conversation, led him to conclude that 'We are living in the greatest revolution in history – a huge spontaneous upheaval of the entire human race.'[49] Merton, looking for an interpretation, turned the spotlight on the inner contradictions, the chaotic forces, to be found within every person.

Merton's theological understanding required him to address a situation in which men and women found themselves increasingly alienated both from their true selves and from the world. He had much to say, for example, about the American dream, the American psyche. He saw his generation as one that had been conditioned by words, slogans and official pronouncements. He spoke of a womb of collective illusions, of false promises, of deceptions. He brought his critical judgement to bear upon what he regarded as 'the mixture of immaturity, size, apparent innocence and depravity, with occasional spasms of guilt, power, self-hate, pugnacity, lapsing into wildness and then apathy, hopped up and wild-eyed and inarticulate and wanting to be popular'.[50]

No less trenchant were his criticisms concerning the international role of the United States. He deplored 'the stupidity and blindness of American power'[51] and the efforts of his adopted country 'to *contain* by violence all revolutionary activity anywhere in the world'.[52] What lay behind many of these criticisms was his concern about the predominant culture: rationalist, activist, ego-centric, acquisitive, aggressive. It was a judgement which he applied no less rigorously to the Soviet Union, to China, to all power blocs caught up in the cycle of technological advance, wealth creation, military might. The abuses of power were a constantly recurring theme: from the manipulations of politicians, generals and the manufacturers of armaments to the pervasive influence of advertising and the mass media; from the denial of civil rights and the oppression of all minorities to the manufacturing, the testing and the stockpiling of nuclear weapons; from the long-feared nightmare of a nuclear holocaust to the actual nightmare of war in Vietnam.

It was, however, a life-affirming, world-embracing discipleship that Merton sought for himself and for others. It was, therefore, axiomatic that the type of holiness he represented was one that sought 'the presence of God *in this present life*.'[53] What he frequently found in Western Christianity, however, was the same 'will-to-power' that characterized the Western world in its relation to the rest of humankind.[54] He bemoaned the emphasis on action, on visible results, on conquest, which obscured a contemplative tradition with its hidden depths, its hidden wisdom.

Merton saw very clearly the changed circumstances in which the church found itself. He rejected the illusions with which churchmen might be tempted to reassure themselves, and his strictures concerning the prevailing model of Catholicism – centralized, bureaucratic, heavy handed – were savage. He confessed to being 'scandalised by (his) own Catholicism',[55] distancing himself from conservatives and progressives alike, and accepting the *diaspora*[56] situation in which the church was required to live out its vocation. Confident in his own Catholic faith and his understanding of the church as the Body of Christ, he looked beyond existing institutional struc-tures, believing that 'events will bring on a crisis that will smash all facades. Maybe in the ruins of the great institutional idol we will recover something of our Christian truth.'[57]

What Merton sought was not withdrawal but open dialogue with the world. He rejoiced in Pope John XXIII's initiative in summoning the Second Vatican Council and interpreted the Council's Constitution on the Church in the Modern World (*Gaudium et Spes*) as a sign of a new spirit of willingness to engage. Mindful of the desert tradition which lay at the heart of his monastic calling, he wanted the church to bring into all discussions the perspective of those who knew themselves to be aliens and exiles. It was in the same spirit that he looked for new forms of monastic life, recovering an earlier emphasis upon solitude, contemplative prayer and manual labour, but incorporating – at least in dialogue – a prophetic dimension that is not easily achieved by any religious community. His appeal for a renewal of monasticism was too ill defined and too often blunted by his own restlessness for a notoriously conservative religious Order to change direction easily, but his determination to think outside the boundaries of established structures and prevailing attitudes ensured that significant changes did eventually take place.

It was in Merton's work as an ecumenist that so many things were drawn together: his monastic and contemplative vocations, his open mind, his emphasis upon the priority of love, his global vision, his understanding of a fast changing world, and the same emphasis upon dialogue: 'Christ is found not in loud and pompous declarations but in humble and fraternal dialogue. He is found less in a truth that is imposed than in a truth that is shared.'[58] He had a profound sense of the indwelling Christ in all people, and he was therefore concerned to look beyond the Christian tradition of the Western world to find a meeting of minds with those who drew upon other traditions of faith. Amiya Chakravarty, the Indian philosopher with whom Merton corresponded during the last two years of his life, recognized the importance of Merton's rootedness in the Christian faith in exploring and interpreting other traditions, and acknowledged his inability 'to deny any authentic scripture or any man of faith'.[59]

Merton would not be constrained by institutions or by conventional definitions of what may constitute religious awareness. It was not intellectual laziness nor was it a doctrine-light liberalism that informed his thinking, but a breadth of imagination, of compassion. The search for God that had taken him out of the world had also brought him back, at least in heart and mind, into the world. It was the religious sensibility that connected his mystical theology, his contemplative prayer, his search for God and for himself. What Merton dared to propose was 'a whole new understanding of the Christian task in our time',[60] a far broader definition – and in his mind a far more Catholic definition – of ecumenism. A fuller awareness in recent years of the great traditions of faith – with their capacity for mutual enrichment and destruction – serves yet again to illuminate Merton's continuing relevance as a thinker, a writer, a teacher, a mystic, an ecumenist.

Merton was first and foremost a man of faith. His abiding passion was the living God, and he refused to hold back from identifying the spiritual vacuum, together with the alienation, that lay at the heart of the human condition. The revolution of which he spoke was, therefore, a spiritual crisis with global dimensions. He could be impetuous in his judgements, but he comes down as a man who has bequeathed a prophetic awareness that continues to resonate. A generation that lives with the accumulated problems of globalization, population explosion, urbanization, migration, environmental hazards, poverty and international terrorism might well judge that his critique is even more pertinent now than it was in his lifetime.

Something of the religious humanism that Merton was feeling after found expression in his commitment to non-violence as the only serious alternative to war. He belonged to a generation that lived in the shadow of Hiroshima and Nagasaki, but a later generation, which knows the extent to which a nuclear balance of power secured the peace of the world throughout the second half of the twentieth century, might therefore look quizzically at his uncompromising campaign against the whole policy of deterrence in a very different age. Merton was not a pacifist, but he came close to embracing the model of non-violent resistance as he argued for the settlement of international disputes by non-violent means. Like Mahatma Gandhi, he knew that religious faith and political action are ultimately inseparable. It may be that a world in which some proliferation of nuclear weapons has already taken place and in which race and politics and religion all too easily inject their poison into each other might yet find in Merton's espousal of effective non-violence a tradition that continues to question the consensus that is so readily accepted on every side.

It was for Merton a matter of supreme importance that the image of God in men and women should be defended and not defaced or destroyed. Few things could more fully serve that end than the contemplative dimension for which he pleaded so consistently. He straddled the divide – so far as his monastic vocation allowed – between contemplation and action, but he knew it was 'a synthesis, always fragile, like life, always to be begun again, always to be rectified'.[61] But in so far as the contemplative life required a depth of awareness, of perception, it enabled him to bring a prophetic dimension into his work, exploring the dynamics of the age, holding in tension the contradictions of his experience, and giving voice to the questions and the concerns of large numbers of people in the middle years of the twentieth century. His independence of mind and spirit, his imagination, his willingness to back his insight and his judgement, his refusal to be constrained: all these personal qualities, underscored by a life in which contemplation and action were inextricably bound together, enabled him to speak for many. He never conformed to any monastic ideal – 'As an ikon, I am not doing too well'[62] – but he can be seen as a man for an age of transition, albeit an age that has not yet fully run its course.

A universal human being

Merton became increasingly aware over the years of the unique situation in which he found himself as he struggled to understand the world's predicament and his own place within it. He described himself as 'the contemporary of Auschwitz, Hiroshima, Vietnam and the Watts Riots' and acknowledged that 'whether I like it or not, I am deeply and personally involved'.[63] This was a world in turmoil, a world in crisis, and in spite of Merton's monastic calling he came to represent for many the struggles of the years in which he lived. 'If one wishes to know where the Western world was in the second half of the twentieth century, Thomas Merton offers considerable enlightenment'.[64]

Friends and interpreters have not hesitated to call Merton 'one of the most remarkable men of our time',[65] even 'a world citizen',[66] or even more 'a universal human being'.[67] He has been rightly seen as 'a man of faith in thoughtful conversation with a faithless age',[68] but it was one of the hallmarks of his conversation that he preferred to be known by his questions rather than his answers. Dan Berrigan, the Jesuit priest with whom Merton was involved in the peace movement in the 1960s, described him as

> … a cosmic nuisance. He asked the questions that crowned heads never ask, church or state. The nature of faith, the secular business of the world, other cultures and religions, music, poetry, photography; and war, war, war, the Bomb, the world becoming a grotesque ossuary. He kept probing, he wouldn't let go.[69]

It is undoubtedly the case that Merton spoke to a deeply troubled age, but his abiding fascination for the twenty-first and not merely the twentieth century lies in the fact that large numbers of people throughout the world continue to find in the man and in his story something of the truth about themselves. Mark Gibbard, an Anglican religious who was irritated in many respects by Merton's spiritual autobiography *The Seven Storey Mountain*, none the less comments: 'But I couldn't put the book down. He was, I felt, just talking to *me*, sharing his feelings with *me*, re-awakening echoes – though we are so different – *within me*'.[70] Robert Lax, a lifelong friend, speaks of meeting people in the course of his travels who have just found Merton's books for the first time and who always say 'He was talking as though he was talking from inside of me'.[71] John Eudes Bamberger, who studied under Merton at Gethsemani in the early 1950s and who subsequently became the Abbot of Our Lady of the Genesee, near

Rochester, New York, tells of the very human way in which Merton wrote about the spiritual life, thereby enabling people to feel that 'Merton understands what I want to be, or what I would like to be, or what I'm trying to be, or what I've gone through, or what I'm coping with.'[72]

Merton did not seek disciples, but, having touched the depths of his own experience, he spoke to the depths of others. His honesty, his humanity, even the contradictions and the discontents he displayed, enabled people, Catholics and non-Catholics alike, to identify with his story and make it their own. His books on the spiritual life, on contemplative prayer, explored in a very accessible way an ideal to which many aspired. His writings on social justice, on war and peace, on the freedom and the dignity of human beings, resonated with many who stood outside all establishments, religious or secular. He had the capacity to raise peoples' sights, to point to what was possible, to what was true, to what mattered; his being able, in spite of his many insecurities, to look life in the face gave others the confidence to find their courage and move forward.

Merton was a man who, even at the end of his life, was still searching. He remained unfinished, incomplete. His many gifts, his personal charm, his ebullience, his search for God: all these he retained, and yet he wrote as one who was never quite able to bring everything together. There were too many loose ends. But Merton knew the central mysteries of Christian faith and had long since acknowledged that 'In order to become myself I must cease to be what I always thought I wanted to be, and in order to find myself I must go out of myself, and in order to live I have to die.'[73]

Paul Quenon, one of the brothers at Gethsemani who knew Merton at the end of his life, spoke of him as 'a gatekeeper: that is to say, a man whose task is to help people set their feet in a larger room, in "vaster spaces of spirit and tradition".'[74] Merton recognized that the appeal of his writing lay partly in the fact that he did not pretend to have all the answers, but he knew the questions, and his approach represented a type of discipleship that is open, questioning, passionate, engaged. What he sought was nothing less than the presence of God in the midst of life, and he pursued his all-too-human journey in the light of a mystical theology that required a complete openness to all other persons because 'ultimately all other persons are Christ'.[75]

Merton presented many faces to the world and the approach that he brought to life has allowed many people to impose on him the Merton that they are looking for. What can be obscured by his preoccupation with the larger issues – political, social, cultural – is the singlemindedness of heart that determined the course of his life. He recognized the need to embrace with a good deal of urgency the challenges afforded by the present moment, but in his search for God and for himself he knew the need 'To go beyond everything, to leave everything and press forward to the End and to the Beginning, to the ever new Beginning that is without End.'[76] The interior journey required 'growth, deepening, and an ever greater surrender to the creative action of love and grace in our hearts.'[77]

The type of discipleship that Merton represented, compromised but compelling, is also an invitation to discipleship. He knew that Christianity must be a religion of dynamic change. Paul Quenon records that 'The most important thing he taught me was how to love God and how to be true and honest in the presence of God. Not to fake it, just to be yourself and live in such a way that you know God accepts you and you go from there.'[78] Beyond Merton's humanity and his delight in the natural world, beyond his parallel vocations and his prophetic awareness, there is his extraordinary capacity to speak to people. Is this perhaps the meaning of the reflection, recorded in his *Journal* some two or three months after he had taken up residence full time in his hermitage at Gethsemani? 'I come here to die and love ... Here, planted as a seed in the cosmos, I will be a Christ seed, and bring fruit for other men. Death and rising in Christ.'[79] Something of what is meant by the continuing fascination of Thomas Merton is captured in his translation of a poem by the Nicaraguan poet, Pablo Antonio Cuadra.

> The flower asked: 'Will my scent,
> Perhaps, survive me?'
>
> The moon asked: 'Shall I keep
> Some light after perishing?'
>
> But man said: 'How is it that I end
> And that my song remains among you?'[80]

The Trappist Monk

I did not come here for myself but for God. God is my order and my cell. He is my religious life and my rule.[1]

I have consistently held that a monk can speak *from the desert*, since there is no other place from which he has a better claim to be heard.[2]

It was in the story and the wisdom of the desert that Thomas Merton found the meaning of monasticism. In the tradition of the Christian Church the desert speaks of the search for God, and the appeal of the desert lies in the fact that it has nothing to offer. It speaks of the abandonment of *everything* in favour of nothing; or, to be more accurate, of the abandonment of everything in favour of God – *and God alone*. The desert is, therefore, a place of withdrawal, of solitude, of testing, but it can also be a place of encounter, a place of truth.

The monastic life, which derives in large measure from the experiences of the Desert Fathers of the fourth and fifth centuries, was shaped by the Rule of St Benedict; but renewal, at least in the Western Church, has been an important element in the story of monasticism. The Cistercian Order had been founded at the end of the eleventh century with a far greater emphasis upon silence, simplicity of life and manual labour; and the Order of Cistercians of the Strict Observance, the Trappists, had been established in the middle years of the seventeenth century by Armand Jean de Rancé, the Abbot of La Trappe in Normandy, in the search for even greater austerity. The dispersion of monasteries following upon the French Revolution led some religious to make their way to the United States, and the first foundation of Trappists in America was made at Gethsemani,[3] in Kentucky, in 1848 by monks who came from Melleray, a daughter house of Citeaux. Few religious communities have interpreted the desert tradition with greater rigour than the Trappists and Merton knew from the outset that 'The monastic vocation … is by its very nature a call to the wilderness.'[4]

The unhappy circumstances of Merton's earliest years, together with the traumas of his time at Cambridge, had left him uncertain and deeply dissatisfied with himself. The years as a student at Columbia (1935–9) and as a teacher at St. Bonaventure (1940–1) were the important years of transition when – alongside his studies, his friendships, his eager participation in the social round, and his early attempts to write and to be published – there was a growing awareness of Catholic Christendom, a discovery of faith and prayer, and the beginning of a life-long exploration of God and of the world in which he found himself. Catholicism began to provide the focus and the discipline he had previously lacked.

This intense phase of discovering the centrality of God led, perhaps inevitably, to an awareness of vocations to the priesthood and to the religious life. Conversations with teachers and friends confirmed and enlarged his sense of compulsion and of the need to pursue the call to holiness. He was fast becoming a young man who in his search for God needed to go the whole way, and the claims of solitude, of poverty, of silence, of contemplative prayer drew him more and more until, acknowledging his need to make an absolute and unequivocal response, he could only say 'I want to give God everything'.[5]

The Jesuits, the Franciscans and the Carthusians all attracted Merton at different times, but his choice of Gethsemani and, therefore, of the Trappists, while it represented the most austere option available for him at that time, also met most fully what he later described as his 'one desire … the desire for solitude – to disappear into God, to be submerged in His peace, to be lost in the secret of His Face'.[6] His first visit to Gethsemani as a retreatant for Holy Week and Easter 1941 was an overwhelming experience, even though later generations might look with some misgiving at his interpretation of what he had found. 'This is the center of America. I had wondered what was holding this country together, what has been keeping the universe from cracking in pieces and falling apart. It is this monastery if only this one'.[7]

His early attempts to live the life of a monk in the world were soon to give way to the far more testing circumstances of living the life of a monk in the monastery. He came to see Gethsemani as the one place where everything must be abandoned, and with his strong sense of the solidarity of humankind he placed great emphasis upon the deprivations of the religious life as an act of atonement for his sin and for the sins of the whole world.[8] But was there something more? Could it be that the decision to become a Trappist was influenced – at least in part – by the guilt and the pain that he carried forward from his year at Cambridge?

Merton presented himself for admission to Gethsemani on the 10 December 1941, a little before his twenty-seventh birthday, and he was accepted by Abbot Frederic Dunne as a postulant to the choir three days later. He was given the name of Louis in the religious life, although his friends outside continued to know him as Tom and his brothers at Gethsemani would invariably refer to him in later years as Louie or Uncle Louie. He received the habit of a novice in the following February, and something of the story and the spirit of the Trappists at Gethsemani was conveyed by Dom Frederic when he counselled that 'we were making a big mistake if we came to Gethsemani expecting anything but the cross, sickness, contradictions, troubles, sorrows, humiliations, fasts, sufferings and, in general, everything that human nature hates'.[9]

Merton's decision did not surprise his closest friends but some wondered if he would stay the course. He recalled in later years 'the lostness and wonder of the first days';[10] but it is here that one of Merton's many contradictions is to be seen most clearly. People mattered. He was companionable. He enjoyed the company of women. Conversation, ideas, argument, laughter were his stock in trade. Yet he was resolved upon a life of solitude and silence. It was an austere vocation, and he took to heart the words of his confessor soon after his admission to Gethsemani that many in the world might depend for their salvation upon his perseverance, upon his fidelity to his vocation. 'You did not come here alone.'[11]

The monastic day began in chapel at 2 a.m. and the choir monks would spend something approaching one third of the day in the liturgical round. The diet was frugal in the extreme. Spiritual reading was confined to one book a week, which was approved by the Master of the Novices. Correspondence was restricted to four half-page letters four times a year, and all mail was customarily read by the Prior or the Master of the Novices. It is true that Merton delighted from the outset in the physical landscape – 'A very wide valley – full of rolling and dipping land, woods, cedars, dark green fields'[12] – but the monks were confined to the enclosure apart from the periods of manual labour in the fields, which would normally occupy five or six hours a day. The monastic day concluded in chapel a little before 7 p.m. and the brothers then withdrew to small partitioned areas in the open dormitory where the beds were little more than wooden benches with pallets and bolsters filled with straw. Merton had no illusions about the life he had embarked upon: 'In the Trappists, it *is* poverty, and labor, and hardship ... [and] ... absolute, unquestioning obedience!'[13]

The abbey at Gethsemani had been built to accommodate between 50 and 70 monks, but by 1946, following upon a remarkable upsurge in vocations, the number of brothers, including novices and postulants, was approaching 200 and was to rise eventually to 270. The problem of accommodating such large numbers was partly addressed by the establishment of new foundations in different parts of the United States;[14] but Merton could justly rejoice in a house that was witnessing a vitality it had not known since its establishment a century before.

Merton's account of his conversion and his entry upon his monastic life[15] continues to stand as a deeply moving record, albeit pious and romanticized; but the threads of discontent, which were to weave their way throughout his adult life, made themselves apparent to himself and to others at an early stage. Monastic formation, which was the primary concern during the years of his novitiate, required periods of instruction some four or five times a week, together with spiritual oversight and direction provided by the Abbot, the Master of the Novices and his confessors. Merton, reflecting on this period some 20 years later, recalled 'years of false fervor, asceticism, intransigence, intolerance'.[16] There is a hint here of the traumas of later times, but he made Simple Profession in March 1944 and proceeded to Solemn Profession on the Feast of St Joseph in March 1947. By then some large questions were beginning to form in his mind. Was it possible to live a life of solitude at Gethsemani? Was the Cistercian Order necessarily the right one for him? Was it not the case that the responsibilities of leading and managing the community would inevitably require the allocation of demanding work – teaching, writing, administration? And what did it mean in any case to be a contemplative? The questions could be subsumed, at least for the time being, in the formal acts of submission, but they would not go away.

The primary vocation

It was none the less Merton's life as a Trappist that was the bedrock of his work as a writer, his experience as a contemplative, his influence as a social critic and an ecumenist. There would be tensions over the years as his vocations struggled with each other, but the different aspects of his life were all contained within his primary vocation. His development was determined during his early years at Gethsemani by the positive response of his superiors to his ability to write. He was encouraged initially by both Dom Frederic and the Master of the Novices to continue with the writing of poetry, but the focus of his writing was influenced initially by the need to respond to the huge increase in vocations to Cistercian monasteries and the consequent demand for books in English about the Order. He spoke of writing as 'the one activity that was born in me and is in my blood'[17] and by the summer of 1947 he could identify no fewer than 12 writing projects in which he was engaged.

It was the publication of *The Seven Storey Mountain* that gave Merton an international reputation. This was his compelling account of one man's search for meaning – subject, of course, to the amendments required by the censors of the Cistercian Order – until the time of Solemn Profession and was an immediate success, with some 600,000 copies being sold during the first year after publication. Merton would be the first to recognize its weaknesses in later years, but the book was hailed by Graham Greene as 'an autobiography with a pattern and meaning valid for all of us',[18] and comparisons have been made over the years with Augustine's *Confessions* and John Henry Newman's *Apologia Pro Vita Sua*.

Merton was already experiencing something of the weariness and self-doubt to which so many writers are susceptible, but the problems he encountered were exacerbated by the consistently heavy-handed approach of the Cistercian censors who, mindful at that time of their responsibilities to determine the appropriateness of what monks might publish, frustrated and enraged him. But there were other considerations. Merton was no longer the man who had embraced the Catholic faith in the late 1930s, finding vocations to the priesthood and the religious life, and entering Gethsemani in December 1941. The transitions he was making are to be found in his *Journals*. Within days of receiving his copy of *Exile Ends in Glory* in June 1948, in which Merton tells the story of one of the pioneers of the Cistercian life in the United States, he complained to himself, 'Where did I get all that pious rhetoric? That was the way I thought a monk was supposed to write, just after I had made Simple Profession.'[19] And within three years this judgement was to be heavily underscored: 'The man who began this journal is dead, just as the man who finished *The Seven Storey Mountain* [is] also dead, and what is more the man who was the central figure in *The Seven Storey Mountain* [is] dead over and over.'[20]

Merton was moving towards an understanding of monasticism in which silence and solitude were the primary requirements. He grasped almost from the beginning the insight of the Desert Fathers that solitude must first be found within oneself. For him, as for all who stand in the monastic tradition, 'The desert of the monk is the monastery – and his own heart.'[21] But Merton feared the relentless encroachment of his writing upon the life of solitude and contemplative prayer. It is true that in his writing Merton entered a private world where he could be alone and free to think for very limited periods of time. There he found the necessary degree of privacy that enabled him to pray as he pursued his reading and his writing, but he also had the opportunity – when his writing programme permitted – to share in the communal task of manual labour.

> How weary I am of being a writer. How necessary it is for monks to work in the fields, in the rain, in the sun, in the mud, in the clay, in the wind: these are our spiritual directors and our novice masters. They form our contemplation. They instil into us virtue. They make us stable as the land we live in. You do not get that out of a typewriter.[22]

Early discontents

It was perhaps inevitable that Merton should become restless as the full meaning of living in community bore down upon him. The daily routines of the monastery, the singing in the choir, the personal characteristics or inadequacies of his brothers all gave him cause for concern at different times. He feared that the Cistercian way of life was being compromised by an activist spirit. He was troubled by the open-door policy, which saw the admission of large numbers of postulants. He questioned the practice of establishing new foundations. He viewed with considerable disdain the commercial operations initiated by Dom James Fox, Merton's second abbot, in his attempt to save Gethsemani from bankruptcy. He mocked the tractors, larger and louder than ever, as they made their way in full fury around the fields of alfalfa, and he scorned the assembly line production of bourbon fruitcake and Gethsemani cheese.

Gethsemani had changed, but Merton had also changed. He was becoming far more focused in his thinking, far less accepting where prevailing attitudes were concerned, critical in his emphasis upon what monasticism, and Cistercian monasticism in particular, should mean. Merton could be hard on himself – and, indeed, on the whole community – for failing to live up to some ideal that was scarcely achievable amidst all the duties and constraints of community life. The initial compulsion that had driven Merton to Gethsemani remained alive, but he struggled to make sense of his vocation.

I wonder more and more to what extent a genuine and deep spiritual life is going to be at all possible in such a community. No question of course that the individual can maintain one on his own, but in order to do so he is going to have to cut his own way through the thicket and not just follow the community.[23]

Merton knew that the perceived problems owed something to his restless spirit, to the unresolved tensions implicit in his vocations, and to his endless capacity to question, to challenge. John Eudes Bamberger, who owed his vocation as a Trappist in part to his reading of *The Seven Storey Mountain*, judged Merton to be 'too creative and too independent and too energetic to fit into any group smoothly for long, in spite of his best intentions'.[24] It is a generous tribute, but Merton also came delightfully close to the truth when he concluded the entry in his journal for Good Shepherd Sunday 1948 by writing: 'Good Shepherd, You have a wild and crazy sheep in love with thorns and brambles. But please don't get tired of looking for me! I know You won't. For You have found me. All I have to do is stay found.'[25]

The life of a Trappist required at the outset three vows: obedience, stability and conversion of manners. In the Rule of St Benedict, poverty and chastity were implicit in the conversion of manners, and so for Merton the three vows represented one inclusive act of commitment. It was the vow of stability, however, which was judged to be so important in monastic formation, binding the monk to one community for the whole of his life, and thereby guarding him against any undue restlessness. The vow of stability was for Merton 'the belly of the whale',[26] the place of withdrawal, of solitude, of truth, but it was also the place at which he stumbled.

Within five years of his going to Gethsemani, Merton had complained in his journal that 'I was not the contemplative or the solitary that I wanted to be, that I (make) no progress in this house and that I ought to be either a Carthusian or an outright hermit'.[27] He was counselled by his confessor that his desire to go elsewhere was nothing more than 'disordered appetite'[28] and he was assured by Dom Frederic that he belonged at Gethsemani. But this reaching out for something different, something new, even something more demanding, never left him. New possibilities were never far from his mind – the Carthusians, the Camaldolese, or even new foundations in the West Indies, in Arizona, in Ecuador, in New Mexico. But what was driving Merton? Was it, as he himself suggested, 'Partly temptation, and partly something more immeasurably solid than that?'[29] His commitment to God remained absolute, and yet the endless search for something different continued.

Merton was a free spirit – impulsive, creative – and he must have wearied his Superiors, and especially Dom James, with his repeated requests to explore new possibilities. Elements of communal self-interest may well have come into play: Merton was too good a teacher and his books represented far too good an income stream for him to be carelessly set aside. But it may also be the case that his Superiors were acting in what they believed to be his own best interests. Dr Gregory Zilboorg, the psychiatrist to whom Merton was referred for a conversation in 1956, was unsympathetic to Merton's dilemmas and thoroughly dismissive of his desire to be a hermit. It may well be that he hardened Dom James's stance by allegedly reporting that Merton 'was likely to take off with a woman and leave the church'.[30]

And yet Merton, torn this way and that, was feeling after something deeper, something more substantial. The rejection in Rome in December 1959 of his application to move to another community found him praying alone in the darkness in chapel: 'Empty, silent, free, opening, into nothing – a little point of nothing that alone is real. What do you ask? Nothing. What do you want? Nothing. Very quiet and dark. The Father. The Father.'[31] There is something profoundly moving about this response after the tormented years of questioning, of complaining. Is it exhaustion? Or is it the work of grace? Is it possible to find here the heart of the true religious? Quietly, in the darkness, in the nothingness, he accepts *at least for the time being* what must now be accepted as the mind of his Order and – dare he say it? – the will of God.

Forming and being formed

Merton tested the patience of his Superiors by his repeated attempts to look elsewhere in pursuit of his monastic calling, but he was none the less fully engaged in the life of the community and entrusted with major responsibilities in shaping the formation of novices and newly professed monks. A visitation of Gethsemani in May 1951 had led to the establishment of the Scholasticate and to Merton's appointment as Master of the Scholastics, where he was required to oversee the programme of formation for young professed monks who had taken simple vows and were preparing for ordination. He had already been providing courses of study on the scriptures, on the contemplative life and on mystical theology, and he would also act now as their spiritual director. In due course classes on patristic theology would be added to the schedule. Merton had received no formal training in theology apart from the instruction he himself had received at Gethsemani, but he had always read widely and, as he remarked with appropriate candour, 'I feel much better mapping out my own approach – from Scripture and the Fathers, Mysticism and Dogma together – blending and culminating in experience.'[32] The demands of teaching and spiritual direction were onerous, and Merton, who had complained even before he had taken up the new appointment that teaching exhausted him, could none the less reflect on the irony of a situation in which, worn out with activity, he could proclaim the virtues of the contemplative life.[33]

It was characteristic of his general approach to those whom he was required to oversee on their monastic journey that he should have recognized at the outset that he would be the one to be most fully formed by the new scholasticate. The questions with which he lived would not disappear, but Merton's work with these young men gave him not only an experience of 'parental' responsibility but also a new understanding of solitude which, at least for the present time, met his continuing need for a deeper experience of withdrawal.

In October 1955, Merton was appointed Master of the Novices. He had made it clear that he was willing to undertake this work, but his appointment might well have surprised the community and it undoubtedly says much for Dom James's discernment in taking the risk of trusting Merton. It would now be his responsibility to present teaching sessions, commonly known as conferences, for the novices on the monastic life and to do so within the approved Cistercian tradition. Courses were provided on scripture, on the history of monasticism, on the Cistercian Fathers, on liturgy and on ascetical theology. Merton taught many of these courses himself throughout his years as Novice Master, and towards the end of his time added conferences on modern literature. Recordings of his conferences with the novices reveal a teacher who is lively, relaxed, well prepared, very human, with a lightness of touch, encouraging participation. But it was *formation* and not *information* that was required, and Merton also brought to his work the empathy of a priest and a pastor.

Merton's strength as a teacher lay in the degree to which he drew upon his own experience. His inquisitive mind was open to the widest possible range of influences: the Fathers of the Western and the Eastern Church, the Cistercian Fathers, the mystics of the later Middle Ages, Russian theologians, Protestant theologians, poets, novelists, social theorists. Dom Aelred Graham, an English Benedictine monk, judged that Merton's early writings lacked not only 'the subtleties of balance and proportion' but also 'the philosopher's intellectual patience and the capacity to handle ideas'. He saw Merton's theology as 'a projection into his writing of a personal experience'.[34] But Merton spoke of himself towards the end of his life as 'a Christian existentialist',[35] and others have reckoned him to be 'a people's theologian ... a great mystical and experiential theologian'.[36]

In spite of the responsibilities he carried for scholastics and novices over a period of 14 years, Merton feared at times that he was failing to take a full part in the life of the community. There is little doubt that at some level he was becoming more detached intellectually and emotionally but he continued to take his place in the liturgical round, teaching his novices, reading as extensively as ever, writing to his innumerable correspondents, and taking an increasingly active part, albeit as a writer, in some of the large issues of the day. And yet the times were changing – in society at large, in the church, in the monastic orders – and Merton was incapable of remaining untouched by all that was happening around him. Just two years or so after he had given up responsibility for the novices, he looked through old notes that he had used in his conferences on the monastic vows. He found them to be 'so legalistic, so rigid, so narrow', and yet, as he remarked, there were many who had thought him to be 'a dangerous radical'. It was the clearest possible indication that 'there really has been something of a revolution'.[37]

The monk and his Abbot

The irritations that disturbed Merton throughout so many of his years at Gethsemani surface at regular intervals in his *Journals*, in his encounters with his Superiors, and in the increasingly activist stance that he took in addressing some of the critical political and social questions of the day. The main focus of his discontents was Dom James Fox, whom Merton had welcomed at the time of his election as 'the Holy Ghost's candidate',[38] but the two men differed greatly in temperament and style, and Merton felt that he was unable to establish a genuine rapport with his Abbot. Dom James was a Harvard graduate who brought to his office a much-needed resolve to place Gethsemani on a secure basis. There were exceptional moments when Merton would acknowledge something of his Superior's achievements, but in the main he wrote as one who despaired of Dom James – the man, his understanding of monasticism, his interpretation of his role as Superior.

Merton could be vitriolic. The Abbot who is portrayed in the *Journals* is often authoritarian, intransigent, untrustworthy and ruthless. He is a man who is convinced of the rightness of his judgement, calculating, anxious at all costs to avoid open conflict, well able to play politics and to indulge in emotional blackmail to secure his ends. There was also a forced heartiness, even perhaps a banality, which could not fail to alienate Merton, who despised the farewell greeting with which the Abbot signed off all his correspondence, together with the rubber stamp bearing the same words with which he gave approval to whatever request required his agreement. 'Tout pour Jésus, tout par Marie, toujours avec un sourire [All for Jesus, all through Mary, always with a smile].'[39] Merton resented any thought that he might contribute to the illusions with which the Abbot consoled himself: 'the illusion of the great, gay, joyous, peppy, optimistic, Jesus-loving, one hundred percent American Trappist monastery'.[40]

But was it perhaps the case that 'Fr. Louis's main villain was Fr. Louis'?[41] It could certainly be argued that Merton was on some kind of emotional roller-coaster, at least where his vow of stability was concerned, throughout the 1950s. Dom James resisted Merton's desire to go elsewhere and live a life of greater solitude. He wrote disparagingly of what he termed 'a lot of poetical fancy and imaginings, a love of adventure', believing that even if he were to leave it would only be a question of time before 'some new idea would hit him and off he would go … a roamer, a gypsy'.[42] Was Dom James merely intransigent, or did he have a greater understanding of Merton's needs than Merton could ever appreciate? Was it a drama driven by Merton's own conflicts as he struggled to work out the meaning of his vocation?

Merton took his vow of obedience very seriously, even though it required a good deal of self-discipline. He resented the opening of conscience letters, the refusal to consider any application that he might go to other communities, the attempt by various Superiors to impose some degree of censorship upon his writings, and the rejection of invitations that he might address conferences or retreats. Merton had chosen a life of withdrawal and obedience, and yet he chose to cast himself in the role of victim. 'I am a sort of reform-school kid who is being punished by being taken off the street.'[43] Differences of personality and perception continued to intrude and to exacerbate a relationship that was undoubtedly strained on both sides. It is possible, reading between the lines, to see something of the truth in Merton's repeated complaints, but the entries in his *Journals* are inevitably subjective, lacking understanding and compassion. Merton wrote as one who appeared to be stuck in a phase of arrested adolescence: headstrong, rebellious, critical of authority, anxious to establish for himself a fair degree of latitude in the interpretation of his monastic life. Perhaps it was his engagement as a writer in the struggle for racial justice in the United States that encouraged him to see himself as one who is 'really like a Negro in the presence of a Southern white man'.[44] And when Dom James presumed to enquire on one occasion about his spiritual life – and he had good reason to do so at that particular time – Merton bridled: 'Yessuh white boss, mighty fine white boss. I'se only a simple ole niggah boy, white boss but de Laud he loves me!'[45]

In his more gracious moments, Merton conceded that Dom James was well intentioned and had done a great deal of good for the community in holding everything together. What was more important from Merton's point of view was the admission that 'He has in fact often left me a great deal of leeway'.[46] There was far more mutual respect and affection than Merton's *Journals* suggest. He relished his arguments with his Superiors, and yet he needed the structure, the stability, the strength of purpose that Dom James supplied.[47] It is certainly the case that Dom James encouraged Merton to persevere with his study and his writing; that he allowed Merton's books to be read in the refectory; that he appointed him Master of the Scholastics and Master of the Novices; that he gave him the title Chief Ranger of the Forest with the responsibility for restoring the woods and, far more significantly, the freedom to roam in the woods and to enter into their silence; that he allowed Merton to pursue step by step what Merton believed to be his vocation to be a hermit, that he enabled him in due course to test his vocation to the eremitical life; and, perhaps most surprisingly, that he used Merton as his confessor over a period of some 15 years. Many might say that Merton's Superiors saved his vocation,[48] and that any objective assessment of Dom James's role is bound to acknowledge that if 'the Abbot held the reins tight, there is small doubt that there was any other way to do it with such a man'.[49]

One of Merton's charges was that Dom James could not face the questions that monasticism was now required to address. Merton's thinking opened out in his later years as he moved beyond his discontents with Gethsemani to wider and far more substantial questions concerning monasticism and the Catholic Church. Merton's ambivalence regarding Gethsemani continued until the end of his life. He wrote of the artificiality, the stupidity and the hypocrisy of the community,[50] and yet he was able at times to acknowledge that 'I have perhaps not really been at all fair with Gethsemani – not really humble enough to accept the life with its limitations.'[51] He found himself increasingly unable to identify with Gethsemani as an institution: the long daily offices, the formal prayers, the frustration and the anger that he felt after so many chapter meetings, the busyness of the place, the constraint of established practices. There were inevitably for Merton large questions about the exercise of authority, not just at Gethsemani but in most religious communities and in the Catholic Church, but there was also a growing sense that 'the strictness of the rule *as we interpret it*' did not necessarily ensure a deepening of the spiritual life of the monks.[52]

Merton was well aware of his capacity to be a disruptive influence in the community. He made a virtue of his self-appointed role as an *enfant terrible*: 'I do not *have* to rock the boat, but I think it is good to do so anyway. I think I really do the community a service by keeping many people unsettled, and raising dangerous questions.'[53] But the questions went far beyond the discontents of everyday life. They were questions about the very nature of monasticism. Merton was persuaded that nothing less than a fundamental renewal would be sufficient. He challenged the notion that structures had any inherent value except in so far as they enabled people to find themselves, and he set his face against any thought that monasticism might unwittingly endorse attitudes of mind that manifestly belonged to another age regarding the place of the church in the world.

Late medieval models of monastic life were no longer relevant. What he sought was more latitude on the part of the established communities in enabling professed members to grow in their monastic formation in different ways. Merton was undoubtedly feeling after forms of monastic life that would speak to his needs, but the emphasis on freedom – freedom to explore, freedom to experiment – was none the less 'the freedom of the desert nomad',[54] which, grounded in the ancient disciplines of silence and solitude, would provide the necessary 'dimension of awareness'.[55] Only then would it be possible for religious to be so attuned to the problems of the contemporary world that they might understand and share in their own distinctive way in the anguish of the world.

There was, therefore, an innate conservatism in the renewal that Merton sought. His complaint was that the simplicity of a true monasticism had gone, and his concern was to make connections which would establish 'a living continuity with the past, and with what is good in the past'.[56] Silence, solitude, obedience, poverty, chastity, penance, liturgical worship, reading, meditation, prayer, productive work: these were the things that mattered. He could not fail to reflect on the anxieties that preoccupied so many communities as the numbers of religious declined and differences of attitude between the generations disturbed whatever general consensus there had previously been about the *raison d'être* of monastic life. But Merton feared that important things were being lost, especially in the liturgical life, and he rejected the relaxations of the Cistercian rule as decreed by the General Chapter of the Order: 'less work, less prayer, less of everything … No sense of any aim, just "make things more bearable". [57]

Some would say that Merton had a profound influence on the life of his community, drawing it back beyond the unremitting rigours associated with the reforms of de Rancé and capturing again something of the spirit of the Cistercian Fathers of the eleventh and the twelfth centuries. [58] Dom Flavian Burns, who was Merton's third abbot, went further and suggested that Merton changed 'a whole generation's attitude toward how to live the monastic life'. [59] But it is perhaps in the questions he asked that Merton's prophetic voice as a Trappist can be heard most clearly. He did not attempt to offer specific guidelines for renewal or to sketch the outlines of a new kind of monasticism. He took note of new developments, but what was evolving as he struggled with the meaning of his own vocation was a new understanding of the monk as 'a marginal person'. [60] Something of the younger Merton who had first found his way to Gethsemani surfaced again: 'The monastic charism is not "for" anything else. It is what it is: the search for God in unconditional renunciation'. [61]

The monk, the church and the world

Merton came to see that the monk in the modern world no longer has any established place in society. He is 'a very strange kind of person, a marginal person'. [62] Perhaps it is here that Merton's genius can be seen most clearly as he speaks of the monk as someone who strives to go beyond the frontiers of everyday experience, transcending 'the ordinary level of existence'. [63] The monk takes his place, therefore, alongside all other marginal persons, and not least those who protest against injustice and inhumanity.

The 1950s saw profound changes in Merton's approach to many things, although the degree to which he had changed only became plain in the writings that finally appeared in the 1960s. His vocation to the religious life, his understanding of a renewed monasticism, his engagement with the critical issues of the day, his wider ecumenical vision: all these informed and illuminated each other. The contempt for the world that had been so prominent in his earlier writings gave way to a compassion for the world and a far greater understanding. He would not deny that his monastic life was a commitment to 'a certain protest and nonacquiescence',[64] but he could no longer accommodate the idea of monasticism as something detached from everyday life. The much-related moment at the heart of the shopping district in Louisville 'at the corner of Fourth and Walnut' where he was 'suddenly overwhelmed with the realization that I loved all those people, that they were mine and I theirs', set the seal upon his discovery of his humanity.[65] He had come to see that the members of his community were in 'the same world as everybody else, the world of the bomb, the world of race hatred, the world of technology, the world of mass media, big business, revolution and all the rest'.[66]

It was, therefore, inevitable that Merton would reject the tradition of *contemptus mundi* (contempt of the world) that he found in Christianity and in many of the world's religions. He distanced himself from any spirit of triumphalism, intolerance or complacency. He challenged the idea of medieval Christendom as 'a unique, timeless norm' which must be recovered with all 'the security and power of the glorious past'.[67]

Merton saw very clearly the severity of the crisis with which the church was now confronted, but he would not allow himself to be seduced by the blandishments of familiar arguments. He sought 'a healthy Catholicism'[68] and would not identify with the different kinds of conformity – equally intolerant, equally empty-headed – that he found in conservatives and progressives. Something important had been lost in the Catholic Church with its centralization of power and its tradition of universal conformity. The idea of the church as a juridical institution, buttressed by the mystique of infallibility and the practice of power politics, had been used to justify too many evils. Merton's depiction of the Catholic Church – or, to be more precise, of the way in which ecclesiastical authority was exercised – took account of the changing circumstances in which the church found itself. He wrote of 'Authority sitting in its office, with all the windows open, trying to hold down, with both hands, all the important papers and briefs, all the bits of red tape, all the documents on all the members of the Body of Christ'.[69] There was no doubt in Merton's mind that it was Pope John XXIII who, in summoning the Second Vatican Council, had dared to open all the windows and to do so knowing what it would mean. What mattered to Merton was the possibility, represented by the Council, that the church

might now engage with the world on the basis of dialogue and reason, and
he welcomed along the way Pope John's encyclical on peace (*Pacem in Terris*)
and the Council's Pastoral Constitution on the Church in the Modern World
(*Gaudium et Spes*) as signs of hope and of a new beginning.

Merton's faith in God and his commitment to Catholicism were never called
in question. He insisted that his conversion began with 'the realization of the
presence of God in *this present life*, in the world and in myself',[70] and it was
this conviction that informed the activities of his later years. In company with
Karl Rahner, he was clear that Christians must accept 'the "diaspora situation"
of the church in the twentieth century' as something that exists and will go on
existing, and it followed for him that the church must therefore be 'a sign of
contradiction to the world'.[71]

Two concepts had become increasingly important in Merton's thinking by
the early 1960s: humanity and freedom. He applauded the humanity of Pope
John, and he looked increasingly for a church which was seen not in institutional terms but rather as 'a living body of interrelated freedoms'.[72] In so far
as the Superiors of religious houses, or the rules and regulations of monastic
foundations, or the way in which the church went about its work, spoke more
of the arrogance of worldly power and pretension, Merton would inevitably find
himself on a collision course. He sought – and would continue to seek until the
end of his life – a theocratic humanism, a Christian humanism, of which an
authentic freedom was an essential requirement, which alone would enable and
encourage an intelligent and wholehearted participation in the life of the world.

Merton's participation would continue to be informed by his vocation
as a religious. His attitude to Gethsemani would remain more than a little
ambivalent, but his understanding of monasticism served only to deepen his
engagement with the world.

> My monastery is not a home. It is not a place where I am rooted and established in the
> earth. It is not an environment in which I become aware of myself as an individual, but
> rather as a place in which I disappear from the world as an object of interest in order
> to be everywhere in it by hiddenness and compassion. To exist everywhere I have to
> be No-One.[73]

The solitude and silence that Merton sought were not easily secured, but
nothing would alter his continuing conviction that at the heart of the monastic
calling lay a degree of awareness, a depth of consciousness, even a dimension of

transcendence which cannot normally be achieved in a secular life.[74] But there was also something more tentative – more tentative and yet potentially more robust – as Merton followed the twists and turns of his vocation: a spirit of openness, a willingness to take risks, a determination to explore whatever truth the present moment might offer.[75] It was in this spirit that Merton addressed the challenges of his day, and in so doing he offered a *type* of discipleship which remains deeply compelling to those who are unpersuaded by over-confident affirmations of faith.

Merton continued to exercise his responsibilities as Master of the Novices, his conferences were largely appreciated, and his writing achieved a new depth and maturity. He found himself in constant demand for articles, reviews, addresses, prefaces, and replies to letters. The desire for greater solitude, the search for a new understanding of monasticism, the feeling after contemplative prayer, the working out of his vocations: all these persisted. But he saw himself increasingly as 'more an independent and a hermit than a community man'[76]; and, capturing the spirit of *aggiornamento*, he engaged with contemporary political and social issues and with the insights afforded by the great non-Christian traditions of faith.

Merton's published writings during the 1960s provide the clearest indication of both the breadth of his reading and the concerns which preoccupied him. He could no longer see the religious life as a rejection of the world. On the contrary, his vocation as a monk to contemplative prayer required a participation in the ideas, the sufferings and the aspirations of people outside the monastery. 'Christianity is concerned with human crises, since Christians are called to manifest the mercy and truth of God in history.'[77] All that he had to say about war and peace and nuclear weapons, about racism and the civil rights movement, about totalitarianism and freedom, and about the tradition of non-violence are underscored by his urgent plea: 'Be human in this most inhuman of ages; guard the image of man for it is the image of God.'[78]

It was, however, the spiritual quest which was of paramount concern. Merton remained at all times rooted in his own tradition of faith. 'Whatever I seek in other traditions is only the truth of Christ expressed in other terms, rejecting all that is *really* contrary to His truth.'[79] It was not a synthesis of religions that he was looking for but a recognition of the insights that might be found in all religions and of their ability to complement and confirm each other. He delighted in the challenge to the world represented by the Desert Fathers of the early Christian centuries. He returned time and again to the theologians and mystics of the medieval church. He was open to the insights to be received from theologians of other Christian traditions. He emphasized the need for men and women to find themselves in God and to engage with all who aspired in the light of their own experience to an apprehension of reality. And so a succession of books spoke of a wider ecumenism, which would include all who seek the meaning of their lives and its ultimate purpose.[80]

Merton could not be easily constrained. His writings and the high profile they had secured ensured that there was necessarily a fair degree of relaxation for him in the rule concerning correspondence. But Merton, obedient in so many respects, was still his own man, and he did not hesitate to initiate and to develop correspondence with increasingly large numbers of men and women all over the world. Freedom mattered: freedom to think, to ask questions, to correspond, to write, to publish. Indeed, it was not the least of his complaints against the censors of the Order that they violated the freedom that he sought as a religious, as a thinker, and as a contributor to contemporary debates. He rarely complained, except in his journals, but confided in a letter something of his disgust at what he judged to be the absurdity of the attitude of the Trappist censors to something he had written: 'I wrote an article on solitude and anyone would think that it was an obscene novel ... I rewrote the thing three times.'[81] His frustration and his contempt did not abate. Two years later he complained that 'if I just wrote out the Our Father and appended the comment "everyone ought to say this prayer," one of the censors of the Order would find fault with my work.'[82]

It was also a matter of some frustration for Merton that permission was never granted for him to attend seminars and conferences or to conduct retreats. He received an increasing number of invitations to speak, but Dom James was determined that he would go outside the monastery only in the most exceptional circumstances, while at the same time requiring Merton to organize the programme and to speak at gatherings which met at Gethsemani, including the ones which Merton himself had brought to the abbey. The meeting of abbots and novice masters held at the abbey in 1962 saw Merton being asked to give the spiritual conferences. He described in self-mocking words what his confinement meant: 'When the canary is asked to sing ... he is expected to sing merrily and with spontaneity ... Everyone can come and see me in my cage, and Dom James can modestly rejoice in the fact that he is in absolute control of a bird that everyone wants to hear sing.'[83]

There is little doubt from his Superiors' point of view that the battle over the vow of stability continued to rage. Merton might feel he was being exploited, but questions concerning other possibilities – in Central or South America, in California, in Alaska – were never far from his mind. As he approached his fiftieth birthday in January 1965, he wrote of 'deep upheavals of impatience, resentment, disquiet',[84] but the passing of the years meant that the possibility of moving elsewhere became increasingly unlikely and – with what seems to be some reluctance – he began to accept that he would remain at Gethsemani.

The hermitage

No less significant than the restlessness that distracted Merton was his increasingly strong sense of vocation to live as a hermit. It was a way of life entirely contrary to the spirit of the age, but he had no doubts about its place within the purposes of God. This was no new development in his thinking. As early as the summer of 1949, Dom James had given him permission to go outside the monastic enclosure and explore the solitude of the woods; and Merton, even at that stage, had played with the idea of arguing the case for a house in the woods where people could go for short periods for silent, solitary, contemplative prayer.[85]

Ten years and more would pass before a small cinder-block house would be built a little less than a mile from the main monastery buildings on the crest of a low knob known as Mount Olivet, with a view of the valley in front and the woods behind. The house, which was known as St. Mary of Carmel, was used originally for discussions with ecumenical visitors. Merton had been a prime mover in urging that such a building might be provided, but it was Dom James who allowed Merton to use it, albeit in a very limited way at the outset, as a place where he might spend some time. Occasional afternoons (from December 1960) gave way in due course to occasional whole days (from March 1962) and eventually to occasional nights (from October 1964). It provided Merton with the necessary breathing space, enabling him to recover some kind of perspective and to deepen his prayer.

By the autumn of 1964 Dom James had agreed to take very seriously Merton's desire to live in full-time seclusion as a hermit, and it was thanks to his Abbot and to the General Chapter of the Cistercian Order that Merton was eventually relieved of his responsibilities as Master of the Novices and permitted from the 20th of August 1965 to live in the hermitage all the time. Merton had been granted what he most desired. He had already found that his limited occupation of the hermitage had enabled him to rediscover a sense of balance, of rhythm. Everything was now given a new context, and the solitude of the woods became 'the chosen locus of freedom' in his life.[86]

Merton's timetable was very simple: rise at 2.30 a.m., say part of the canonical office, meditation, Bible reading, simple breakfast, study, routine domestic chores, another office, a few letters, say Mass at the monastery, a cooked meal, return to the hermitage, see the Abbot once a week, light reading, another office, meditation, writing, another office, light supper, meditation, bed about 7.30 p.m.[87] The ideal he held before him was one of living for God alone – 'Love of God in Himself, for Himself, sought only in His will, in total surrender'[88] – and he spoke unsurprisingly at the outset of 'the immense relief' of his new life.[89] And yet the evidence suggests that the hermitage also provided a way of coming to terms with Gethsemani. The dichotomy between the ideal that he sought and the reality of his daily life continued. His discontents were focused on the monastery; and the hermitage, which provided the necessary degree of solitude and detachment, served also as the means by which he regularized *on his terms* his relationship with the community.

Merton's life as a hermit was not to be free of anxiety, restlessness, wilful rebellion. How could it be? He remained persuaded of the beauty and the necessity of the solitary life but developments in his thinking served only to strengthen his conviction that 'True solitude is deeply aware of the world's needs.'[90] This meant for him a participation in the torments of humankind: 'The contemplative must assume the universal anguish … The solitary, far from enclosing himself in himself, becomes every man. He dwells in the solitude, the poverty, the indigence of every man.'[91] But what illuminates the depths of solitude and of contemplative prayer is the experience of love: being 'in love with all, with everyone, with everything'.[92]

Merton acknowledged his continuing indebtedness to St John of the Cross. It was in his writings that he found echoes of his own experience in which darkness and light, suffering and joy, sacrifice and love are so closely united with each other that they seem at times to be identical. 'It is not so much that we come through darkness to light, as that the darkness itself is light.'[93] But the end to which solitude, silence and contemplation must move is an awareness of the oneness of all things in love – and in God.[94]

There is no reason to question the integrity of Merton's approach to all these things, but the reality of his life at the hermitage proved to be somewhat different. The demands of his work had left him exhausted long before he was given permission to live full-time at the hermitage. 'I am simply surfeited with words and typescript and print, surfeited to the point of utter nausea. Surfeited with letters, too.'[95] But Merton was unable to do a great deal about it. 'I feel like a drunk and incontinent man falling into bed with another whore, in spite of himself. The awful thing is that I *can't* stop.'[96] When he gave up his responsibilities as Master of the Novices, he was asked by the Abbot to continue giving a conference every Sunday and at the same time to prepare in a matter of weeks a new guide for postulants. Within two months of going to the hermitage he was complaining that his prayer lacked depth, and that reading and writing – fed by 'a kind of intellectual gluttony' – loomed far too large.[97]

Merton failed from the beginning to conform to any stereotype of what a hermit might be. He continued to pursue his literary activities, his wide-ranging correspondence, and his various personal and professional friendships. He could not fail to be aware of what was happening: 'Merely living alone, but continuing to engage in a lot of projects, is not yet an authentic hermit life. The projects must go.'[98] The aspiration was unexceptionable, but there is little reason to believe that it was ever a serious option for Merton.

He needed solitude, but he also needed people. He had complained over the years about the artificiality of community life, but honesty required him to admit that there was something equally artificial and arbitrary about the hermitage. The solitary life mattered, and yet he was aware from the beginning of some loneliness at the hermitage, and his far-too-numerous visitors were all persuaded of his need to see people. An early and most welcome visitor one Sunday evening had been Brother Clement, the cellarer who, acting as Merton expressed it in the noblest tradition of monastic cellarers, brought with him a six-pack of beer. The early months in the hermitage brought visits from Dom Jean Leclercq, the Benedictine scholar with whom Merton had corresponded over many years; Ernesto Cardenal, the Nicaraguan priest and poet who had been in the novitiate under Merton in the late 1950s; Victor and Carolyn Hammer, long-established friends with whom Merton was regularly in touch; Naomi Burton Stone, his literary agent; and Ed Rice, a photographer and writer and long-standing friend from Merton's days at Columbia.

The desire for solitude was genuine, but the hermitage became a cloak for a degree of independence that Merton had not previously achieved. His account of a day in Louisville in December 1965 with Jim Wygal, the psychologist who had also become a friend, provides an intriguing insight into the way in which his mind was beginning to turn. He had visited the University Library, met with Wygal for lunch, and then gone on to his house to watch on television the meeting in space of Gemini 6 and Gemini 7. He records: 'All this I went into as a deliberate exercise of the new "worldliness" – in other words to be able to see these things without defensiveness and criticism, though also without ga-ga optimism. This is the world I live in and I am part of it.'[99] But scarcely a month was to pass before he commented in his *Journal*, 'I see, once again, how muddled and distracted I am. Not free!'[100]

It was about this time – four months into living full-time at the hermitage – that Merton listed in his *Journal* the various physical afflictions that had troubled him over the years.

> An arthritic hip; a case of chronic dermatitis on my hands for a year and a half (so that I have to wear gloves); sinusitis, chronic ever since I came to Kentucky; lungs always showing up some funny shadow or other on ex-rays (though not lately); perpetual diarrhea and a bleeding anus; most of my teeth gone; most of my hair gone; a chewed-up vertebra in my neck which causes my hands to go numb and my shoulder to ache – and for which I sometimes need traction.

This was a sad catalogue for a man who had scarcely turned 50, and he was mindful of the intrusions that these various ailments represented. 'There is no moment any more when I am not *aware* that I have something wrong with me and have to be careful.'[101]

There are repeated references in his *Journals* to ailments and infirmities of one kind or another. The meeting with Dr. Gregory Zilboorg, a psychiatrist, in the summer of 1956 had proved to be unhelpful, and in 1960 Merton had been given permission to go to Louisville to see Dr. James Wygal, a psychologist, for a course of sessions. The professional consultations gave way to a good deal of friendly socializing in later years which Merton thoroughly enjoyed. But students of holistic medicine might want to ask with reference to some of Merton's afflictions: Why did *this* person have *this* condition at *this* time? There was, however, one other condition which was about to overtake Merton: an affair of the heart, which would test to the limit every vocation he had ever espoused.

Falling in love

There are occasional – at times erotic – references in Merton's *Journals* to the feminine and perhaps by inference to the sexual fantasies that delight and torment. He records dreams at one period of a young Jewish girl whom he called 'Proverb' and by whom he was 'embraced with determined and virginal passion'.[102] He enjoyed being with young women and acknowledged the sexual frisson that was most certainly present on some occasions.[103] He had an affectionate but entirely appropriate relationship with Naomi Burton Stone – a long-standing friend, his agent, and in due course one of his literary trustees – about whom he could not fail to acknowledge some degree of ambivalence as he reflected upon 'a curious, somewhat sexual dream'.[104] He undoubtedly regretted the selfishness and the emptiness of his sexual encounters in earlier years[105] and he wrote at one point of 'chastity … [as] my most radical poverty' and of the 'irreparable loss which I have not fully accepted'.[106]

Merton persuaded himself that only solitude could provide the perspective that would enable him to engage with life – critically, compassionately. He identified *discernment* as 'one of the most important virtues of the solitary',[107] but it was discernment that was most conspicuously absent from his relationship with 'M',[108] a student nurse within months of graduation, who was assigned to care for Merton as he recovered in hospital in the last few days of March 1966 after surgery on his back. 'M' remains an unknown person who can only be seen through Merton's eyes. His account of the relationship – and he wrote fully and with great candour – is to be found in his *Journal*, in his *Midsummer Diary*, and in the *Eighteen Poems* he wrote for 'M'. Letters that 'M' wrote to Merton were destroyed by him in August 1968 on the eve of his departure for Asia.

Merton's telling of the story suggests that he and 'M' were both eager to love and to be loved. 'M' was already engaged to a serviceman on active duty in Vietnam, but – while it lasted – the relationship was intense and all consuming. Merton acknowledged that they had become too friendly with each other by the time 'M' left Louisville for her Easter vacation, and admitted that he should have confined himself to a letter or two. The weeks that followed saw a flowering of their relationship: telephone calls, letters, visits, occasional meals, times together, and occasionally several hours alone, assisted by the collusion of a handful of friends. There were moments of tenderness, of delight; times of passion, of ecstasy; periods of self-doubt, of anguish, of anxiety. He wrote in his journal of a determination 'to stay pure, according to our obligations',[109] but he gave himself a good deal of latitude in his interpretation of his vows.

Merton's closest friends responded with varying degrees of approbation, anxiety and foreboding. Ron Seitz, who claimed Merton as the dearest of friends, reckoned that 'what had happened was "all too human" and that he was a better man for it',[110] but this somewhat complacent judgement ought not to stand uncontested. Merton was deeply torn, but what is so disquieting is the way in which he wrote about the relationship *from his point of view*.

> Here is someone who, because I exist, has been made much happier … and revealed to me something I never thought to see so intimately again – the beauty of a girl's heart and of her gift of herself.[111]

> I simply have no business being (in) love and playing around with a girl, however innocently. It is true I do sincerely love her and I know she loves me too, and we do owe each other something – but all in all it is simply a game, a fascinating, pleasurable exciting game that she plays perfectly and I have enjoyed it almost to ecstasy.[112]

Merton subsequently referred to this last passage as 'a shameful evasion',[113] a denial of what he actually felt, but the entry in his *Journal* stands and speaks all too eloquently of a troubled spirit.

It may well be as several commentators have suggested that Merton discovered in this relationship not merely his capacity to give and receive love, but also a greater depth, a greater wholeness. But these observations cannot entirely justify the situation in which Merton found himself. It is not merely that he was twice 'M''s age, that he was a priest, a religious and a hermit. It is far more that he was aware from the outset of her vulnerability. He wrote of her need to 'believe in herself and get free from some destructive patterns and attachments that are likely to wreck her'.[114] It is a judgement to which he returned at a later date: 'She is a mixed up person with many conflicting trends.'[115] Merton had come to believe that his 'response of love to M was *right*',[116] and yet he confided in his *Journal* within a month that 'I am a solitary and that's that. Sure, I love M but [that] can never interfere with my main purpose in life – and that is that. God knows!'[117]

Merton struggled to reconcile the hermit and the lover, the life of solitude and the interludes of intense lovemaking. He tried hard to persuade himself that his love for 'M' – to the degree that it was pure and unselfish – could be part of his love for God, of his self-offering to God.[118] But did he seriously believe that the love represented no denial of his chosen life of solitude? Was it really the case that his love for 'M' could be accommodated without conflict in his interior life of meditation and prayer?

It was Merton's impetuous behaviour that eventually betrayed them, and Dom James, while being entirely firm in his decision that the relationship must end, displayed a kindness and a degree of understanding that took Merton by surprise. But Merton could never surrender the moral high ground to Dom James, and when some weeks later his Superior jested that 'I am thinking of writing a book on how to get hermits into heaven' Merton's anger got the better of his judgement and – without the slightest foundation for any anxiety – retorted 'When the baby is born you can be its godfather.' At least Merton had the grace to comment in his *Journal* 'We are a pair of damned cats.'[119]

It was inevitably a long and tortuous process of detachment, dominated by changing moods, fluctuating and ambivalent feelings. Merton tried to reassure himself that he did not want to hurt 'M' unnecessarily, although his official biographer reached the conclusion that Merton had led 'M' on to believe that there was some possibility of his leaving Gethsemani and marrying her.[120] By the autumn of 1966, he acknowledged that he had behaved at the outset 'like a drunken driver going through every red light'.[121] The contradictions that were exposed by Merton's relationship with 'M' went deep and penetrated all parts of his life. 'M' had been an eager and passionate participant in the unfolding drama, but she had also been caught up unwittingly in all the ambiguities with which Merton was wrestling:

> living as an absurd kind of hermit when I am not really a hermit. Living as a writer when I am not sure I want to write any more, or *what* I want to write, living as someone who is identified as a typical monk when I have the most serious reservations about everything that is going on in the monastic life.[122]

Merton had been struggling from the beginning to make sense of the hermitage. The frequency with which he received visitors, or responded to requests for articles, or took advantage of the hospitality of friends, raises questions about the seriousness of his avowed intention to live in solitude and in silence. He claimed for himself a degree of personal autonomy which was at variance with his vocation, and 'M' was caught in the crossfire of his conflicting needs and aspirations. Perhaps he recognized something of the truth about himself when he wrote in his *Midsummer Diary for 'M'*: 'I just cannot be tied ... I am a wild animal, and I know you know it … I know in fact that you love me for it … You are in love with a fox, or a deer, or a squirrel. Freedom, darling.'[123]

Steering his own course

It was freedom that Merton seemed to renounce most conspicuously when he signed an agreement in September 1966, having completed a year in the hermitage, that he would spend the rest of his life in solitude. Merton was unable to forego the observation that Dom James had countersigned the agreement, 'content that he now had me in the bank as an asset that would not go out and lose itself in some crap game'.[124] The truth of the matter is that his Abbot, in the light of the previous six months, was probably more concerned to save Merton from himself. Certainly there is precious little evidence that the remaining 27 months of Merton's life would see him seriously inhibited by this formal commitment.

Merton struggled with himself and with the community as he attempted to make sense of his life at the hermitage. He tried to recover the priorities that had first taken him to Gethsemani: 'All the old desires, the deep ones, the ones that are truly mine, come back now. Desire of silence, peace, depth, light … I know where my roots really are – in the mystical tradition, not in the active and anxious secular city business.'[125] But these things are not so easily achieved as his words might suggest. His commitment to contemporary social issues, both as a religious and as a writer, continued, together with his ever-growing awareness of the depths to be explored in other religious traditions. He shared something of the fruits of his reading and writing with the increasing numbers who came to his Sunday afternoon conferences, although by the summer of 1967 these informal talks had become something of a chore: 'these performances, these Sunday amusements, entertainments of the bored … Is the fact that "people like them" a good enough reason? I feel the whole business is a bit phoney. I am no longer in touch with the community or very much in sympathy with it.'[126]

But it was not only the inadequacies of life at Gethsemani that oppressed him. A spirit of helplessness surfaced from time to time as he reflected upon a sense of decay in society in general, in the church and in the monastery. He looked with distaste at 'the gasping of a culture that is rotting in its own garbage', and yet he could add without a moment's hesitation: 'I know, all this is too pessi-mistic – I am trying to salvage something in myself by saying "I am not that, at least!" Yet I am part of it – and I must try to bring life back into it, along with the others.'[127]

In July 1967 he was permitted to say Mass at the hermitage for the first time and to prepare his own food. It meant that his links with the community became increasingly tenuous. Dom James continued to resist attempts to secure his presence at various external engagements, but Merton was well able to find his own diversions, and he acknowledged that he was failing to achieve what he had hoped for from the hermitage. 'I am careless, untrue to myself, undisciplined, free with the wrong kind of freedom, drink and talk too much.'[128]

It was at this period of his life that Merton found so much delight and self-expression in photography, in calligraphy, in the music of Joan Baez and Bob Dylan, and – his old love – in jazz. He complained from time to time of the visitors, invited or uninvited, who came to see him at the hermitage, but his increasingly frequent visits to Louisville, especially to see the doctors, gave him the necessary cover to meet with friends. Frank and Thomasine (Tommie) O'Callaghan and their young children provided him with the home and family scene he had never known; other friends – Thompson and Virginia Willett, Jim Wygal and James Laughlin – entertained him at home, or at the Pendennis Club, or at the Embassy Club. Merton delighted in picnics with friends in the monastery grounds, and even more so in his occasional visits to hear jazz in Louisville. Few people enjoyed more than Merton the times when he could break out in thoroughly self-indulgent ways: friends, picnics, drink, jazz, the right kind of conversation.

But questions remain. Was Merton using the freedom of the hermitage to distance himself from Gethsemani and from the constraints of the religious life? Was he merely taking from life the things he wanted? Was he making up for lost time? Had his vocation run its course? Or could it be that his God-given humanity was merely imposing itself upon his chosen calling? There were certainly occasions when his sociability got the better of his judgement, and his extended visits to town unquestionably went far beyond the letter and the spirit of his vocation, but he was aware of the artificiality of so much that he encountered. 'The quiet of the hermitage is good. The sound of the jazz was good. In between – a vast morass of nonsense, babble, riding, talking, pretending.'[129] The feeling of being torn, of being compromised, remained: 'I have a sense of untruth and ambiguity in all my "social" existence, from my conferences in the monastery to visits with people from outside.'[130]

Dom James's decision to stand down as Superior in January 1968 took Merton by surprise. He did not know how his brothers would vote in the ensuing election and, completely misreading the mind and the mood of the community, he issued a statement – 'MY CAMPAIGN PLATFORM for non-Abbot and permanent keeper of the present doghouse' – in which he made it plain that he would not be a candidate. Merton's facetious attempt at humour served only to alienate the community. He acknowledged that he was ill equipped 'to spend the rest of my life arguing about trivialities with 125 slightly confused and anxiety ridden monks … You would probably be voting for me on the grounds that I would grant you plenty of beer. Well I would, but it takes more than that to make a good Abbot.'[131] In the event, Merton was delighted by the election of Dom Flavian Burns, a former student from his time as Master of the Scholastics, who had been testing his vocation to the eremitical life since 1966. It symbolized for Merton a break with the past, a rejection of all that Dom James had represented. He saw Dom Flavian as 'a man we can talk to, work with frankly, exchange ideas with, propose real experiments to'.[132]

Dom Flavian's election brought to the forefront of Merton's mind the hope that he might be allowed to travel. There had only been three official journeys outside the monastery during his years at Gethsemani,[133] but Merton responded with a good deal of enthusiasm to journeys to California and New Mexico in May 1968. He had been allowed to conduct a series of conferences for the Trappist nuns at Our Lady of the Redwoods, at Whitehorn in California, but he had also been asked by Dom Flavian to explore the possibility of a hermitage on some isolated part of the Californian coast. It was for Merton a voyage of exploration, having been set free from the institutional constraints of the last 26 years. He was able to look at the world with new eyes and explore new places, new possibilities. He had been troubled by the contradictions of the life he was living prior to his visit, but the meaning of what he had found in California remained, and he saw, although not for the first time, the need for serious adjustment.

It was the Asian journey in the autumn of 1968 that brought together for Merton so many of the things he had been feeling after over so many years. He had been invited to attend a meeting of Asian abbots that was scheduled to take place in Bangkok in December 1968. But Dom Flavian was clearly open to other possibilities for Merton: time in California and Alaska – to be quiet, to lead retreats and conferences, and to consider places for a new foundation of hermitages; but also time in the course of an extended tour of the Far East to visit some Buddhist centres. Merton responded with unrestrained happiness: 'It is so utterly new to have an abbot here who is completely open to new possibilities! ... Here I am suddenly on the edge of something totally new, completely unplanned and unforeseen.'[134]

Merton went with an open mind. His concern was 'to enjoy the long journey, profit by it, learn, change, and perhaps find something or someone who will help me advance in my own spiritual quest'.[135] Questions concerning Gethsemani could be put on hold: 'I am not starting out with a firm plan never to return or with an absolute determination to return at all costs. I do feel there is not much for me here at the moment and that I need to be open to lots of new possibilities.'[136] Merton was still seeking, still journeying.

His travels took him initially to New Mexico, California, Alaska and Chicago; but then, leaving the United States on the 15th of October 1968, he went to Thailand (Bangkok), to India (Calcutta, New Delhi, the Himalayas, Madras), to Ceylon or Sri Lanka (Colombo, Kandy, Polonnaruwa), to Singapore, and finally back to Thailand for the conference in Bangkok. His journal, his poems and the posthumously published *Asian Journal* provide all that could be asked for: gloriously evocative accounts of all that he saw, the people whom he met, the conversations that took place, the books he read, the ideas he explored, the priorities in his thinking.

Merton had prepared in advance the various papers he would give at different times, although he invariably departed from the text. The Temple of Understanding Conference in South Calcutta a week after his leaving the United States took as its theme 'The Relevance of Religion in the Modern World'. Merton took his place as a speaker alongside rabbis from New York and Jerusalem, Chinese scholars from Taiwan, Sufis and Jains – representatives of ten world religions in all – who met over four days. Merton returned to his familiar theme of the monk as a marginal person, sharing with poets and hippies the vocation to be irrelevant so that they might see the world from a different perspective. He shared his anxieties concerning monasticism in the Western and Christian world, urging his brothers in the East to keep faith with their ancient traditions of monasticism and contemplative wisdom.[137]

Life opened up for Merton in these final weeks of his life, but it was above all the conversations that were so important: the discussions with Buddhist monks in Thailand; the conversations with Amiya Chakravarty, the Indian philosopher and poet with whom Merton had corresponded in recent years; the chance meeting in Calcutta with Chogyam Trungpa Rimpoche, one of the

exiled lamas from Tibet; and above all his three interviews with the Dalai Lama
at Dharamsala. The religious culture of the East, with its traditions of mysticism,
contemplative prayer and monasticism, was reaching into the heart of Merton's
vocations as a religious, as a priest, as a hermit and as a human being. His visits
to Mahabalipuram (in India) and Polonnaruwa (in Ceylon) led him to conclude
that

> … my Asian pilgrimage has come clear … I know and have seen what I was obscurely
> looking for. I don't know what else remains but I … have got beyond the shadow and
> the disguise. This is Asia in its purity … It says everything; it needs nothing. And
> because it needs nothing it can afford to be silent, unnoticed, undiscovered.[138]

There was a coming together in Merton's mind of the Christian mysticism of
Western Europe in the medieval world and the age-old contemplative wisdom
of Asia. He was mindful of the pitfalls inseparable from the journey he had
undertaken: 'Too much movement. Too much "looking for" something: an
answer, a vision, "something other".'[139] His discussions with the Dalai Lama led
him to reflect again on the contemplative life as 'a space of liberty, of silence, in
which possibilities are allowed to surface and new choices … become manifest',
but implicit in his awareness of the possibilities was an openness to others in
what he called '*compassionate* time'.[140] It was an exposition of the contemplative
life, and yet it was something more: a confession – almost a joyful celebration –
of all that he had been seeking during the long years at Gethsemani.

Merton brought with him to Asia a determination to enter wholeheartedly
into every experience, every encounter. What he found confirmed his Christian
faith, and his reflections upon the meaning of what he saw and heard served
only to emphasize his continuing indebtedness to the mystics of the later middle
ages with their understanding of darkness and light, of being and non-being.
One reflection – was it a dream? a meditation? – required him to explore the
three doors which are one door: the door of emptiness, the door without sign,
and the door without wish. It was this third door – 'The unplanned door. The
door never expected. Never wanted' – through which Merton was required
to enter.[141]

Merton's intention had been to go on after the Bangkok conference to
Indonesia and to Lantao Island, Hong Kong, and he had already raised the
possibility of extending his tour so that he could visit monastic communities
in several parts of Europe. Gethsemani remained an open question: 'Though I

fully appreciate the many advantages of the hermitage at Gethsemani, I still have the feeling that the lack of quiet and the general turbulence there, external and internal, last summer are indications that I ought to move'. And yet there was a renewed commitment: 'I do not think I ought to separate myself completely from Gethsemani ... I suppose I ought eventually to end my days there ... There is no problem of my simply wanting to "leave Gethsemani". It is my monastery and being away has helped me see it in perspective and love it more.'[142]

Merton travelled to Bangkok for the AIM (Aide à l'Implantation Monastique) Conference on 8 December. This had been organized by abbots of Benedictine communities and drew a fair number of people, including 36 priest monks from every part of Asia. Merton's paper on 'Marxist and Monastic Perspectives' was given on the morning of 10 December and at the end he remarked with characteristic informality, 'So I will disappear from view and we can all have a Coke or something. Thank you very much.'[143]

There was a Mass at 12 noon and Merton then retired to his room after lunch, where his body was found a few hours later. He had apparently taken a shower and had probably slipped or suffered a heart attack and in the fall had pulled a faulty electric fan on to him. The precise circumstances in which he died could not be established, although the cause of death was electrocution and heart failure. Questions have inevitably been asked, but Merton's official biographer was persuaded that 'the evidence still speaks overwhelmingly of an accidental death'.[144] Merton had died on 10 December, the 27th anniversary of his arrival at Gethsemani seeking admission. His body was returned to Gethsemani and the funeral ceremonies, together with his burial in the monastic enclosure, took place on 17 December. The ever-searching, provocative, independent-minded and yet obedient son of Gethsemani had returned home.

Merton had long since believed that he would die at a relatively early age. 1967 had seen the death of three friends,[145] and 1968 had begun badly for him with the death of Sy Freedgood, one of his closest friends from the Columbia years. Merton had observed at the time 'It is already a hard year, but I have a feeling it is going to be hard all the way and for everybody.'[146] The year had seen the assassinations of Martin Luther King in April and Robert Kennedy in June. Merton saw their deaths as further indications of the tragic despair that possessed the country. It's easy to go back and, in the light of events, read some deep meaning into what were serious, or half-serious, or scarcely fully formed reflections. As he left the United States for Bangkok in mid-October, Merton had written 'I am going home, to the home where I have never been in this body';[147] and – perhaps more presciently – in recounting his conversation with Chatral Rimpoche in Calcutta in mid-November, he had spoken of 'our complete understanding of each other as people who were somehow *on the edge* of great realization and knew it and were trying, somehow or other, to go out and get lost in it'.[148]

Few words capture more succinctly all that Merton had been feeling after throughout his adult life: the fundamental mystery of God; self-abandonment; pressing at the boundaries of knowing and not knowing; the glad anticipation of all that might be. The Asian journey had set the seal on the questions that had excited and tormented him for so long. It is impossible to say what might have happened if he had returned from the Far East. His life and his vocation had run their course. His experience at first hand of the wisdom and the holiness of Asia had enriched all that he had lived for. Twenty years before, he had concluded *The Seven Storey Mountain* with words that captured all that might now be said. He had tasted the solitude of God's anguish and God's poverty, he had been led into the high places of God's joy, and it remained only for him to die in God and find all things in His Mercy.[149]

The Writer

I am less and less aware of myself simply as this individual who is a monk and a writer, and who as monk and writer, sees this or writes that. It is my task to see and speak for many, even when I seem to be speaking only for myself.[1]

It is the perennial task of all artists to see and speak for many, even when it might appear to them that they speak only for themselves. Merton was the child of artists and he brought to his work as a writer the awareness, the vulnerability and the compulsion of all true artists. But there was an additional ingredient: Merton had been identified at the end of his student years at Columbia University as a writer who was 'aware of the living present and all it may hold of pain and purpose'.[2] This was a surprisingly apposite statement and it captured the quality that is most discernible in his writing as it developed over the years within the austere framework of his monastic calling.

Merton had good reason to reflect at various times upon his vocations as a monk, a writer and a contemplative. The element of self-doubt was never far away, but he was ever mindful of the necessity of his work as a writer. He might live with questions concerning the monastic life to which he had committed himself; he had no questions about his vocation as a writer.[3] But writing is a solitary vocation, and it might well be inferred that it was through his writing that Merton pursued from his earliest years the solitude that he required. Solitude represented for him a deeper awareness of the present and, as he negotiated his way through the frustrations and the discontents, so he came to see that the religious life enabled him 'to live fully and completely in the present, praying when I pray, and writing and praying when I write'.[4]

Merton was troubled at times by the thought that his writing was merely an exercise in self-absorption. He was undoubtedly a man who needed to write – addiction was his word, on one occasion – and he was clearly best able to think things through when he was writing about them. But in the midst of the self-doubt, the weariness and the complaints about censors and superiors, there was his need to find a proper degree of freedom and personal responsibility for the development of his monastic life and his writing. It might be a step too far to say that he achieved wholeness through his writing, but he was able to grow beyond a journey of self-discovery into a robust and compassionate exploration of the questions and the torments of his world.

Merton came to see that true art – like contemplation – is inseparable from life, and that the poet, like the mystic, requires a prophetic intuition. It is in all these areas – the inter-relatedness of his vocations, the journey beyond himself, the prophetic intuition – that Merton's fascination as a writer is to be found. And yet for Merton writing was required to serve one other end: 'My typewriter is an essential factor in my asceticism.'[5] Writing was a necessary part of his vocation to holiness.

Early writings

Something of Merton's early ambition to write can be seen during his years as a boy at Oakham and as a student at Columbia. At Oakham, he had edited the school magazine and contributed short stories, poems and drawings. At Columbia, he was the Art Editor of *The Jester* for one year and more than 30 issues included stories and cartoons he had submitted. He went on to edit the Year Book for 1937, and by the late 1930s was writing book reviews for *The New York Herald Tribune* and *The New York Times*. He was increasingly seen as someone who would go on to write and be published, although attempts to secure publishers for four early novels[6] were unsuccessful. By the end of his time at Columbia he had abandoned earlier thoughts of a career in journalism. His ambition now was to be 'a writer, a poet, a critic, a professor'.[7]

Columbia had been a new beginning for Merton. He became part of a small group of teachers and fellow students – Mark van Doren, Daniel Walsh, Robert Lax, Edward Rice, Seymour Freedgood, Robert Gibney, Robert Giroux, John Berryman and Ad Reinhardt – who were to be influential in the development of his vocations as monk and writer. It is certainly the case that the writing of poetry took on a new significance after his conversion, and he was guided in that – as in other things – by Mark van Doren, even though he failed at the time to find a publisher for his poems.

During the time when Merton was teaching at the Columbia Extension School and St Bonaventure (1939–41), he was looking for a way in which he could combine a life devoted to God with his writing. But his religious vocation was running apace and by December 1941, with the prospect of a second medical examination for the Draft Board and the very serious possibility of military service or non-combatant duties in the armed forces confronting him, Merton brought forward by several days his decision to go to Gethsemani. He confined to the incinerator the manuscripts of three finished and one half-finished novels; he retained and despatched to Mark van Doren the poems he had written, the carbon copy of his most recent novel, *The Journal of My Escape from the Nazis*,[8] and a journal – presumably the *Perry Street Journal* or the *Cuban Interlude* – together with some material for an anthology of religious verse; he sent other papers to Robert Lax and Edward Rice.

Merton therefore brought with him to Gethsemani his vocations as a monk and a writer. He was a young man who had found God and who was embracing the life of a Trappist with all the deprivations for which Cistercians of the Strict Observance were renowned. He had come to see Gethsemani as the place where he could surrender everything, but in his writing, in so far as it might be permitted, he was determined to explore the depths within himself. It would never be sufficient for him merely to observe and to relate. He had the eye and the ear, the instinct and the intuition, of an artist. He knew that words have an integrity, a vitality, and he was beginning in his life and in his writing to plumb the depths of God. He saw the writer as a craftsman, but for him the ability to write was far more than a matter of technique, of application. It was a virtue 'nourished, and infused and entertained by God'.[9]

Merton's potential as a writer was recognized from the beginning of his time at Gethsemani. Trappist houses had not always been sympathetic to writers, and Merton acknowledged that 'An author in a Trappist monastery is like a duck in a chicken coop. And he would give anything in the world to be a chicken instead of a duck.'[10] Dom Frederic Dunne, his first Abbot, encouraged Merton to continue with the writing of poetry, and three collections – *Thirty Poems* (1944), *A Man in the Divided Sea* (1946) and *Figures for an Apocalypse* (1947) – appeared before he had made Solemn Profession in March 1947. Meanwhile Merton, with his great competence in languages, was being used by his Superiors to translate into English various Latin and French books on Cistercian spirituality and he was also beginning – over and above his spiritual autobiography – to write a range of books relating to Cistercian life, Gethsemani and contemplative prayer. The manuscript of *The Seven Storey Mountain* had been sent to his literary agent as early as October 1946, and whatever encouragement he had received at Gethsemani to persevere with writing – from the Abbot, the Novice Master and his confessors – was confirmed by the Abbot General, who told Merton that it was entirely right for him to continue writing.

Dom Frederic had been at pains to suggest to Merton that his writing should not interfere with his life of prayer. On the contrary, 'it demanded a life of more intimate union with God'.[11] Merton's feelings fluctuated a good deal. He saw only too clearly the contradiction between what he wrote about contemplative prayer and the way he lived. 'It seems to me to be a great indecency for me to pass in the opinion of men as one who thinks he knows something about contemplation. The thing makes me feel as if I needed a bath and a change of clothing.'[12] It was the voice of the solitary or the would-be solitary trying to secure a hearing. But Merton understood the truth of the situation: 'It is not much fun to live the spiritual life with the spiritual equipment of an artist.'[13] If it is the case that the artist is one who is compelled to look beyond the constraints of convention, to make new and unexpected connections, to explore the hidden depths, then Merton, confined within the monastic enclosure, had no need to wonder 'why I read so much, why I write so much, why I talk so much, and why I get too excited about the things that only affect the surface of my life'.[14] There were certainly times when it felt as though he had learned nothing during these formative years; yet he could bounce back and assert that 'my work is my hermitage because it is *writing* that helps me most of all to be a solitary and a contemplative here at Gethsemani'.[15]

Merton had been allowed to use the community's rare book vault for his writing from the beginning of 1949, but insisted that prayer was his first priority and that everything else, including writing, was accidental. He wrote – as he himself acknowledged – because writing was in his blood, but there were depths in him that cried out for solitude, for the freedom and the silence of the woods, and it was there that he found the meaning of what he attempted to say in his writing.

The weariness Merton was experiencing went far beyond the volume of work to which he was committed. He remained convinced of the rightness of his vocation as a writer, but the consequences – administrative and pastoral – left him feeling exhausted. 'I believe God wants me to write *something*, but to be always up to my neck in censors and contracts and royalties and letters all around the world and reviews and correspondence with my dear readers … I don't know.'[16] He had been more than a little troubled by the strictures of the censors regarding *The Seven Storey Mountain*: too much self-exposure (drink and sex) and, even more unhappily, negative comments about his ability to write. He had been unprepared for the sheer quantity of fan mail that followed the publication of his autobiography: 'I knew I would have crosses, but I never expected that one of the biggest would be mail. I am getting something like seven to ten letters a day.'[17] There were also the rumours, although in Merton's case they seemed to be more a matter for wry smiles than another burden to be borne: 'As soon as a religious writes a book and gets it published the rumor starts traveling around: "He has left the monastery, you know."'[18]

The range and the quantity of Merton's writing over so many years could easily give the impression that words simply poured out of him, but this was not invariably so and he admitted that his preparatory work, while stimulating, could also be very laborious. He read widely; he made extensive notes which he kept beside him in a large number of notebooks; but he could then find himself terrified by the many ways in which his material could be brought together, even before – having completed the writing – he undertook wide-ranging revisions.

The situation was exacerbated for Merton by the awareness that in his early years at Gethsemani he had written too readily in the way he thought a monk was expected to write. An early casualty of this period of transition was *The Cloud and the Fire*, which was eventually published in 1951 as *The Ascent to Truth*. The book attempted to provide an introduction to the writings of St John of the Cross, and it was a subject therefore with which Merton should have been very comfortable, but his assessment of what he was doing makes sombre reading:

> I had been worrying and bothering for two months about being unable to get anywhere with this new book … There were some forty pages of it, written mostly in blood … And they were terrible. Great confusion. Too long-winded, involved, badly written, badly thought out and with great torture, too.[19]

But the aspiring novelist and poet of the Columbia years were giving place gradually to the mature writer who, in the space of little more than a decade, would establish an international reputation as biographer, historian, diarist, essayist, poet, correspondent, translator, spiritual writer, social commentator and critic.

The journals

There are five distinct types of literary activity to which the student of Merton's writings must turn: his journals, his letters, his books, his articles and mimeographs, and his poems. The journals, the letters and the poems have been brought together – or very largely brought together – in comprehensive editions of his work, but the desire to track down everything he wrote continues. These are the archives where it is possible to find the man and the monk, the conversationalist and the contemplative, the lover and the hermit, the campaigner and the man of prayer, the social critic and the ecumenist. They are also the archives where it is possible to trace the developments in his thinking, the transitions he was required to make as he rediscovered himself and the world around him, the continual reaching out for new horizons, and the endless search for God.

Merton's *Journals*, brought together in seven volumes and published between 1995 and 1998, cover a period of nearly 30 years. Extracts from some of these journals appear in one form or another in several other books published during his lifetime or since his death. The journals tell of his day to day life; his changing moods; the individuals who impinged upon him at one time or another; his reading, his thoughts, his ideas; the questions that clamoured for attention; his writing; the frustrations, the discontents; the endless self-questioning, self-criticism; the ebullience, the irreverence, the humanity.

Some two years before he entered Gethsemani, Merton wrote 'Journals take for granted that every day in our life there is something new and important.'[20] Certainly, he poured himself into his journals. They served as diary, as spiritual journal, as therapist's couch, as confessional. As a literary genre, they possess immense versatility. Allowances have to be made for judgements that should not always be taken at face value: for his capacity to over-simplify, to dramatize, to lose all sense of proportion, to denigrate himself and others. What they reveal, however, is a man who is endlessly fascinating: thoughtful, passionate, frivolous, provocative, restless, a bundle of contradictions, but someone who returned time and again to the things that had first taken him to Gethsemani.

Merton's journals provide ample evidence of his descriptive powers as a writer. He brought a clear eye to all that he observed, but he was also well able to turn the spotlight upon himself and the traumas that afflicted him. The community at Gethsemani became all too often the focus of the anguish he felt, and his personal anxieties became symptomatic of wider concerns. He was well aware of the contradictions with which he wrestled, but his vocation as a religious was always at the forefront of his mind, even as he addressed the political and social issues of the day. His position could not be one of neutrality, and nor could it ever permit complaisance or collusion. The concern of much of his writing in the 1960s was his critique of power, together with an overriding anxiety concerning the possibility of nuclear war. As the United States threatened to tear itself apart over the question of racial justice and as the war in Vietnam pursued its course, Merton feared for a world that was out of control and possibly on the brink of unparalleled disaster.

It was no small part of the freedom that Merton claimed for himself in the pursuit of his vocations that he should have become so open in his later years to the insights of the other great world religions. But Merton had no illusions about the hard realities of the contemporary scene. For men and women of faith, Christian and non-Christian faith, the world had become an uncomfortable place: 'We must adjust our attitude … In the west we are in the post-Christian age – and all over the world it will soon be the same. The religions will be for the minority. The world as a whole is going to be not pagan but irreligious.'[21] For Merton, writing as a Christian, the inescapable vocation to be exiles or aliens served only to strengthen his commitment to Christ and his dependence upon the message of the Gospel.

The self-abandonment that had been there at the outset remained: 'To be open to the nothingness which I am is to grasp the all, in whom I am.'[22] He returned constantly to the times of quiet recollection, of waiting upon God, of losing himself in God: 'God, my God, God whom I meet in the darkness, with You it is always the same thing! Always the same question that nobody knows how to answer.'[23] The questions continued until the day he died, but, as he wrestled with the discontents that haunted him throughout his years at Gethsemani, he did not fail to ask himself the important question: 'I have found myself a very good cross. Question: just because a cross is a cross, is it the one God wants for you?'[24]

It was when he checked the galley proofs for *The Secular Journal* in the late summer of 1958 that Merton came to feel that his best writing had always been in his journals. Extracts indicate the quality and the concerns of much of the writing, but they also reveal the character of the man: reflective, good-humoured, searching, at times tortured, and yet alive with a love for God. An earlier judgement, based upon a reading of his journal entries, had left him embarrassed and apologetic: 'I am wondering what I thought I was talking about. The first thing that impresses me is that practically all I wrote about myself and my trials was stupid because I was trying to express what I thought I *ought* to think … rather than what I actually did think.'[25]

Merton knew at an early stage that his journals would eventually be published and yet he was determined that they should tell the whole story. Nothing is more illuminating than the approach he adopted to those sections of his journals which concerned his relationship with 'M'. He was entirely clear in his own mind that the affair was an important part of his story, demonstrating his loneliness, his need for love, the inner conflict, and the predicament in which solitude was both a solution and a problem.[26]

It is in the journals that Merton makes himself so readily available. But what was the compulsion that required him to write so much about himself? Was it an endless journey of self-discovery that he was embarked upon? Did he write in order to find himself, to contain himself, even perhaps to learn to grow beyond himself? Did he write for himself alone, or is it the case that he wrote *from his earliest years* with an eye to publication? An entry in December 1940 is explicit: 'Why would I write anything, if not to be read? This journal is written for publication. It is about time I realized that, and wrote it with some art.'[27]

Although the traditions of the Cistercian Order were not sympathetic to the idea of publishing personal journals, Dom James had encouraged Merton to continue with his writing. He recognized Merton's literary temperament and feared that to deny him the outlets he needed might precipitate some mental disturbance,[28] and yet he expressed to Sister Thérèse Lentfoehr, one of Merton's closest confidants, the anxiety that in the keeping and the publishing of a journal 'there is so much, necessarily and unavoidably of the I, I, I …'[29]

Merton might pursue the question 'Who is this self?' and go on to propose his own justification for the writing of a journal – 'to keep honestly situated'[30] – but once the idea of publication has taken root in the mind of a writer, the exercise takes on a different character. There is an editorial footnote in the second volume of Merton's *Journals* which is pertinent. Merton had written to Naomi Burton Stone to tell her he was working on a journal for publication. The editor suggests that from that date 'Merton's journals are becoming artifacts of conscious self-presentation for a future audience'; and he infers that thereafter 'Merton begins blurring any line that might have previously existed between his journals as spontaneous diaries of remembrance and as conscious, semi-fictional reconstructions of the self, autobiography as a work of art.'[31] It is a cautionary footnote. The extent to which Merton kept everything – journals, copies of letters and drafts of articles – lends substance to any suggestion that

Merton was not merely writing for himself. One of his brothers at Gethsemani, reflecting on Merton's response to the establishment of the Thomas Merton Room at Bellarmine College in the early 1960s, spoke of being 'just a little taken aback that [Merton] felt that everything he wrote was significant'.[32] But why should a writer not keep everything? It is entirely proper for a writer to write for others. Yet a question remains when consideration is given to the story of a man who chooses a life of withdrawal, silence and solitude, and who then writes so compulsively and so extensively *about himself*.

The letters

Second only in importance to the *Journals* in any understanding of Merton are the letters he wrote to a very large number of correspondents all over the world. A credible estimate is that he wrote something like 10,000 letters[33] to more than 2,000 correspondents in the course of 20 years. The initial constraint on the writing of letters was relaxed for Merton as his publications generated correspondence that had to be attended to, and in his final years at Gethsemani there were no serious inhibitions as he struggled to maintain a wide-ranging and exhausting correspondence. Like the journals, his letters enabled him to write – at least during the last decade of his life – unsupervised and uninhibited by the censors.

A letter is an encounter between two individuals. It is personal, direct, immediate. It will often have a context – a background of friendship, of experience, of common concerns, of shared ideals. It can provide an opportunity for the free exchange of thoughts and ideas, and in so far as it invites a response, there is an openness, an incompleteness about a letter. What a good letter can never conceal is the personality of the writer. The General Editor of Merton's *Letters*, while speaking of Merton's ability to address issues of substance and to do so with a telling phrase and an ever-ready wit, writes also of 'the impish smile that lights up so many of his photographs [looking] out through the letters, too'.[34]

Merton complained at regular intervals that he received far too many letters, that the burden of correspondence was oppressive. The letters were none the less the means whereby he maintained and – from time to time – initiated friendships. Letters meant a great deal to him. They were his lifeline to the outside world. But was there another consideration? Sister Thérèse Lentfoehr, who typed manuscripts for Merton, accumulated in the course of her life a large collection of Merton's papers. Her typing of his manuscripts enabled Merton to correspond with her with very great frequency and to use her as an outlet for letters which would not otherwise have been permitted. It is once again an editorial comment that,

> Another factor in their long and voluminous correspondence may be that Merton was aware that these letters would be preserved. He may not have been sure that other correspondents kept or would keep his letters, but he *knew* that Sister Thérèse kept every page, every sheet, every scrap that issued from his hand or typewriter. These letters in fact became an alternate form of journal keeping for Merton, another facet of the autobiographical exercise in which he was continually engaged.[35]

Evelyn Waugh, who prepared *The Seven Storey Mountain* for publication in the United Kingdom in a revised and abridged form in the late 1940s under the title *Elected Silence*, encouraged Merton to confine himself to correspondence. It was an early acknowledgement of a young writer's potential as a letter writer, and one that has been more than justified by the scope and content of his correspondence. Michael Mott judged Merton to be 'one of the few great letter writers' of the twentieth century.[36] His volume of correspondence trebled, and perhaps at times quadrupled, between the late 1940s and the years immediately prior to his death. He had his fair share of bread-and-butter letters: dealing with publishers and literary agents, refusing invitations to speak at conferences or workshops, ignoring wherever possible letters that he judged to be from fanatics. But his friends, together with an increasingly large circle of religious, literary and serious-minded colleagues and contemporaries, provided him with an arena in which he could engage with all his literary skills. What is revealed in his letters is a multi-faceted personality: intimate, serious, passionate, penetrating, bubbling with ideas, light-hearted, witty.

A very large number of Merton's letters, published in five volumes between 1985 and 1994, have been grouped together in broad categories: letters on religious experience and social issues; letters to new and old friends; letters on religious renewal and spiritual direction; letters to writers; and letters in times of crisis. The letters to be found in these volumes have also been reproduced (in some instances) and complemented (in others) in several publications which bring together the two-way exchange of letters between Merton and individual writers, including among others Boris Pasternak, the Russian writer and dissident;[37] Robert Lax, a friend from Columbia days and a freelance writer;[38] Wilbur H. Ferry, the Vice-President of the Center for the Study of Democratic Institutions at Santa Barbara, California;[39] Daisetz Suzuki, a Zen scholar;[40] Rosemary Radford Ruether, a theologian who was deeply involved in urban churches working on issues of poverty, racism and militarism;[41] James Laughlin, publisher and friend;[42] Czesław Miłosz, poet, Nobel Prize winner and a former resistance fighter in Poland in the Second World War;[43] and Jean Leclercq, the Benedictine scholar.[44] And subsumed in these various collections are not only some of the mimeographed letters which, for the sake of convenience, Merton sent to various friends in the 1960s, but also – and far more importantly – the Cold War Letters,[45] written between October 1961 and October 1962, mimeographed and distributed privately among friends in order to escape the ever-watchful eye of the censors of the Cistercian Order, in which Merton shared his thoughts on questions of war and peace.

Some indication of the character and diversity of Merton's correspondence can be found, by way of example, in his initial approach to Boris Pasternak; in Rosemary Radford Ruether's observation on the exchange of letters she maintained with Merton over a period of 18 months; in an editorial comment on the correspondence that passed between Merton and Czesław Miłosz; in Merton's last letter to Jean Leclercq in which he encapsulates in two short sentences the vocation of the religious in the modern world; and – not to be overlooked – in the playful, zany letters that Merton and Robert Lax exchanged with each other.

Merton, prompted by his reading of Pasternak's autobiography, wrote in August 1958: 'With other writers I can share ideas, but you seem to communicate something deeper. It is as if we met on a deeper level of life on which individuals are not separate beings. In the language familiar to me as a Catholic monk, it is as if we were known to one another in God.'[46] It is a passage which speaks eloquently of the spirituality of the writer and which places the correspondence on an elevated plane from the beginning.

Merton's exchange of letters with Rosemary Radford Ruether between August 1966 and February 1968 was a robust, no-holds-barred correspondence. Ruether, who had initiated the correspondence, challenged Merton, albeit without success, to reconsider his monastic life and to find his vocation in the world. She likened Merton and herself to 'two ships that happened to pass each other on our respective journeys. For a brief moment we turned our search lights on each other with blazing intensity. Then, when we sensed that we were indeed going in different directions, we began to pass each other by.'[47]

The exchange of letters with Czesław Miłosz – 40 letters during the last decade of Merton's life – touched upon the large questions of the day, but they spoke also of a shared commitment to religious faith in a troubled world. An editorial comment speaks of 'a dialogue between two powerful voices seeking to maintain faith in some of the most turbulent years of the late twentieth century. They recognized totalitarianism, scientism, atomic war, and racism as among the greatest threats to mankind's ability to sustain belief in a just God and in Providence.'[48]

The correspondence between Merton and Jean Leclercq continued over 20 years. Their letters went beyond early preoccupations with monastic texts to some of the large questions that both men were concerned to address: the place of the monk in the modern world, ecumenism, and the possibility of dialogue with the non-Christian traditions of monasticism in the Far East. But it was Merton, writing what was to be his last letter to Leclercq, who expressed so succinctly their common understanding of the monastic vocation: 'Those who question the structures of contemporary society at least look to monks for a certain distance and critical perspective ... The vocation of the monk in the modern world ... is not survival but prophecy.'[49]

If Merton's initial approach to Pasternak was marked by grace and sensitivity, if the exchanges with Ruether were mutually respectful but hard-hitting, if the correspondence with Miłosz displayed a shared commitment to faith in uncertain times, if the letters that passed between Merton and Leclercq derived from their mutual concern to see a renewal of monasticism on the basis of prophetic witness, it is also important to take account of the entirely different character of the letters that passed between Merton and Robert Lax. When Prophecy Still Had A Voice consists of 346 letters between June 1938 and December 1968. They touch on all the concerns to be found in other correspondence – world events, the banalities of modern life, their spiritual journeys – but the concern in the earliest letters to talk about friends and books and writing projects is never lost. They wrote as old friends, intimate friends. They played with words. They sat lightly – if the fancy took them – to spelling, grammar, syntax. They resorted to puns, to double-talk, to allusions, to avant-garde poetry. 'Friends in a playful mood' is one description of a volume of their later letters, A Catch of Anti-Letters, and Merton and Lax, comfortable with each other, make it possible to see Merton as the monk who is perennially boyish.

Beyond the many concerns to be found in his correspondence, there is the central theme to which Merton constantly returned: his vocations as a religious, as a contemplative. A letter to Sister Emmanuel, a Brazilian nun, in January 1962, spoke of the role of the Christian contemplative in attempting to discern God's working in history: 'I think at least some contemplatives must try to understand the providential events of the day. God works in history, therefore a contemplative who has no sense of history, no sense of historical responsibility, is not a fully Christian contemplative.'[50]

But Merton's prophetic awareness went beyond the confines of his Christian faith and enabled him to hold together his social concerns within a wider ecumenical vision. In a letter to Dona Luisa Coomaraswamy, who was actively compiling a collection of her late husband's writings on Hinduism and Buddhism, Merton shared his conviction that the task of men and women of faith – in so far as they are able to unite in themselves the great spiritual traditions of humankind – is to move life forward in the direction of world peace. It was not something that would always be understood or valued, but it was none the less a pioneering work undertaken by men and women whose lives are signs or sacraments of peace.[51]

The books

It is, however, through his books that Merton is best known and judged to be one of the great spiritual writers – even, perhaps, one of the prophetic voices – of the twentieth century. Like his journals and his letters, his books demonstrate his evolution as a man, a monk and a writer. The compulsion to write remained to the end, and it was there – in all his writings – that Merton engaged with himself, with the world and with God. He knew that 'The work of writing can be for me, or very close to, the simple job of *being*.' It was the means whereby he might 'pay [his] debt to life, to the world, to other men.'[52]

Merton's published works include pamphlets, illustrated booklets and extended essays as well as far more substantial pieces of writing. Essays which have served a particular purpose – an article for a journal, a conference address for religious – will appear in a wider context in later publications. A study of monasticism will slip into a meditation on the contemplative life. What are properly designated spiritual writings might address subjects as diverse as the sayings of the Desert Fathers, the mystical theology of St John of the Cross, the use of scripture, and the praying of the psalms. Writings that come under the broad heading of social issues will move, and sometimes move very freely without any strong sense of continuity, from ideas of personal freedom, to the use and abuse of language, to mythology, to literature, to the role of the church, to questions of war and peace. Posthumously published writings will often draw upon earlier publications and may or may not include new and hitherto-unknown material.

The developments in Merton's writing in both subject matter and style have led some to speak of the earlier and the later Mertons. Merton himself distinguished three phases in his writing: from the time of his conversion in 1938 until his ordination in 1949; from the time of his ordination until the early 1960s; and then the final years of his life. The first phase was caricatured by Merton as 'first fervor stuff': unworldly, intransigent (*The Secular Journal*, *The Seven Storey Mountain*, *Seeds of Contemplation* and the first two volumes of poetry – *Thirty Poems* and *Man in the Divided Sea*). The second phase was a time of transition when Merton turned again towards the world and drew increasingly upon the insights of secular writers (*The Sign of Jonas*, *No Man Is an Island*, *Thoughts in Solitude*, *The Silent Life* and the volume of poems entitled *Strange Islands*). The third phase saw a far more wholehearted engagement with the world (*Disputed Questions*, *Gandhi on Non-Violence*, *Seeds of Destruction*, *Raids on the Unspeakable*, *Conjectures of a Guilty Bystander* and the poetry to be found in *Emblems of a Season of Fury* and *The Way of Chuang Tzu*).[53]

The transitions Merton made in understanding himself and his several vocations during his years at Gethsemani are reflected in his books. Critics have drawn attention to the unevenness of his writing; to a tendency, especially in the earlier years, to be far too impressionistic; to a disconnectedness as essays and articles, drawn from different sources, are brought together in one volume. But the predominant impression is of 'a man churning with ideas' who has the capacity to touch minds and hearts.[54] The imperfections of treatment and style tell of a mind that was open, exploratory, acquisitive and eager to share.

Merton's writing in so many of his chosen areas was at variance with the traditions of the Trappists and few of the discontents that related specifically to his writing weighed more heavily than the strictures of the censors of his Order. Anyone less committed to his work would have abandoned writing altogether. But he had also to contend with the negative comments of some of his readers and as his range of interests broadened he knew he was being judged by his earlier writings. 'Either I am rejected entirely because the "monasticism" is unacceptable, or my later work is rejected for not being "spiritual" and "unworldly" like the earlier ones.'[55] Merton was more than happy to stand his ground: 'I will resolutely continue to be me, and say what seems to me to be true ... I think there are quite a few people who are glad to have someone say what I am saying.'[56]

Merton could be very dismissive of his work and it is not too surprising to find that he looked quizzically at many of his books as he began to move beyond his earliest years at Gethsemani. *Exile Ends in Glory* was dismissed as 'pious rhetoric'.[57] *Seeds of Contemplation* was found on reflection to be 'cold and cerebral'.[58] *The Seven Storey Mountain* was described within three years of publication as 'the work of a man I never even heard of'.[59] *Bread in the Wilderness* looked to Merton even before publication like 'a botched piece of work'.[60] *No Man Is an Island* was 'too glib'.[61] By the mid-1960s, taking as his starting point Rilke's conviction that 'a work of art is good only if it has sprung from necessity'[62] and reflecting on all his publications to date, Merton was persuaded that only a handful of books, together with some of his poems and one or two other pieces of writing, passed the test: *The Seven Storey Mountain* (1948), *The Sign of Jonas* (1953), *Thoughts in Solitude* (1958), the essay entitled *Notes for a Philosophy of Solitude* which had appeared in *Disputed Questions* (1960), parts of *The Behaviour of Titans* (1961), *The Way of Chuang Tzu* (1965), the soon-to-be-published *Conjectures of a Guilty Bystander* (1966), his writings on Zen, and something like 30 of his poems. These were all judged to have come from 'a kind of necessity ... The rest is trash ... Or rather the rest is journalism.'[63]

Merton was embarrassed by the continuing popularity of *The Seven Storey Mountain*. He described it in retrospect as 'a kind of edifying legend', but it was one that he tried hard to live down.[64] Personal transformation was no longer sufficient. He claimed for himself a fair degree of freedom in the interpretation of his monastic calling, and by the same token he argued for a full recognition of men and women's inherent freedom in relation to society and to the structures of power by which they were so frequently oppressed. But authentic human freedom requires an open dialogue and it was this that Merton provided in so many of his later books.

Merton was always mindful of the obligations of conscience and he therefore often appeared to be too dogmatic, too uncompromising, when he wrote about the renewal of monasticism, the inability of the Catholic Church to adapt to the demands of a changing world, the artificiality of life in the United States, the question of racial justice, the ever-present anxiety concerning nuclear weapons and the war in Vietnam. But the change in style and presentation in so many of his books from the mid-1950s suggests a far more open approach and calls for an active participation on the part of the reader.

Some of Merton's later books read as though they are an assortment of notes, reflections and articles that have been written in the first instance for other purposes. It is as though Merton could not write and publish fast enough, and yet the principle of open dialogue became increasingly important. William Shannon suggests that it was from the time of the publication of *No Man Is an Island* in 1955 that Merton began to ask questions of his readers in the light of religious experience. *Disputed Questions* (1960) speaks of controversies which demand the attention of those who think and care.[65] *Conjectures of a Guilty Bystander* (1965) consists of personal observations on his reading and on events, but it is essentially a dialogue with his readers in which questions are raised for private reflection and response. 'I do have questions, and, as a matter of fact, I think a man is known better by his questions than by his answers.'[66]

It is, however, in *Raids on the Unspeakable* (1966) that this method of working is to be seen most clearly. Merton's address to the book in the Prologue demonstrates the position he has now reached, but it represents also an approach to Christian witness that is principled and pragmatic. 'You are not so much concerned with … traditional answers to traditional questions, for many men have decided no longer to ask themselves these questions. Your main interest is not in formal answers or accurate definitions, but in difficult insights at a moment of human crisis.'[67]

This is the sense in which the book might be seen as a series of *Raids*, but the *Unspeakable* was for Merton an eschatological image. Merton had no illusions about the magnitude of the task or the likely response, but the indestructibility of hope, Christian hope, was the ground of his whole being, and it provided the base from which he made his final appeal. He wrote still as one who was giving advice to his book, but he was speaking of himself and to himself. 'You are not big enough to accuse the whole age effectively, but let us say you are in dissent. You are in no position to issue commands, but you can speak words of hope.'[68] The authenticity for which Merton pleaded left his reader free to make the necessary response.

It is here that the monk, the contemplative and the writer come together. What connects so much of Merton's writing – his experience of contemplative prayer, his critique of the contemporary scene, his dialogue with the East – is his desire to draw people into depths which may not have been previously identified or explored. He wrote of contemplative wisdom as 'a knowledge beyond knowledge in emptiness and unknowing'.[69] The corruptions of power, which in their varying forms were his primary targets in his social criticism, must also be rejected by all who follow the path of contemplation. 'The contemplative way requires first of all and above all renunciation of this obsession with the triumph of the individual or collective will to power'.[70]

But the contemplative way does not by-pass the contradictions of ordinary experience; rather, it is the way that leads through self-abandonment to wisdom. 'This way of wisdom is no dream, no temptation and no evasion … It is not an escape from contradiction and confusion for it finds unity and clarity by plunging into the very midst of contradiction, by the acceptance of emptiness and suffering.'[71] It might well be asked – bearing in mind the contradictions and the confusions with which Merton lived – if this is where and how the human discontents make the transition and take on something of the character of divine discontent. The unifying theme in all his activities, all his concerns, is provided by Merton's continual return to the desert tradition and to the foundations of Christian hope which are the events of Good Friday and Easter Day, the mysteries of death and resurrection.

In his Preface to *My Argument with the Gestapo* (1969), the novel first written in 1941 and subsequently revised and prepared for publication by Merton, he introduced the book by describing it as 'a kind of sardonic meditation on the world in which I then found myself: an attempt to define its predicament and my own place in it'.[72] If other words could be substituted for sardonic – questioning, searching, tentative, critical – then the sentence might well stand as a summary statement for many of his later writings, because what he was so frequently attempting was a portrayal of the predicament of the world in which he found himself and *as always* of his place within it. He might well have moved far beyond his earlier style of writing and the preoccupations that seemed then to be so important; and yet, writing of himself and his brothers at Gethsemani, he had captured correctly at the beginning something of the truth of the human condition: 'The life of each one in this abbey is part of a mystery … In one sense we are always travelling, and travelling as if we did not know where we were going. In another sense we have already arrived.'[73]

The articles

One literary form which conveys the idea of someone who is 'always travelling' is the short piece of writing: the article, the lecture, the introduction to someone else's book, the preface, the review. Such writings are necessarily limited in scope, focused, similar or different in subject matter to each other as the case may be, but none the less taking their place – certainly where Merton is concerned – alongside quite literally hundreds of similar exercises in the same genre. They constitute the fourth body of material where Merton's literary genius can be found. All the familiar preoccupations are to be discovered in the vast resource of short (and not so short) articles, prefaces, reviews.

These articles have much to say about the breadth of Merton's reading, the range of his correspondence and his ability to revise his thinking and his writing as life moved on and opportunities presented themselves. Many of Merton's books – *Disputed Questions* (1960), *Life and Holiness* (1963), *Seeds of Destruction* (1964), *Seasons of Celebration* (1965), *Raids on the Unspeakable* (1966), *Mystics and Zen Masters* (1967), *Faith and Violence* (1968), *Zen and the Birds of Appetite* (1968), together with several posthumously published books – *Contemplation in a World of Action* (1971), *Thomas Merton On Peace* (1971), *Ishi Means Man* (1976), *The Monastic Journey* (1977), *Love and Living* (1979) and *Passion for Peace* (1995) – are largely collections of essays that have previously appeared in journals or been delivered as addresses to particular groups.

Merton's *Literary Essays* considered the work of some of the writers who had influenced him: William Blake, James Joyce, Edwin Muir, Boris Pasternak, William Faulkner, Albert Camus, together with a number of Latin American poets for whom he had a special regard. But one of the chief merits of the *Literary Essays* is that they reveal something of Merton's understanding of the role of the artist in society. His Master's thesis at Columbia on William Blake and his initial hope that any doctoral research might have explored the writings of Gerard Manley Hopkins had established in his mind some sense of the prophetic role of the writer. William Blake had seen 'official Christendom as a *narrowing* of vision, a foreclosure of experience and of future expansion, a locking up and securing of the doors of perception'.[74] That was not a road down which Merton was prepared to travel. On the contrary, he identified himself far more with Albert Camus in his determination to 'fashion an art of living in times of catastrophe, to be reborn by fighting openly against the death instinct at work in our society'.[75]

The words could serve as a description of the position Merton was establishing for himself. His reading of James Joyce brought Merton back to his commitment to non-violence and to his belief, in common with Mahatma Gandhi, that non-violence matters because it is 'a power for real change'.[76] Its concern is not revelation or proclamation but conversion of minds and hearts. It is not surprising that Merton should therefore embrace the ideal that Boris Pasternak had come to represent: namely, the freedom against oppression that is essential not only for the artist but for the dignity of humankind. Merton defined the role that Pasternak had played and claimed it for himself: 'I seek only to do what Pasternak himself did: to speak my mind out of love for man.'[77]

The prophetic role of the artist that Merton was identifying and appropriating for himself found a significant outlet in the articles he wrote in several journals from the mid-1950s. He had played a small part in the launching of *Jubilee* in 1953, a monthly journal that carried the subtitle *A Magazine for the Church and Her People*. It was a reputable journal that secured recognition in the national press and won no fewer than seven prizes in its first three years from the Catholic Press Association. Merton was a regular contributor and his involvement served to strengthen his reputation as a household name in Catholic families. Something of what *Jubilee* had been looking for – the centrality of the church's liturgy, questions concerning authority and collegiality, the importance of dialogue between the church and the world – found some acknowledgement in the work of the Second Vatican Council. But Merton found other outlets and by the early 1960s he was also contributing regularly to *The Catholic Worker*, *Commonweal* and *Blackfriars*. It was there in a succession of articles, free or largely free from the eye of the censors, that Merton's writing as a social critic – civil rights, nuclear weapons, non-violence, Vietnam – so often found expression.

Throughout these years many of Merton's books appeared in translation in different countries, and his Prefaces for these publications enabled him to reflect upon what he had previously written and to focus on a particular question.[78] These Prefaces demonstrate both the degree to which he had moved on in his thinking and the priorities which he continued to hold. His Preface to the French edition of *Monastic Peace* (1960) made connections between the life of the religious and the needs of the world: 'the monk's vocation is not an evasion of the Modern Age ... There is no truth, no life, in an existence which refuses to face the realities of our time.'[79] Such an emphasis could be maintained by Merton within a tradition of mystical theology and contemplative prayer, and so his Preface to the Korean edition of *Life and Holiness* (1965) addressed the question of Christian discipleship: 'To be a Christian is then not only to believe in Christ, but to live as Christ and, in a mysterious way, to become united with Christ. This is both Christian life and Christian holiness.'[80]

But the particular vocation that Merton increasingly marked out for himself was the voice of protest. It found expression in his writing, but it derived from his monasticism. His Preface to the Japanese edition of *The Seven Storey Mountain* (1963) spoke of radical dissent:

> By my monastic life and vows I am saying NO to all the concentration camps, the aerial bombardments, the staged political trials, the judicial murders, the racial injustices, the economic tyrannies, and the whole socio-economic apparatus which seems geared for nothing but global destruction in spite of all its fair words in favour of peace. I make monastic silence a protest against the lies of politicians, propagandists and agitators, and when I speak it is to deny that my faith and my Church can ever seriously be aligned with these forces of injustice and destruction.[81]

This is a distinctive interpretation of the monastic life and it has to be inferred from all that is known about Merton that he would have taken that position whatever his primary vocation had been. But the prophetic awareness that is so obviously present in his critique of the contemporary scene gives way at times to a prophetic voice. This voice is never more insightful, more prescient, than in his treatment in his *Literary Essays* of the work of the young black writers Melvin Kelley and James Baldwin.[82] He portrays the evil of racism – outspoken and violent in the southern states, hidden but implicit in other parts of the United States – but Merton then moves forward in unexpected ways as he identifies the anticipation in the African American community of the decline of Western civilization and the end of the white domination of the world. Is it therefore a matter of great surprise, Merton asks, if the African American can no longer be content with integration into a situation that has had its day?[83]

And yet Merton – in a moment of profound creativity – is able move on and comprehend black and white in one *kairos*, one moment of truth, one hour of salvation. And so he continues: 'There is one *kairos* for everybody ... The white man, if he can possibly open the ears of his heart and listen intently enough to hear what the [African American] is now hearing, can recognize that he is himself called to freedom and to salvation in the same *kairos* of events which he is now, in so many different ways, opposing or resisting.'[84]

What Merton referred to disparagingly as 'this writing job'[85] kept him alert, informed and eager to participate. He was regularly oppressed by the burden of writing – 'I will forever be a lackey of pious journalists and editors; the right-thinking rabbit who gives birth to litters of editorials every morning before breakfast'[86] – but few steps were taken to restore any kind of balance. He knew the responsibility could only rest with himself; but little was ever done, although there is just a hint towards the end of his life that the *need* to write was beginning to diminish.[87]

The poetry

Merton's poetry, the fifth of his literary archives, represents a thread that runs through his work as a writer. Some would say that Merton saw himself primarily as a poet rather than a theologian or a philosopher. He had few illusions about his competence as a poet, but he saw 'the emergence of an occasional poetic word into consciousness' as a vital ingredient in his monastic life.[88] What his poetry reveals is not merely the familiar preoccupations, but also something of the character of the man. He wanted, like his beloved William Blake, to look beyond the things immediately to hand; and, ever attentive to life's deepest rhythms, he drew upon his great gift with words to go beyond the constraints of language.

Poetry commended itself to Merton as an art form because it spoke of 'the flowering of ordinary possibilities'[89] and, disciplined by his monastic formation, he knew the necessity of listening, as St Benedict had required, with the ear of the heart. But that was exactly where the intuition and the awareness and the voice of the prophet could come into play, because the poet is bound to attend to voices that are not yet heard by the generality of humankind.[90]

The Collected Poems of Thomas Merton brings together the ten volumes of poetry published during his lifetime and in the years immediately after his death. There are important omissions – most notably many of the *Eighteen Poems* written for 'M' – and previously unknown poems have appeared from time to time. What is to be found in Merton's poetry are the variations and the transitions in subject matter and in style that characterized so much of his writing. Critics have not always been enthusiastic, but there is delight, tenderness, humour, passion, anguish, pain. Merton – writing as observer, or participant, or pilgrim, or lover, or critic, or voice of conscience – holds up a mirror to his world and to ours.

Robert Lowell, reviewing *Thirty Poems*, the first collection of Merton's poetry to be published, while remaining somewhat agnostic about Merton's writing, saw him none the less as 'easily the most promising of our American Catholic poets'.[91] Later volumes of poetry often received a less-positive welcome. Critical comments acknowledged his use of words and striking images, his intellectual energy, his capacity to surprise and challenge, but there was a broad consensus that the quality of his writing was uneven. Reviewers observed that Merton lacked 'the discipline of the true artist';[92] that something of the original freshness had been lost;[93] that too much of the poetry was derivative;[94] that what was presented often amounted to little more than 'Merton's personal outrage against the sins of his generation'.[95] It may be that Merton's compulsion to write and to publish was so overpowering that his poetry was rushed out with little time allowed for editing and revising.[96] And yet Merton as a poet continued to intrigue and one critic judged that *The Collected Poems* imaged the man and his life: 'maddeningly disparate, full of surprises, probing, zany, revealing yet concealing, confronting and challenging our conventional attitudes'.[97]

Such poetry cannot easily be classified; but it might be most helpful to speak of the poetry of the cloister, the poetry of the heart and the poetry of the abyss.[98] These categories have a broad definition: some poems might properly appear in more than one place; some poems demand to stand alone. Subject matter will often indicate the cloister, the heart or the abyss; yet questions of language, of style, of poetic treatment and presentation will also arise as progressions are made from one classification to another.

Some of Merton's early poems focus inevitably on Gethsemani. He speaks of solitude: the Abbey is the holy desert where the brothers, hidden in their disguises, come by night as separate strangers to meet the quiet Christ.[99] He tells of the liturgical round: of Matins, calling his soul to wake in the cloisters of the lonely night;[100] of the Night Office, as brothers touch the rays they cannot see, and feel the light that seems to sing.[101] He writes of the monks working in the woods and the fields, singing a different office with their saws and axes, or turning the country white with grain.[102]

These early poems have a gentle, reflective, 'first-love' quality, but *the poetry of the cloister* goes beyond the routine of the monastic day at Gethsemani. It speaks of the search for God, of the desert experience, of monasticism, of the tradition of faith, of the variations of religious experience. Poems such as 'Aubade – The Annunciation', 'St. John Baptist' and 'Clairvaux' (from *A Man in the Divided Sea* [1946]); and 'Spring: Monastery Farm' and 'The Transformation:

For the Sacred Heart' (from *Figures for an Apocalypse* [1947]); and *'The Quickening of St. John the Baptist'* (from *The Tears of the Blind Lion* [1949]); and *'Macarius the Younger'*, *'Song: If You Seek ...'* and *'Hagia Sophia'* (from *Emblems of a Season of Fury* [1962]) all belong in this category. It is here – and in many other poems – that Merton treats of the mysteries of faith: of prayers flying like larks (*'Aubade – the Annunciation'*), of receiving in the desert the keys of our deliverance (*'St. John Baptist'*), of singing the grain that dies and triumphs in the secret ground (*'Spring: Monastery Farm'*).

But the poetry of the cloister did not exclude other traditions of faith in which Merton saw something of his own search for God. His study of the poetry of Chuang Tzu, the Chinese Taoist Master of the fourth century BC, led him to make connections with the mystical theologians of the late middle ages. What Merton found in solitude and in a Christian tradition of contemplative prayer was also found by him in his translation of Chuang Tzu's poems with their emphasis upon being and non-being (perhaps most especially *'Action and Non-Action'*, *'In My End is My Beginning'*, *'Tao'* and *'Where is Tao?'* from *The Way Of Chuang Tzu* [1965]). And, even more surprisingly, in his poem *'The Night of Destiny'*, which marks the end of Ramadan, Merton saw in the gift of the Quran to Mohammed something of the mystery of Christmas when the Incarnate Word is revealed.

Midnight!
Kissed with flame!

See! See!
My love is darkness!

Only in the night
Are all the lost
Found.

In my ending is my meaning.[103]

The poetry of the heart encompasses a smaller group of poems in which Merton writes out of a rich, warm humanity, with tenderness, with good humour, and at times with pain. They come from all periods of his life, and they include poems for a brother lost in action (*'For My Brother: Reported Missing in Action 1943'* from *Thirty Poems* [1944]); for a child by way of response to a picture she had drawn of a house and subsequently sent to Merton by her father ('*Grace's House*' from *Emblems of a Season Of Fury* [1963]); for a lover (*Eighteen Poems* [1985]); for an old friend, Robert Lax, and for whom poems sent by Merton had many of the characteristics of the letters they had exchanged over the years ('*Proverbs*', '*Twenty Three Point Prospectus*' and '*Western Fellow Students Salute*');[104] and for Gethsemani, if the '*Fire Watch*' with which he concluded *The Sign of Jonas* can be admitted as a prose poem.

Something of Merton's feeling for the departed can be found in '*The Trappist Cemetery: Gethsemani*' (from *A Man in the Divided Sea* [1946]), when he wrote with more than pious affection of the continuing dependence of the living upon those who have died, and again in his '*Elegy for a Trappist*' (from *Sensation Time at the Home* [1968]), in which he tells simply of his admiration for an old monk, Father Stephen, who cared for the garden, displaying boundless love, and whose monastic journey was now completed. But few poems display a greater anguish than the one written by Merton on hearing of the death of his younger brother, John Paul, in April 1943, scarcely two months after his marriage, while on an expedition with the Royal Canadian Air Force over the English Channel. It is a poem that speaks of a brother's love, of a quiet solidarity in death, and of Christian hope.

> Come, in my labor find a resting place
> And in my sorrows lay your head.
>
> For in the wreckage of your April Christ lies slain,
> And Christ weeps in the ruins of my spring:
>
> The silence of Whose tears shall fall
> Like bells upon your alien tomb
> Hear them and come: they call you home.[105]

An entirely different kind of love is explored by Merton in *Eighteen Poems*.[106] The poems trace the romantic relationship with 'M' from its first beginnings until the separation required by Merton's vocation. He speaks of tenderness, of anxiety, of divided loyalties, of what might be, and of the pain of letting go. There is delight: lying beneath the fragrant tent of 'M's dark hair ('*May Song*'), four wet eyes and cool lips and worshipping hands ('*Louisville Airport*').

There is the eagerness of the lover: pacing up and down, waiting in his uneasy lonely place (*'Aubade on a Cloudy Morning'*). There is the time of desolation: the voice in the night, trembling with sorrow, separate in strange places, two half-persons wandering in two lost worlds (*'Evening: Long Distance Call'*). And there is the last cry of despair: 'If only you and I were possible' (*'For "M". In October'*).

But the monk, the contemplative and the writer can never be entirely disentangled from each other, and the most affectionate of all tributes, in which Merton is undoubtedly speaking from the heart, is the prose poem *'Fire Watch'*, in which he enters freely into the silence of the night: keeping watch as he moves through the monastic buildings, exploring with every step the depths of his own vocation, meeting with God in the darkness, mindful of those entrusted to his charge, standing alone and yet not alone before the mystery of life and death – 'Thou in me and I in Thee and Thou in them and they in me.'[107]

It is, however, in *the poetry of the abyss* that Merton articulates so clearly the developments in his thinking. The abyss speaks of the depths of human experience – the emptiness, the chaos, the torment – and for Merton these archetypal images find expression in the contemporary scene, in the corruption and the tyrannies of power, in the holocaust, in questions of peace and war, in nuclear weapons, in the battle for civil rights. A political dimension had never been entirely absent from his poetry. As early as 1939, when Merton was far more preoccupied with the turn of events in Europe than with any vocation to the religious life, he was writing of a rare ugly bird, screeching a sour song in the German tongue, and with a heavy sense of foreboding depicted Europe as 'a feast / For every bloody beast' (*'Fable for a War'*).[108] Seven years later, he concluded his second volume of published poems pondering 'the story of our monstrous century' in which, starting with two world wars, the doors of hell had been bombed from their hinges, the cage of the antichrist burst open (*'La Salette'*).[109]

By the mid-1950s James Laughlin, who published so much of Merton's poetry, was aware of new directions in his writing. It was what he called 'the secularization of Merton's poetry'.[110] *The Strange Islands*, Merton's fifth volume of poetry and his first for eight years, was published in 1957. It marked an important transition for Merton with a greater openness to the world, a deeper sense of identification with people, and a far greater simplicity in language and style (*'How to Enter a Big City'*, *'The Guns of Fort Knox'*, *'Whether There is Enjoyment in Bitterness'*, *'The Tower of Babel'*). Changes of subject matter were more than matched by changes of style in Merton's later collections (*Original Child Bomb* [1962], *Emblems of a Season of Fury* [1963], *Cables to the Ace* [1968]) and in the undated poem *'Epitaph for a Public Servant'* as he brought a prophetic voice – increasingly dominant, increasingly shrill – to bear upon his social concerns. Experimental forms provided a presentation of the facts interpreted by a brutal irony. Image, symbol and satire came together as he moved between poetry and prose.

'Original Child Bomb' (1962) is a prose poem on the dropping of the first atomic bomb on Hiroshima. It purports to present a narrative account of events between 12 April 1945 (the accession of Harry S. Truman to the Presidency) and 14 August 1945 (the end of the Second World War), but Merton's matter-of-fact style is heavy with irony. 'In the year 1945 an Original Child was born. The name Original Child was given to it (the bomb) by the Japanese people, who recognized that it was the first of its kind.' The subtitle of the poem – 'Points for Meditation to be Scratched on the Walls of a Cave' – expresses the foreboding that motivated Merton in all his writing about war and peace. With careful calculation, Merton describes the dropping of the bomb, the temperature, the total devastation, the horrendous loss of civilian life, and then, 'As to the Original Child that was now born, President Truman summed up the philosophy of the situation in a few words. "We found the bomb", he said, "and we used it."'[111]

It was a matter of great concern to Merton that Western civilization was in irreversible decline, destroyed by a barbarism from within itself, and in that context he was persuaded that poets were 'almost the only ones who have anything to say ... [because] ... they have the courage to disbelieve what is shouted ... from every loudspeaker.'[112] *'Gloss on the Sin of Ixion'* addresses the grotesque consequences of war and the corruptions of power in the lives of individuals caught up in the system.

> Heavy war bums
> Political wheels and copper generals
> Drink nuclear smoke
> And lose manhood.
> Shameless, unintelligent,
> But shrewd enough
> To spill sun power,
> Spin the planets,
> Ravish sacred man![113]

This is a theme that is picked up in Merton's *'Epitaph for a Public Servant'*, a poem that is subtitled *'In Memoriam – Adolf Eichmann'*. Here is a man who might well have said 'I entered life on earth / in the aspect of a human being / and believed / in the higher meaning' and who yet, in settling for the party, for the leader, for official orders, learned 'to forget / The undesirable Jew', granting a so-called 'mercy death / With institutional / Care.'[114] The holocaust represented for Merton the barbarities that are inflicted time and again by the powerful upon the powerless, and so in his 'Chant to be Used Around a Site with Furnaces', having described in a succession of short sentences the sequence of events in the death camps, he turns to the predicament in which he and his contemporaries are now placed: 'Do not think yourself better because you burn up friends and enemies with long-range missiles without ever seeing what you have done.'[115]

For Merton, one of the latter-day equivalents of the holocaust was to be found in the oppression of black people, and not least of all in the southern states of America. He identified himself fully with the civil rights movement, and his poem *'And the Children of Birmingham'*, drawing upon the fable of Little Red Riding Hood, is a melancholy commentary upon the Birmingham, Alabama, scene of black children – walking into 'the story of Grandma's pointed teeth', into 'the shadow of Grandma's devil', into 'the fury of Grandma's hug' – being confronted by police dogs, fire hoses and the hatred of a white mob.[116]

The changes in style which had become so evident in the 1960s are made most explicit in *Cables to the Ace* (1968) and in *The Geography of Lograire* (1969). *Cables*, which employs poetry and prose, concerns itself largely with the use and the abuse of language in a world that no longer understands the integrity of words and the coherence of a cultural identity. *The Geography*, which may well be the author's preferred work when all his poetry is taken into account, is described by Merton as a 'wide-angle mosaic of poems and dreams' into which he has brought his own experience and everybody else's.[117] So much of Merton's reading is to be found in this work as he draws freely upon myth and legend, symbolic names, the echoes and the resonances of words, of ideas. It is an obtuse, even an obscure, work, as he attempts to speak of the unity of humankind, of the many ways in which that unity is destroyed, and not least of all by the assumption of some kind of moral superiority by the Western powers. What Merton is, therefore, feeling after is a global vision in which his continuing search for identity and meaning can now be set.

Merton's later poetry displays a determination to go beyond the conventional use of language and to adopt an approach that is experimental, idiosyncratic.

It is 'a kind of anti-poetry',[118] surreal, disconnected, ironic, satirical. Is this the measure of the abyss that, with the abuse of language, he believes a conventional dialogue is no longer possible, and that his writing must therefore assume the form of anti-writing?[119] What is being presented, then, in Merton's anti-poetry is 'a method of writing for a post-Christian world',[120] and yet the monastic perspective remains. It is 'a poetry of dissent';[121] but the writer, who is also monk and contemplative and social critic, continues to plead even in a situation of profound alienation for the integrity and value of all people.

The monk and the writer

It was the monastic vocation, in spite of its many frustrations, that illuminated and enlarged Merton's writing. Jean Leclercq's judgement was that Merton 'saw everything through a monk's eyes'.[122] Writing was burdensome, but Merton knew himself well enough to jest 'I shall continue writing on my deathbed, and even take some asbestos paper with me in order to go on writing in purgatory'.[123] And yet he was tested repeatedly as he pursued his vocation as a writer: the culture of a Cistercian house which gave permission to write and then erected a series of obstacles; the difficulty of finding anyone with whom to discuss his work; the endless routine of sitting at his typewriter day after day; the dissipation of his creative energies by responding far too frequently to requests for reviews, prefaces, articles, contributions to other people's books; the suspicion, even at times the hostility, of Catholic groups to his later writings.

Nothing enraged Merton more than the behaviour of the censors of the Order, especially when he came to address questions of war and peace in the early 1960s. Disregarding everything implicit in the common understanding of the word, he rejected the argument that his *Trappist* vocation required him to be silent. The gravity of the situation throughout the world required in Merton's judgement whatever monastic perspective he might bring. All too often the religious life took on in his experience the appearance of 'a cold war between Superiors and subjects'[124] and Merton resolved to chart his own course between obedience and freedom. He railed, therefore, against the 'culpable silence' to which Superiors and censors would condemn him[125] and he battled through to a position of positive and passionate dissent, of critical non-conformity.

Merton was confirmed in this stance by the high view he held of the role of the artist, the writer, the thinker, the man of prayer. For Merton, it was poets in particular who had the prophetic task, because 'they have the keys of the subconscious and of the great secrets of real life', but their power to speak required freedom, 'the freedom of conscience and of creation'.[126] It is none the less no small part of Merton's achievement that he could contain within himself the diarist, the correspondent, the spiritual writer, the poet, the social commentator, and could hold these identities as a writer within his particular complex of vocations. It was Naomi Burton Stone's judgement that Merton's 'heroism ... had been in learning to live with this ever-present conflict of interests, in never giving up'.[127]

It may be that the explanation is to be found in the transitions that Merton made throughout his life. References to the poetry of the cloister, of the heart, and of the abyss, do not speak of a rigid chronological progression, but they do tell of very significant and very discernible changes of perception, of priority, as he moved beyond the discovery of faith and vocation to an active participation as a writer in the torments of his world. Merton remained the monk, the contemplative, but he would have shared Martin Luther King's judgement that 'A person has not started living until they cease identifying with their own personal problems and begin identifying with the problems of all humanity'.[128] Was it here that the many discontents which persisted throughout his life took to themselves new points of reference, a wider range of meaning, even perhaps something of the divine compassion and the divine purpose? Certainly he knew that *for him* a monastic calling required a serious engagement with 'the big issues, the life-and-death issues';[129] and the boundary markers were the priority of God, the priority of the person, the priority of conscience, and the priority of freedom.

Merton was aware of his limitations as a writer. He was conscious at times of the need 'to write better, write less, go deeper'.[130] He acknowledged the danger of trying to say something about everything.[131] He recognized that too much of his writing had been 'provisional, inconclusive, half-baked'.[132] T. S. Eliot's judgement on Merton's early volumes of poetry was that he 'wrote too much and revised too little'.[133] It may be that Merton was simply in too much of a hurry: 'I have been a man without silence, / A man without patience, with too many / Questions'.[134] But something of the truth might also be found in the observation that he looked at the world through 'a wide-angle lens'.[135] He was well able to come in close, to focus on a specific question, but there was a tendency in his discussion of critical political questions to be too sweeping, too facile.

There was also a diffidence, even an ambivalence, in Merton about his writing. He saw the danger of what he called 'my persistent desire to be somebody',[136] but there can be little doubt that he wrote with an eye to posterity, and worked hard to ensure that his papers would be preserved.[137] He cooperated in the establishment of the Thomas Merton Room at Bellarmine College in November 1963, now the Thomas Merton Center at Bellarmine University, Louisville, and saw it as a guarantee that his work would survive. 'The Merton Room is a kind of escape from Gethsemani, a protest against their messing up, destroying, losing, frittering away, dispersing, rotting, canning, feeding to mice everything I have put my heart into.'[138] But he saw the ambiguity of such a place: 'A place where I store away endless papers, in which a paper-self builds its nest to be visited by strangers in a strange land of unreal intimacy.'[139] Was it, therefore, some sense of unreality that Merton was expressing when on his final visit to the Merton Room the day before he left Gethsemani for his journey to Asia he quipped to a friend, 'A good place to cut a fart and run?'[140]

But was there something more: about his writing, about the Merton Room, about himself? He confided in his Author's Preface to *A Thomas Merton Reader* that 'When a thought is done with, let go of it. When something has been written, publish it and go on to something else.'[141] His writing mattered enormously, but one of his brothers at Gethsemani observed that 'He did not make a big thing of his writings, and once they came out he never read them again.'[142] Was it the discipline of his monastic formation that enabled him to write and then let go? Or was it the knowledge of what had been said and yet remained unspoken? His reflections in his journal on the Merton Room spoke of the 'ambiguity of an open door that is closed. Of a cell where I don't really live. Where my papers live. Where my papers are more than I am.'[143] But then he acknowledged, 'I myself am open and closed. When I reveal most I hide most. There is still something I have not said: but what it is I don't know, and maybe I have to say it by not saying.'[144]

The Contemplative

The contemplative is not just a man who sits under a tree with his legs crossed, or one who edifies himself with the answer to ultimate and spiritual problems. He is one who seeks to know the meaning of life not only with his head but with his whole being, by living it in depth and in purity, and thus uniting himself to the very Source of Life – a Source which is ... too real to be contained satisfactorily inside any word or concept or name assigned by man ... Contemplation is the intuitive perception of life in its Source ... it is an obscure intuition of God Himself, and this intuition is a gift of God Who reveals Himself in His very hiddenness as One unknown.[1]

Contemplation was the heartbeat of Thomas Merton's life. He wrote early in his monastic life that 'My vocation is contemplative and I simply *must* fulfill it.'[2] He knew the contradictions with which he wrestled, but he found some resolution in interior solitude, and he acknowledged towards the end of his life 'the absolute primacy and necessity of silent, hidden, poor, apparently fruitless prayer.'[3] The contemplative life was central to all that Merton had to say. It was a constant point of reference.

It is perhaps as a contemplative that Merton is best known. He was concerned to affirm the importance of the contemplative dimension in human experience and to plead for a far greater contemplative orientation in the life of the church. Contemplative living and contemplative prayer were directly related in his understanding to the identity, the integrity, the freedom of each individual; they represented 'a sudden gift of awareness, an awakening to the Real within all that is real.'[4]

Merton's approach to the contemplative life was in large measure a response to the all-important questions: 'What are we here for? What does God intend for His world and for the men He has placed in it?'[5] He rejected any idea of the contemplative life as 'esoteric knowledge or experience,'[6] or even in his later years any thought that it was something removed from the realities of daily life. It would be necessary to secure an appropriate degree of detachment from the confusions of the world, but Merton's appetite for life and for God was too generous, too extravagant, to permit any distortion. He was emphatic that 'The true contemplative is not less interested than others in normal life, not less concerned with what goes on in the world, but *more* interested, more concerned.'[7] Contemplation provides an entirely different perspective. Awareness, intuition, apprehension, perception: these are the words that captured for Merton something of the meaning of the contemplative life.

He was clear that the first priority is not living for contemplation but living for God.[8] In contemplation, Merton went far beyond the formalities of public worship and established patterns of private prayer, entering an unfamiliar world where words and concepts and images and feelings fall away. Contemplative prayer is necessarily a gradual process and one that can only develop as it secures a place within the rhythm of a person's life; but as the journey continues, there is a growing awareness that what is being encountered is not an idea of God, nor even a desire for God, but God Himself. Contemplation is about knowing God in an entirely new way – not by instruction, but by experience. It requires listening to God in silence, but it is hearing without hearing, seeing without seeing, knowing without knowing. Those who take the risk of discovering what it means to be alone with the Alone will perceive God as light and love and life. What matters, therefore, is not what we *do*, but what we *receive*. It is no longer a question of knowing about God, but of knowing God. It is to be possessed in the depths of our being by a realization of God, and of ourselves in God, and of all humankind with ourselves in God – in love.

But Merton's was an austere vocation. His life was lived in the light of the conviction that 'There is an absolute need for the solitary, bare, dark, beyond-concept, beyond-feeling type of prayer.'[9] Contemplative prayer represented for him the preference for the desert that lay at the heart of his monastic calling. Prayer and meditation and contemplation involve 'a kind of descent into our own nothingness',[10] but it is only there in the darkness that God can be perceived as the One who is 'All in All'. And yet there is in all these things a wider dimension. The real journey in life may be interior, but for Merton the discovery of a more profound identity could only be the springboard for seeing the world in its entirety in the light of God.

Stepping stones

Merton returned repeatedly in his writing to the subject of contemplation, although he tells us little about his own practice of contemplative prayer. There are hints but little more, and yet, bearing in mind his emphasis upon grace and vocation in his exposition of the contemplative life, it is possible to identify three important places – Rome, Columbia, Gethsemani – and the formative influences that they constituted in shaping his life as a contemplative.

Merton's discovery of prayer, which he described as 'a great grace',[11] preceded his conversion by several years. His visit to Rome in February 1933, immediately after his 18th birthday, took place at a time of transition in his life. He had just left Oakham, having secured his scholarship place at Cambridge for the ensuing autumn. The visit enabled him to explore the churches, the frescoes, the mosaics, and – far more importantly – something of what they represented. It is difficult, as Merton tells the story, to separate the compulsion to pray from an awareness of the presence of his father who had died two years before, but there was also, as Merton recounted the experience 15 years later, a profound initiation into the life of prayer as he began to pray, perhaps for the first time in his life, not only with his lips and his intellect and his imagination but out of the depths of his being. Merton was quick to add that he had been praying to the God whom he had never known, but what he had received was the grace to pray and he describes how on the next day he made his way to Santa Sabina and walked into the church with the sole purpose of kneeling down and praying to God.[12]

Merton's years at Columbia as a student and a teacher saw his discovery of Catholic faith and of vocations to the priesthood and the religious life. The influence of teachers and friends was enormous as he considered all the possibilities that life presented. He delighted in the freedom that the university provided, and he later described himself as 'being turned on like a pinball machine' by writers as diverse as Augustine of Hippo, Thomas Aquinas, Meister Eckhart, Thomas Traherne, William Blake, Gerard Manley Hopkins, and – beyond the Christian tradition – Ananda K. Coomaraswamy.[13] A meeting with Bramachari, a Hindu monk who visited Columbia in the summer of 1938 at the invitation of one of Merton's closest friends, served to point him back to the Western and Christian tradition of philosophical and mystical writing.

Merton's dissertation on William Blake for his master's degree in 1939[14] gave him an appreciation of the place of allegory, symbolism, mysticism, contemplation and transcendence in Blake's work as an artist, and of the relation of all these things to a mainstream Catholic tradition which had its roots deep in the story of the Western world. It may be that it was through his study of Blake that Merton developed an early understanding of the relevance of a contemplative approach to art and to life. It was certainly the case that his reading for his dissertation coincided with his reception into the Catholic Church, his taking on board the prescribed practices of Catholic piety and the first stirrings of his vocations.

It was, however, Gethsemani which gave Merton the formation and the discipline which enabled him to find his vocation as a contemplative. He confided in his journal that everything in him cried out for solitude and for God alone,[15] but the desire for solitude and silence, which persisted for the rest of his life, was not entirely free of personal considerations. He admitted in later years as he began to live increasingly at the hermitage that 'my solitude is partly that of an intellectual and poet', and even more that the hermitage provided an acceptable solution where his relationship with the community was concerned. But solitude also represented 'a deepening of the present',[16] and even while he continued with his work as Master of the Novices, quite apart from his writing and his correspondence, he attempted to find three hours a day for simple meditative prayer and another three hours for study. His mind was ever alert and active, and yet in solitude – and above all in contemplative prayer – he sought depths which his enquiring mind could never entirely encompass or possess. 'Our interior prayer is simply the most intimate and personal way in which we seek the Face of God.'[17]

The struggle to make sense of his vocations as monk, contemplative and prolific writer caused him a good deal of distress, but Gethsemani afforded opportunities for reading, translating, writing and teaching. New influences therefore shaped Merton's understanding of contemplation: the Desert Fathers of the fourth and fifth centuries, the Cistercian Fathers of the twelfth century, the mystics, English and continental, of the fourteenth, fifteenth and sixteenth centuries. But Merton's probing mind and broad human sympathies enabled him to draw also upon the thoughts of writers as diverse as Chuang Tzu, the Chinese Taoist mystic of the fourth century BC, mystics of the Jewish, Islamic and Hindu traditions of faith, Max Picard, the twentieth-century philosopher, and Mahatma Gandhi. He knew, however, at an early stage that the contemplative life required – at least for him – the freedom and the rhythms of the natural world. In the changing of the seasons, in the silence of the woods where he was allowed to walk and work, in the vibrant life of the fields and the trees, he touched new depths. 'All you do is breathe, and look around.'[18]

It was no small achievement on Merton's part to secure the priority of contemplative prayer against the background of the prevailing culture of Cistercian houses. But the desire to be 'interiorly alone'[19] did not mean that his solitude could become a refuge from the world, and Merton, who lived with the contradictions that his temperament and his vocations imposed upon him, found that in entering the depths within, he was also entering the depths with others.

Merton refused to confine the contemplative life to those who shared his monastic vocation and he was quick to concede that not every religious is called to be, at least to an advanced degree, a true contemplative. But monasticism is founded upon the paschal mystery of death and resurrection; it embraces the habits of silence and solitude so necessary to the contemplative life; and the daily routine – the recitation of the psalms, the reading of the scriptures, meditation and liturgical prayer – provides a framework within which contemplative prayer might properly grow. What the monastery seeks to create for the monk with its rules and its observances is 'something of a spiritual desert of silence, solitude, detachment, poverty, austerity, labor and prayer.'[20]

It was the desert tradition that compelled Merton to look in the first place to the monastery as the place where the contemplative life might be encountered. In an early poem, 'St. John Baptist', he provided what might almost be an exposition of contemplative prayer.

I went into the desert to receive
The keys of my deliverance
From image and from concept and from desire.
I learned not wrath but love,
Waiting in darkness for the secret stranger
Who, like an inward fire,
Would try me in the crucible of His unconquerable Law.

And Merton – not reticent in this instance in making proprietorial claims – hailed the Baptist, by virtue of his being a 'Desert-dweller', as 'the first Cistercian and the greatest Trappist.'[21]

The austerity of contemplative prayer is a recurring theme in Merton's books, and so in another poem, 'The Quickening of St. John the Baptist', he wrote of:

The speechless Trappist, or the grey, granite Carthusian,
The quiet Carmelite, the barefoot Clare,
Planted in the night of contemplation,
Sealed in the dark and waiting to be born.

They are religious – both men and women – for whom 'Night is our diocese and silence is our ministry', and whose vocation is to be:

... exiles in the far end of solitude, living as listeners
With hearts attending to the skies we cannot understand.[22]

Throughout his years at Gethsemani, Merton saw contemplative prayer as the primary service that religious might offer the world, and in pleading for a renewed monasticism he was asking that monastic communities might be more open to the possibilities of contemplative experience. But what was Merton saying when he spoke of the religious as one who lives at 'the far end of solitude'? Was he holding up an ideal of monasticism from which monastic communities must inevitably fall short? Did he fail to take account of the institutional responsibilities that are inseparable from community life? Was he concerned to recover something that had been lost and that he believed to be essential to a true understanding of monasticism? Or was he merely identifying and commending a type of monasticism that would be more congenial to himself?

Necessary preconditions

Merton's commitment to the contemplative life was never an end in itself. It was always for the church and for the world. It may be that seclusion and silence and solitude would enable the religious to find union with God in contemplative prayer, but in contemplation the religious goes beyond personal illumination and finds commitment and empathy, taking to himself something of the pain of the whole world. It was, therefore, no small part of Merton's journey that contemplative prayer and contemplative living (and the theological presuppositions on which they rested) should inform his vocations as social critic and ecumenist.

Merton's insistence that his identity as a person could only be found in the free response he had made to God's call should not, therefore, be seen as a bid for personal autonomy. It was both his reading of the times and his understanding of the role of the religious that were so important in the discussion. He protested, especially in his later years, against any implicit suggestion on the part of his Superiors that the contemplative life might be used as a device for keeping monks under control, entirely detached from the world's problems. It was the fact that the religious lives in 'an ingrained irrelevance'[23] that equipped him for the critical questioning that constituted for Merton his distinctive vocation. 'For the monk searches not only his own heart: he plunges deep into the heart of that world of which he remains a part although he seems to have "left" it.'[24]

The two necessary preconditions for the contemplative life both inside and outside the monastery are solitude and silence, but it is *interior* solitude, *interior* silence. Merton wrote as one who, in spite of his many-sided personality, was both a solitary and a contemplative. There are times in his writings when the two words seem to be interchangeable. There is certainly a good deal of overlap, but there will be some who, gregarious by nature and living in the world, will have a contemplative dimension that requires something of the interior solitude of which Merton wrote so frequently. Solitude and silence belong together: they are not a retreat from life, nor do they constitute a self-indulgence, 'a narcissistic dialogue of the ego with itself'.[25] What they make possible is the authentic freedom, the authentic living, which Merton sought. They represent nothing less than a 'serious return to the center of our own nothingness before God'.[26]

The desert as a place of testing and a place of truth is central to Merton's understanding of the contemplative life. The person who responds freely to the call to solitude 'falls into the desert the way a ripe fruit falls out of a tree', but – with or without other people – it is still 'the one vast desert of emptiness … the place of silence where one word is spoken by God'.[27] The gifts of the desert are, therefore, the necessary degree of detachment, a proper perspective, a self-abandonment, and then – and perhaps only then – it is possible to stumble upon the mystery of the divine love.

The interior solitude to which the contemplative is called is a universal possession or, to be more accurate, a universal possibility. Merton believed that 'All men are solitary. Only most of them are so averse to being alone, or to feeling alone, that they do everything they can to forget their solitude.'[28] But it is only through the solitude that is born of emptiness, of nothingness, that a person comes to maturity. Only then can the fictions and the delusions that men and women construct be abandoned.[29] Only then can reality be faced and life be dealt with as it is. What matters is not achieving degrees of excellence in the contemplative life but the recovering of a person's true self.

There is nothing self-contained about the true or deepest self. Contemplation has a social and not merely a personal character. For Merton, it is in solitude that a person meets with the solitude of others and with the solitude of God. A deeper awareness of the world's needs is one of the first fruits of the contemplative life. But even more: the test of true solitude is the degree to which a person is 'wide open to heaven and earth and closed to no one'.[30] The degree of solitude to which a person might aspire will vary a great deal, but solitude remains – in the experience of the contemplative – 'the doorway … into the mystery of God'.[31]

Merton conceded that few are called to the contemplative life, or, rather, to a contemplative life with its heavy monastic resonances as he had portrayed it in his earliest writings. What mattered was the contemplative orientation: 'Prayer must penetrate and enliven every department of our life, including that which is most temporal and transient.'[32] He looked to the monastery to hold the contemplative experience for the whole church, recognizing the difficulties of practising contemplative prayer in the world; and yet he pleaded for the contemplative dimension as a necessary ingredient in the completeness of any person.

Merton recognized that many would feel the need for an interior silence in order to sustain their discipleship, but he became impatient with mystical writings that were out of touch with ordinary life: 'Mysticism flourishes most purely right in the middle of the ordinary.'[33] He had learned as a young Trappist that he could pray as he wrote, and in his later years new art forms came to his aid. Photography – with its focus upon the detail, the simplicity and the innate beauty of the ordinary – became an important aspect of his contemplative life; and calligraphy, or a form of calligraphy depicting abstract images in black ink, captured something of the silence he was eager to explore. More and more he sought a contemplative awareness in the routines of everyday life: 'Learn how to pray in the streets or in the country. Know how to meditate not only when you have a book in your hand but when you are waiting for a bus or riding in a train.'[34]

Merton's openness to life led him to appreciate the simplicity and the solidity of a living faith. Love of God and love of people: these were the priorities, and they were sufficient to guarantee the religious meaning with which all life might be invested. Contemplation was ultimately tested in the familiar routine of everyday life: 'walking down a street, sweeping a floor, washing dishes, hoeing beans, reading a book, taking a stroll in the woods – all can be enriched with contemplation and with the obscure sense of the presence of God'.[35]

The contemplative writings

Contemplation was the subject to which Merton continually returned in his writings, and his books signal the different stages through which he passed in his maturity as a monk and a contemplative. *What is Contemplation?*, published in 1948, was a small booklet which explored the meaning and the practice of contemplative prayer, drawing freely upon the scriptures and the Fathers of the church, especially Thomas Aquinas and John of the Cross. *Seeds of Contemplation* appeared the following year and was described by Merton as 'a collection of notes and personal reflections'.[36] It possessed many of the weaknesses of *The Seven Storey Mountain*, and Merton felt even at the time of publication that it lacked 'warmth and human affection',[37] but modest revisions for subsequent editions softened the general approach, and the book has the merit of introducing many of the themes – discovery, freedom and the darkness – that mattered so much to Merton in his understanding of contemplative prayer. *The Ascent to Truth*, over which Merton laboured long and hard, was eventually published in 1951. It was a book in which Merton drew freely upon the writings of John of the Cross, and it represented his only attempt to speak of the contemplative life in the light of dogmatic theology rather than personal experience. It is a distinction that was to count for a good deal in Merton's later writings.

Merton's early books on contemplation had their value, even though he came in due course to deride them as the writings of his younger years when as 'a rip-roaring Trappist' he had been too superficial, too cerebral.[38] *The Inner Experience*, although its publication was not finally authorized until 2003, was very largely completed in 1959 with the exception of a handful of additions and amendments that Merton made in 1968. It marked the transition in his writing about the contemplative life. Merton continued to seek the inner self in the desert of self-abandonment, but it was also there, beyond words and ideas, that the true self might find in the darkness of unknowing the unity of the whole creation in God. Merton knew that there was much in the contemporary world that was deeply destructive of all that was sought by contemplatives, and yet contemplation did not represent a life of withdrawal. It remained for men and women the ground of personal freedom, the ground of being in God. And it was there – perhaps for the first time – that Merton allowed the reader to see the degree to which he was beginning to draw upon the insights of Eastern thought, as he acknowledged the phenomenon of contemplative experience at different times and in different places.

A succession of books followed in which Merton shared his developing thinking: *The New Man* (1961), *New Seeds of Contemplation* (1962), *The Way of Chuang Tzu* (1965), *Zen and the Birds of Appetite* (1968), *Contemplative Prayer* (1969) and *Contemplation in a World of Action* (1971). *New Seeds of Contemplation*, which retained the substance of its predecessor, was none the less seen by Merton as a new book. He explained in the Preface that, whereas *Seeds* had come out of his own solitude, the writing of *New Seeds* had been informed by a growing awareness of other people: the loneliness and the perplexity of the scholastics and the novices for whom he had been responsible; the loneliness of people outside the monastery; the loneliness of people outside the church. Merton had changed in his understanding of himself and of contemplation. The difference was the degree to which he could now identify with the questions and the pain of the world: 'contemplation is out of the question for anyone who does not try to cultivate compassion for other men'.[39] Merton drew upon the language and the spirit of Zen as he expounded his understanding of contemplation as awareness; his appreciation of contemplation in distinguishing between the true and the false self; and his emphasis upon contemplation as the means whereby God, who transcends all ideas about Him, 'utters Himself ... speaks His own name in the center of your soul'.[40]

It was Merton's emphasis upon experience that made him so responsive to Zen, which speaks of consciousness rather than systematic teaching. *Zen and the Birds of Appetite* was published little more than a month before his death. It consists in large part of essays that had been published in previous years, and it conveys Merton's appreciation of Zen as an awareness of reality: 'simply [seeing] what is right there and [not adding] any comment, any interpretation, any judgement, any conclusion'.[41] Zen can therefore inform all situations, all traditions of faith, all experiences. The enlightenment to which Zen looks is to be experienced in the circumstances of everyday life, but the way that leads to enlightenment is – as in the Christian tradition – the way of self-emptying, of self-abandonment.

Contemplative Prayer, which was published the year after Merton's death, is a general essay on the nature of prayer. Its starting point was an attempt to get to grips with the personal prayer of the religious, but Merton had moved beyond the monastery in his thinking and his concern was to provide a study of monastic prayer, practical and non-academic, which might be of interest to all Christian people. He captured the meditative and contemplative aspects of personal prayer, the praying of the heart, in which every Christian can enter a tradition of praying – what Merton called 'the Church of the Desert' – in which light comes from the darkness and life from death.[42] Christian mystics and contemporary existentialists both informed his thinking as he considered the element of risk that is necessarily present, because it is only beyond the 'dark night of faith' that the light and love of God can be apprehended.[43] And so he turned again to the teaching of John of the Cross, for whom the soul must be like to 'a blind man leaning upon dark faith, taking it for guide and light, and leaning upon none of the things that he understands, experiences, feels and imagines'.[44] But Merton also offered a word of hope, because it is only when everything has been abandoned – 'all desire to see, to know, to taste and to experience the presence of God' – that God's presence can actually be experienced.[45]

Merton's increasingly important emphasis upon experience informed the connections he made between contemplation and action. There are passages in his writings where words such as solitude and mental prayer and meditation and contemplation seem to carry similar meanings. There are none the less important differences of emphasis and meaning, but the connections are strong and all these contemplative or quasi-contemplative activities are directed to one end: the realization of God and of our common humanity in a life of abandonment and self-giving.

Contemplation, like meditation, is not concerned with achieving a knowledge of God. It is, rather, the awareness that our whole being is penetrated by God's knowledge of us and His love for us. Love is the key word. Merton moved over the years far beyond any simplistic distinction between contemplation and action. He came to see the profound interconnectedness of all life. Contemplation might be the pure gift of God, but it is tested by the degree to which it leads individuals beyond themselves. If 'contemplation is charity drawn inward to its own divine source', there could be no question but that 'action is charity looking outward to other men'.[46]

A contemplative dimension

Merton saw the need to recover a contemplative dimension which had been almost obliterated by the prevailing culture – activist, technological, confused.

He rejected what passes so easily for contemplation but actually amounts to little more than self-love, and he dissented from specious assumptions about how God speaks. Indeed, he questioned 'the whole mentality that creates the impression that He has to be constantly speaking to people. Those who are the loudest to affirm they hear Him are people not to be trusted.'[47]

There may be a partial explanation here of Merton's reticence in writing about his own prayer life, but one rare insight is provided in his response to Abdul Aziz, a Sufi scholar with whom he corresponded during the last eight years of his life, concerning his method of meditation. He wrote of a way of prayer that is focused entirely upon the presence of God and His will and His love. There was no question of using any image of God. It was, rather, a matter of adoring God as One who is entirely beyond all comprehension. Merton's prayer could then be properly described as 'a kind of praise rising up out of the center of Nothing and Silence'. It was for him nothing less than seeking the Face of the One who, being invisible, makes Himself known to those who lose themselves in Him.[48]

Merton was mindful of the danger that contemplation might be seen as 'a spiritual commodity that one can procure, something that is good to have'.[49] He doubted if it is possible to teach people how they might become contemplatives. He knew the path that he must take for himself – 'a straight line into the void and the wilderness'[50] – but he held back from laying down clear ground rules for others to follow. There is, therefore, no template to which the reader might turn for a step by step guide to the practice of contemplative prayer.

Nor could there be! What becomes clear is that there is no hard and fast distinction in Merton's thinking between contemplative prayer and contemplative living. Contemplative prayer could certainly not be considered as prayer in any restricted use of the word – time, place, method, subject matter. For Merton, it is in contemplation that God makes Himself known as the ground and centre of our innermost being. The contemplative life is nurtured by contemplative prayer, but contemplative prayer remains *the coming into consciousness of what is already there. God is so close!*[51] It is helpful, however, to identify the significant reflections and experiences scattered throughout Merton's books, which, considered in relation to each other and in a way consistent with the main thrust of his thinking over a period of 20 years, make it possible to indicate the direction in which those who seek the path of contemplative prayer and contemplative living might move forward.

The contemplative way

The starting point is faith

Merton speaks of contemplation as 'an experience of divine things', and he goes on to insist that we can only experience what we have already begun to possess.[52] It is necessary in the practice of contemplative prayer to move beyond the convictions and the consolations of faith, but he is clear that 'You start where you are and deepen what you already have.'[53] The stories, the symbols of faith, the sacraments are primary points of reference, but the contemplative journey requires a good deal of openness as to where God might be found. There are none the less pitfalls for the unwary, and those who approach the contemplative life with nothing more than a spirit of curiosity or an appetite for new experiences are seriously mistaken.

The call to contemplation

Contemplative experience is 'a pure gift of God'.[54] It is in the nature of Christian faith that there is an awareness of the work of the Holy Spirit, and it is the activity of the Spirit that becomes increasingly important as progress is made in the life of interior prayer. Merton writes of being found by solitude, of being invited to enter it, but the vocation to interior solitude – and, therefore, to contemplation – requires a response. Many other gifts will be required: compassion, self-denial and a capacity 'to see the value and the beauty in ordinary things'.[55] The possibilities and the risks are considerable. Contemplation is gift and grace – and costly discipleship.

The desire to pray

It might be thought that the desire to pray can be taken for granted on the part of those who would pursue the contemplative way; but it is here – and at an early stage – that serious mistakes can be made. The problem is largely one of self-deception. What passes for interior dialogue can easily become 'a smoke screen and an evasion'[56] if the desire for God in prayer becomes a desire for the consolations of prayer. Contemplative prayer does not set a person free from the struggles of everyday life. It is John of the Cross who indicates the character of contemplative prayer.

> In order to have pleasure in everything
> Desire to have pleasure in nothing.
>
> In order to arrive at possessing everything
> Desire to possess nothing.
>
> In order to arrive at being everything
> Desire to be nothing.
>
> In order to arrive at knowing everything
> Desire to know nothing.[57]

What matters is not desire but the desire for God.

Entering the silence

Physical solitude may well be helpful, the absence of noise will almost certainly be essential, but it is interior solitude and silence that prepare the way for a contemplative life. A conscious effort is required, even in the midst of life's routines, to withdraw from the preoccupations and the cares that are the stuff of life. But times of solitude and silence must never be ends in themselves. The challenge is 'to become *fully awake*'.[58] What is, therefore, required is a recognition of our dependence upon God and of our poverty and weakness. Something of what these words might entail is to be found when Merton writes of the solitary as one who has gone beyond all horizons: 'There are no directions left in which he can travel. This is a country whose center is everywhere and whose circumference is nowhere. You do not find it by traveling but by standing still.'[59] This is a prospect that will mean different things to different people, but it requires an openness to the things that are not yet known, a slow and gradual preparation for the day when it will be possible to reach out to an entirely new way of being with God.[60]

Letting go

The absence – or the apparent absence – of activity is not in itself sufficient. 'There is no such thing as a kind of prayer in which you do absolutely nothing.'[61] The mind and the will must learn to rest in God. There must be a letting go of the familiar landmarks of faith and prayer, together with the attachments that constitute so much of our well-being. What is to be abandoned is not merely any reliance upon these things but also any perception of ourselves, any inappropriate self-image. 'Once you become aware of yourself as seeker, you are lost. But if you are content to be lost you will be found without knowing it, precisely because you are lost, for you are, at last, nowhere.'[62] The presence of God can only be experienced by those who let go of everything. Only then is it possible to receive God's gift of Himself and to find one's true self in Him. It is the ancient paradox of dying and behold we live. 'God Himself, bearing in Himself the secret of who I am, begins to live in me not only as my Creator but as my other and true self.'[63]

In the darkness

The phases that might be identified in the contemplative life move almost imperceptibly from one to another – the desire to pray, entering the silence, letting go – until any progress that has been made is overtaken by darkness. Merton draws freely upon the apophatic tradition as he insists that 'the way to God lies through deep darkness.'[64] It is a sombre note, and Merton brings into play his great skill with words in expounding the life of the solitary and of the contemplative. 'What prayer! What meditation! Nothing more like bread and water than this interior prayer of his! Utter poverty. Often an incapacity to pray, to see, to hope. Not the sweet passivity which the books extol, but a bitter, arid struggle to press forward through a blinding sandstorm.'[65] Merton is writing out of a desert tradition informed by his own psychology, but what he portrays all too vividly is the experience of interior conflict – of anxiety, doubt, poverty of spirit – as the solitary, the contemplative, finds that all familiar patterns of thought and action must be left behind. 'If nothing that can be seen can either be God or represent Him to us as He is, then to find God we must pass beyond everything that can be seen and enter into darkness.'[66]

The temptation is to doubt, but the experience of the contemplative speaks of a deeper truth. 'God, Who is everywhere, never leaves us. Yet He seems sometimes to be present, sometimes absent. If we do not know Him well, we do not realize that He may be more present to us when He is absent than when He is present.'[67] It may be that God can only be experienced as darkness, but penetrating the darkness is a new awareness, a new apprehension. The gift, the grace, if it can be received, is the presence of God, the knowledge of God, in uncertainty, in nothingness.

Nothingness

Darkness, emptiness, nothingness: the words speak of what is experienced 'when we have left all ways, forgotten ourselves and taken the invisible Christ as our way'.[68] Hitherto God has been known through concepts, images, symbols, but with the letting go of all these things, the contemplative moves beyond what is known to what is not known. What has, therefore, been entered upon is 'one vast desert of emptiness which belongs to no one and to everyone'.[69] It is in his exploration of nothingness that Merton draws most obviously upon the mystical traditions of both the Christian West and the non-Christian East. The hidden depths of the contemplative life remain mysterious and inexplicable, but what lies beyond all knowing and all unknowing is an awareness of a mutual indwelling, a recognition that the mystery of the deepest self and the mystery of God are one.

Loving and being loved

For the contemplative, the Christian contemplative, love is the only unfailing source of light and life. 'We do not see God in contemplation – we *know* Him by love.'[70] The solitude and the silence, the darkness of un-knowing, the experience of nothingness, serve one end: an awareness that the ground of all being is Love. It is a 'love that is free of everything, not determined by any thing, or held down by any special relationship. It is love for love's sake.'[71] Love and the freedom of love have no boundaries, and Merton, drawing out the meaning of these things, speaks of the paradox that to love God perfectly requires that we love ourselves perfectly as He loves us.

Discovering the true self

It is here that the contemplative is brought to the heart of contemplative prayer and contemplative living. Merton writes of 'a door [that] opens in the center of our being and we seem to fall through it into immense depths ... all eternity seems to have become ours'.[72] What is now within reach is the end towards which contemplation moves: it is the discovery of the true self in God, where there is no division or separation between subject and object, where the being of God – He IS – becomes the only reality, and where to find God is to find one's self.

Discovering all humankind

There can be no separation, however, between the discovery of one's true self and the discovery of all humankind in God. 'The more we are alone with Him, the more we are with one another.'[73] It is in the solitude of contemporary prayer that the contemplative moves beyond awareness to an identification with other people. What is, then, asked of the contemplative is an acceptance of responsibility for our world, and any refusal to engage is to ensure that the contemplative life becomes an illusion, an escape. Contemplative prayer and contemplative living are one, and both demand some sharing in 'the universal anguish and the inescapable condition of mortal man'.[74]

Discovering God

But whether Merton's emphasis falls upon the discovery of one's true self or the discovery of all humankind, it is always a discovery in God and a discovery of God. Beyond the contemplative experience of seeing and not seeing, of hearing and not hearing, of knowing and not knowing, there is the encounter with God in which He is loved and known and seen as One who is unseen and unknown and unpossessed. But this is the life to which the children of God are called. It is the sharing in the divine nature for which we are made.[75]

Few quotations from other writers in Merton's books are more telling than the words of Abbé Monchanin in which, capturing the spirit of the monastic calling and monastic prayer, he portrays the experience of the solitary and the contemplative. 'Now is the hour of the garden and the night, the hour of silent offering:

therefore the hour of hope: God alone. Faceless, unknown, unfelt, yet undeniable: God.[76] The many phases that might be identified in Merton's writings about the contemplative life and contemplative prayer – from the starting point of faith to the discovery of God – do not constitute a spiritual exercise that is complete and entire in itself. Merton was concerned, and especially in his later years, to draw out the *prophetic character*, the prophetic witness, of the contemplative life. He wanted solitude and silence to be informed by love, so that a first-hand experience of human suffering might give contemplative prayer greater reality and depth.

Claiming a full humanity

Merton judged the contemplative dimension to be necessary for the world as well as the church. It was one of his complaints in the 1960s that contemporary society was failing to give people lives that were fully and authentically human. Claiming a full humanity was an important part of the contemplative vocation. The ideal to which he pointed was 'one complete man who is in God and with God and from God and for God. One man in whom God is all in all.'[77] Merton was, therefore, persuaded that the contemplative life was to be pursued for the sake of others. The prophetic vocation of the solitary, the contemplative, was to withdraw so that they might contribute to the healing of the nations. Contemplatives, who have found their own freedom in God, cannot therefore fail to be a voice of protest, reminding all humanity of 'its true capacity for maturity, liberty and peace'.[78]

An austere vocation

It is possible to discern a sequence in Merton's writings about contemplation, but it is not a sequence that can be replicated in all circumstances. The phases that have been identified might serve as a guide for those who want to realize a contemplative dimension, but it has to be asked if Merton's emphasis upon the austerity of the contemplative vocation might be too heavy handed to be entirely helpful.

The apophatic tradition from which Merton drew freely throughout much of his monastic life placed great emphasis upon the phases that have been identified as *letting go, in the darkness* and *nothingness*; and yet he was quick to reject any caricature of his position based upon too great an identification with these things. 'Please don't think that I am for a whole lot of introversion and introspection … True, in the past I have been much more inclined to that kind of "contemplation" … but one learns over a period of years to go beyond the limits of a narrow and subjective absorption in one's own "interiority".'[79]

But even in his later years Merton returned time and again to the rugged sternness of the contemplative life. It is 'a life of deep sorrow and contrition'.[80] It offers nothing more than 'an arid, rocky, dark land of the soul',[81] and contemplation, because it is to be lived in 'the age of Auschwitz and Dachau, Solovky and Karaganda is something darker and more fearsome than contemplation in the age of the Church Fathers'.[82] It is possible to identify the traditions – philosophical, mystical, experiential – that informed Merton's thinking, but what were the other considerations, personal to Merton and his own psychology, that coloured his understanding of the solitary life, the contemplative life? His undoubted vocation as a contemplative was the bedrock of his life; but how much did it matter that for him the call to holiness could only be an austere vocation? that the rigours of the Trappist life represented the only response he could make? that discontents continually welled up within him? that his several vocations lived in an uneasy relationship with one another? These questions do not begin to hint at the whole story or point to one conclusion. There is a lightness of touch, a delight, a joy and an abundant good humour; but the dominant impression is of one who – at some unavoidable personal cost – dared to risk 'his mind in the desert beyond language and beyond ideas where God is encountered in the nakedness of pure trust'.[83]

A mystical theology

Merton's teaching about the contemplative life derived from his awareness of the church as the mystical body of Christ. A sentence in passing, written in a letter to a friend with whom he had corresponded over several years, spoke briefly of his conviction that 'We cannot get too deep into the mystery of our oneness in Christ.'[84] Merton looked to the transformation of all things in Christ, and his understanding of what this might mean fell within the parameters of the church's mystical theology. 'When you and I become what we are really meant to be, we will discover not only that we love one another perfectly but that we are both living in Christ and Christ in us, and we are all One Christ. We will see that it is He Who loves in us.'[85]

For Merton, the contemplative life represented nothing less than a continual rediscovery of Christ. His understanding of Christology and eschatology, with its strong emphasis upon what these core doctrines might mean for people in the present time, was central to his thinking. He was mindful of all the dimensions of Christian mysticism – biblical, patristic, liturgical – and implicit in his exposition of Christian contemplation, what he called *theoria*, was the central mystery of death and resurrection. The phases identified in his thinking as *letting go, in the darkness* and *nothingness* tell of God's self-emptying, of God's *kenosis*, in Christ. The phases identified as *loving and being loved*, the *discovery of the true self and of all humankind* and the *discovery of God* speak of the prophetic dimension which required an awareness of the mystery of God at work in history.

Merton stood firmly within the Western tradition of prayer – Catholic and monastic – but he knew that contemplation is not only a Christian phenomenon and he found it far beyond the confines of the Christian church. It was 'theology as *experienced*' rather than 'theology as *formulated*' that Merton was feeling after in contemplative prayer,[86] and this perhaps gives the clue to the broader and far more inclusive understanding of contemplation to which he aspired. He wrote to Amiya Chakravarty of 'the reality that is present to us and in us: call it Being, call it Atman, call it Pneuma ... or Silence', and went on to speak of 'the happiness of being at one with everything in that hidden ground of Love for which there can be no explanations'.[87] The mystical writings of the Sufis, together with Taoist, Zen and Buddhist influences, enabled Merton to make connections with his own understanding of the contemplative life and to incorporate insights from other traditions of faith and experience within a Christian frame. Merton, the Christian Trappist, might see contemplation as a mark of maturity in the Christian life, but the maturity he was looking for required a total inner transformation, and his mind was too open, his spirit too generous, to fail to recognize the points of consonance.

The transformation that he sought presupposed a contemplative journey in which, penetrating the depths of our own existence, there is a discovery of the God in whom we find ourselves in Christ. But the experience of God in contemplation is not for ourselves alone but also for others. This is the test by which the integrity of contemplative prayer stands or falls.

> The closer the contemplative is to God, the closer he is to other men. The more he loves God, the more he can love the men he lives with. He does not withdraw from them to shake them off, to get away from them, but, in the truest sense to *find* them. *Omnes in Christo unum sumus* [All are one in Christ].[88]

But transformation, which must take place in the depths of interior solitude, of contemplative prayer, can only be accomplished by love. Beyond the darkness, beyond the experience of nothingness, there is the awareness of loving and being loved which can now become the one true guide. 'He who is alone, and is conscious of what his solitude means, finds himself simply in the ground of life. He is "in Love." He is in love with all, with everyone, with everything … One disappears into Love, in order to "be Love." '[89]

Transformation has a broad remit, and so for Merton there must also be at the heart of love 'a contemplative grasp of the political, intellectual, artistic and social movements in this world'.[90] This emphasis, expressed so cogently in a letter to Pope John XXIII, can be seen in his unsuccessful attempt to secure papal recognition for a new kind of monastic community which, while it would be essentially contemplative in character, would welcome writers and intellectuals for retreats and discussions. What Merton was envisaging was an interpretation of the monastic and the contemplative life, which would be appropriate for him with his particular gifts and which might pioneer an entirely new kind of monastic foundation. And yet, leaving Merton's special pleading on one side, there continued to be in his interpretation of the contemplative life the need for a Christian understanding of society, a Christian interpretation of all that was happening in the world events of the day. It was an understanding which would find expression more and more in his writing as the contemplative informed the writer and the social critic. The prophetic dimension, which became increasingly pronounced in his thinking over the years, required the solitary person, the hermit, the contemplative, to realize and to inform a global consciousness.

Few passages in Merton's writings come closer to what he had been exploring in the contemplative life than the questions he posed to his readers in Contemplative Prayer. 'Does God impose a meaning on my life from the outside, through event, custom, routine, law, system, impact with others in society? Or am I called to create from within, with Him, with His grace, a meaning which reflects His truth and makes me His "word" spoken freely in my personal situation?'[91] For Merton, the contemplative life was the guarantee of his identity and integrity as a person, but breadth of vision ensured that as a contemplative he had a word of hope to offer: 'Whether you understand or not, God loves you, is present in you, dwells in you, calls you, saves you, and offers you an understanding and light which are like nothing you ever found in books or heard in sermons.'[92] In that word there lay not only Merton's convictions about God but also the invitation to find beyond solitude and silence the grace of an 'intimate union in the depths of your own inmost self, so that you and He are all in truth One Spirit'.[93]

The Social Critic

The monk retains his own perspective and his own horizons, which are those of the desert and of exile. But this in itself should enable him to have a special understanding of his fellow men in an age of alienation.[1]

The Christian cannot be fully what he is meant to be in the modern world, if he is not in some way interested in building a better society free of war, of racial and social injustice, of poverty, and of discrimination.[2]

Nothing demonstrates more dramatically Thomas Merton's capacity to change than his emergence in the 1960s as a social critic who was informed, engaged, articulate and passionate. He became during the last decade of his life one of the most outspoken social critics in the United States, but this was not a development that could have been foreseen during his early years as a religious. The desert traditions of withdrawal, solitude and contemplative prayer had taken Merton to Gethsemani, and it was there in the midst of his many preoccupations that he came to embrace the world, addressing the critical political and social issues of the day, and deploying from his distinctive standpoint his skills as a writer.

He recalled in the early 1960s that there had been an earlier time when the large questions had impinged upon him. He described himself as 'a survivor of the shipwrecked thirties',[3] although the radicalism of his student years had subsequently been obscured by a contempt for the world. The transition in his thinking had come shortly after the publication of *The Seven Storey Mountain* in 1948. It was then that he had come to see not merely that it was no longer possible for him to *write* as he had thought a monk ought to write; he could no longer *think* as he had believed a monk ought to think. He continued to reject the deceptions of the world, but he acknowledged that his earlier judgements had been too undiscriminating, too disdainful. The world most certainly represented at one level values with which he could not identify, but it was no longer an adequate, let alone a compassionate, response for the world 'to be first ridiculed, then spat upon, and at last formally cursed'.[4]

A deeper maturity, a wider experience, brought with them a greater clarity: 'The only essential is ... God Himself, Who cannot be found by weighing the present against the future or the past, but only by sinking into the heart of the present as it is'.[5] Step by step, year by year, it is possible to trace the developments: a changing attitude to the world; a rejection of any false dividing line between the sacred and the secular; a distinctive understanding of the role of the monk in society; an awareness of the perspectives that solitude could provide; a broad and deep compassion. All these were the necessary pre-requisites, but he had yet to find his voice. Prayer continued to be the first priority, but he saw increasingly the need to speak clearly and without any possibility of being misunderstood.

The earlier contempt for the world gave way to a growing conviction that he had come to Gethsemani in order to find his place in the world. In spite of his many discontents, he remained persuaded of the relevance of the monastic vocation. Religious may well be people who have separated themselves from society, but for Merton it was necessary that they should remain open to the needs of the world and in critical dialogue with it.

It was no longer possible for Merton to see the monastery as a place that was detached from the life of the world. It was 'the *whole* world' that was reconciled to God in Christ, 'not just the monastery, nor only the convents, the churches, and the good Catholic schools'.[6] And there was something more: the pretensions of Catholic Christendom, which had given the monk an assured place in society, no longer had any meaning. The monk was called once again to become 'a stranger and wanderer on the earth', but there was nothing constrained about Merton's understanding of the monastic calling. Conscious of feeling something of an outsider where his fellow countrymen were concerned, he could only emphasize the necessity of being 'an alien everywhere, to help the world become one, and deliver it from its obsession with small definitions and limited boundaries'.[7]

The idea of separation from all establishments was one that easily commended itself to Merton. It was on the margins that the monk would find his integrity, holding the vision and exploring the depths of human experience. It is not surprising that Merton should, therefore, make connections in his thinking between the monk and the poet, the displaced person, the prisoner, the protester against injustice. For him, they were all set apart by their vocations from the world, open to the possibility of suffering, and yet raising fundamental questions about the meaning of life. Merton spoke of himself as a revolutionist – 'in a broad, non-violent sense of the word' – and he believed that the revolution he sought would be achieved slowly and painfully not only through the initiative of the oppressed, but also through the work of intellectuals, artists, and men and women of prayer.[8] It was there that the monk must find his place.

The urgency of the situation persuaded Merton that the monk had a contribution to make *as a contemplative* in the discussions of his day. Solitude and silence, the foundations of a monastic life, should encourage religious to bring their awareness of God into all contemporary situations, but the monastic perspective would be enlarged for contemplatives who could enter into the universal experience of alienation, identifying with the solitude and the poverty of people everywhere. The monastery, therefore, became for Merton 'a place in which I disappear from the world as an object of interest in order to be everywhere in it by hiddenness and compassion'.[9] Yet there was nothing enclosed about the solitude that Merton sought. It served as the springboard for his work, enabling him to secure a hearing as a radical Christian social critic, and yet remaining – as his monastic calling required – at arm's length: 'halfway between in and out of the action'.[10]

It is entirely consistent with the man who is to be found in his several vocations that life should have been for Merton a struggle, courageous but costly, to seek the truth. Against the backcloth of what he feared most – a nuclear holocaust – Merton was clear that it was no longer sufficient merely to write about monasticism and the life of prayer. He judged the situation to be deeply serious, perhaps 'the most serious crisis in Christian history'.[11] An early poem, written in his first years at Gethsemani when the spirit of *contemptus mundi* was strong, spoke of 'the winter of our hateful century'.[12] What he now feared was a relapse into a collective barbarism in which both the individual and the freedom that alone can secure our humanity would lose their meaning.[13] The mass conformity he observed led him to explore the idea of alienation. The world was at crisis point: 'in turmoil, spiritually, morally, socially. We are sitting on a thin crust above an immense lake of molten lava that is stirring and getting ready to erupt.'[14]

Merton came to see that any contribution he might make was bound to be circumscribed by his being removed from the centre of political debate. It meant that he was confined to questions of principle; but through his writings

– mimeographed letters, articles and books – he secured a new constituency of readers as he spoke for a younger generation, giving voice to their concerns, their radical questioning. His affirmation was also theirs:

> Against the mass brutality of war and police oppression, solidarity with the victims of that oppression. Against the inhumanity of organized affluence, solidarity with those who are excluded from any participation in the benefits of almost unlimited plenty. Where 'the world' means in fact 'military power', 'wealth', 'greed', then the Christian remains against it. When the world means those who are concretely victims of these demonic abstractions (and even the rich and mighty are their victims too) then the Christian must be for it and in it and with it.[15]

Theological foundations

Merton saw the times in which he lived as a post-Christian age, and it was therefore proper that he should draw in his thinking upon a great diversity of sources. His starting point was the Christian gospel and the Christian conscience, but over and above the predictable sources – the Old Testament prophets and the Desert Fathers – he owed much to the writings of Erich Fromm, Czesław Miłosz, Albert Camus and Simone Weil, and to the far more conspicuously present influences of the Zen Masters, of Mahatma Gandhi and Boris Pasternak. What he found in them and many others through reading and correspondence was a confirmation of the contemplative vocation, in nurturing the freedom of the individual in the face of the forces of collective irresponsibility.

It was the *social* consequences of the monastic and the contemplative vocations that were so important for Merton in his later years. What followed, therefore, was the conviction that 'one cannot live and die for himself alone. My life and death are not purely and simply my own business. I live by and for others'.[16] No other rationale would be required for the social critique, wide ranging and hard hitting, that he felt compelled to make, but two primary Christian theological affirmations – *incarnation* and *eschatology* – underscored everything he had to say.

It was the doctrine of the incarnation, informed by Merton's mystical theology, that enabled him to see men and women in an entirely new light. 'In Christ, God became not only "this" man, but also in a broader and more mystical sense ... "every man". [17] It followed, therefore, that no Christian could be indifferent to the fate of any other person, because every person must be seen in some sense as Christ. But the insights Merton drew from his theology were reinforced by an understanding of the realities of life. The interdependence of nations and peoples required a new sense of mutual solidarity and mutual responsibility. The dynamics of a new world order served only to strengthen his theological presuppositions. 'It is no longer even a question of "my brother" being a citizen in the same country. From the moment the economy of another country is subservient to the business interests of my country I am responsible to those of the other country who are "in need". [18]

If it is the case that everyone is bound up in the lives of everyone else, then there are connections to be made with a Christian understanding of Christ's mystical body, the church. From the beginning, there had been somewhere near the heart of Merton's understanding of mystical theology the conviction that 'Christ suffers in the Church: and there is nothing suffered on earth that Christ Himself does not suffer. Everything that happens to the poor, the meek, the desolate, the mourners, the despised, happens to Christ.'[19] The softening of the hard edges of Merton's earlier way of thinking about the church and the world did not lead him, however, to abandon his emphasis upon the Christ who, having taken to Himself the fullness of our humanity, suffers now with those who are the victims of oppression. Merton's increasing awareness of the world as a single organism and of humankind as one family, one world, inevitably brought to the forefront of his concerns the priority of the poor and the dispossessed. 'The people of God are the poor of the world.'[20]

The present age was for Merton 'a time of finality and of fulfilment'.[21] Christ had come proclaiming the Kingdom of God, and it was the task of the Christian 'to build the Kingdom of God in this world'.[22] Christian people might continue to look for the transformation of all things at the end of time in God's final act of sovereign power, but *nothing* could abrogate the responsibility to build 'a better world here and now'.[23] Merton had not only left behind the old superficial boundaries between the secular and the sacred, he had also grown beyond earlier distinctions in eschatological thinking between *now* (what is) and *then* (what shall be). He wrestled, in common with others, with 'a new sense of eschatology: not the traditional hope of the second coming of Christ *at the end*, but of the revelation of eschatological finality *worked out within history* itself.'[24] For Merton, the Kingdom, although it could not yet be seen, had already been established, and it followed that Christians were therefore required to live in a time when choices must be made and decisions taken.

But incarnational faith and eschatological hope could not be separated, and together they required a deep involvement in all the concerns of the contemporary scene. Merton took his cue from the Russian philosopher, Nicolas Berdyaev: 'Eschatology is not an invitation to escape into a private heaven: it is a call to transform the evil and stricken world.'[25] The challenge for Merton was irresistible: 'If History is in God's hands, then what in God's name are we sitting on our fat rumps for, doing nothing, blind, deaf and dumb, waiting for God to prevent history from happening?'[26]

Monastic vocation, contemplative prayer, mystical theology, wide and instructive reading, extensive correspondence, and above all a mind that was open to what was happening in the world: all these combined to ensure that Merton offered a critique which continues to be pertinent. He spoke of his faith as an eschatological faith, but it was earthed in contemplation, and – with both feet planted firmly on the ground – he would insist that the Christian cannot realize his or her vocation in the modern world if he or she is not actively engaged in building a better society.

It was not the least of Merton's discontents that the limitations imposed on him at Gethsemani had very nearly stifled his vocation as a contemplative. His Christian formation – the Scriptures, the Fathers, the mystics – were complemented by the writings and the prophetic witness of Mahatma Gandhi, who spoke of the power of truth and love to transform the human scene. Truth (or his perception of the truth) and love (or his understanding of the claims of love) gave Merton's work as a social critic an integrity and a passion which it might not otherwise have had. Merton needed no persuading that 'Love is the only answer.'[27] The Kingdom of God was pre-eminently for him a kingdom of love and it is by love, God's love, that the Christian is called to transform the world. But love is not merely the ground of personal salvation, the key to the meaning of a person's own existence, it is also – for Merton – 'the key to the meaning of the entire creation.'[28]

He knew that predictable words about the meaning of love could easily be vacuous, but truth and love were not abstract concepts for Merton. They had meaning only in so far as there was a proper emphasis upon the integrity and the freedom of men and women as *persons*, and the freedom of the person was fundamental to all that he had to say. He distinguished in his use of words between the individual and the person, calling in question the cult of the individual that had dominated thinking in the Western world since the age of the Enlightenment. Individuals represented for him nothing less than 'the social atomism' that had led to inertia and decay.[29] What was required was a transformation of the present order and, because the progress of the person and the progress of society could only go hand in hand, nothing could be accomplished without the free participation of the person – all persons – in the life of the world.

It was one of the attractions of the writings of Boris Pasternak that Merton found there a confirmation of so much that he wanted to say. Pasternak did not write from a tradition of formal Christian faith, but he spoke out of a profoundly Christian tradition of spirituality. Merton applauded Pasternak's emphasis upon the nobility of the individual person, and – even more – his courageous challenge to 'the chaotic meaninglessness of all twentieth century life'.[30] The lesson that had to be learned applied to the West and the East, to capitalist as well as communist societies. *Dr. Zhivago* – to take the most obvious instance – was from Merton's point of view a protest not merely against Russian totalitarianism but against 'most of the gross, pervasive and accepted structures of thought and life which go to make up our changing world'.[31]

The church as a sign of contradiction

It was one of Merton's chief complaints that the church, and especially the Catholic Church, failed consistently to ask the questions, to voice the protests, he believed to be necessary. His judgement was that the church had become too conformist, too compliant. He wanted the church – indeed, all religious groups – to be centres of dissent whenever they found that political programmes and government policies called in question fundamental Christian principles. He saw the need for a Christian witness in political life but seriously doubted the wisdom of any so-called Christian policy which required the church to collude with 'the decadent structures of warfare states'.[32] He pleaded for a church that ceased merely to embody the past but actually embraced the future.

Merton was well aware of his capacity for impatience, for anger, when the church failed to respond to the needs of the times, but his criticism went beyond any suggestion that the church was just 'slow and stolid and inert'.[33] Accusations of something approaching culpable guilt are to be found, certainly in one journal entry, as he linked together in one broad sweep the behaviour

of German Catholics under Hitler, Pope Pius XII and the Jews, the Church in
South America, the treatment of Blacks in the United States, and the French
Right in the Algerian conflict.[34] Merton knew how easily the church could
'make an idol of itself, or identify too closely with other idols: nation, region,
race, political theory.'[35]

He bemoaned the timidity of so many Catholic thinkers and teachers and
writers. His personal faith and his high doctrine of the church remained
unimpaired, but he rejected the idea that fidelity to God and fidelity to the
institutional church are one and the same thing. His experience at the hands of
the censors of his Order led him to believe that any good he might do would
only be achieved in spite of his Superiors rather than with their assistance.[36] By
temperament, he continued throughout his life to be suspicious of the undue
influence that vested interests – secular or ecclesial – might bring to bear.
The robust Catholicism he sought had little room for church bureaucracies.
Merton wanted a church that would be less of an organization and more of a
community of persons united in freedom, in love – and in Christ. That was for
him the only basis for informed and critical discussion, for the free exchange
of ideas, for open dialogue. What Merton called 'centuries of triumphalist
self-deception'[37] had to give place to entirely new ways of being and thinking
and engaging. 'The Church needs Christians with independent and original
thought, with new solutions, and with the capacity to take risks.'[38] It was a need
that Merton was eager to meet.

It was only to be expected that Merton would be encouraged by the new
spirit of openness and dialogue, which characterized for him the pontificate
of Pope John XXIII. He welcomed Pope John's encyclicals on social justice and
on war and peace, and he was broadly appreciative of the work of the Second
Vatican Council, but he had no illusions about the situation in which the church
found itself in the middle years of the twentieth century. It was a time of crisis
for the church, but *crisis*, as Merton was quick to point out, meant *judgement*,
and 'the present is always being judged as it gives way to what was, yesterday,
the future.'[39] The crisis was one of identity and vocation, but any denial of the
truth of the situation would render the church incapable of making sense of the
claims that a new and unfamiliar world was making upon it.

Karl Rahner was one of the theologians who enabled Merton to see so clearly
the *diaspora* situation in which the church was now placed and to accept it
as the inescapable starting point for any engagement with the world. Merton
refused, therefore, to look for scapegoats – the secularity of modern thought,

or the infidelity of Christians; nor did he seek quick and easy solutions – a new outpouring of apostolic zeal. The diaspora was to be seen as 'a "must" in terms of the history of salvation',[40] and this emphasis enabled Merton to distance himself from those who looked back to a mythical golden age which must be recovered at all costs and to strengthen his conviction concerning the church's prophetic vocation.

It was certainly Merton's concern to keep alive in the world what he called 'the presence of a spiritual and intelligent consciousness'.[41] Social questions – poverty, the class structure, social justice, and especially non-violence – had preoccupied him at various times in the 1930s. He had flirted with campus communism at Columbia without allowing himself to be drawn fully on board, but as his vocations developed he saw the need to integrate his political convictions with his theology. Beneath the pious spirit of *contemptus mundi* of his early monastic years, there lay – somewhat submerged but ready to be called back into life – the familiar student tradition of being questioning, socially concerned, and in political terms Left-inclined.

It was only in the late 1950s, however, that Merton's interpretation of his vocation as a religious took on an entirely new dimension. Alongside his thinking about the meaning of monasticism, his expressed wish to live as a hermit, and his exploration of contemplative prayer, it becomes necessary to set his concern 'to discover *all* the social implications of the Gospel', joining with those who look for a transformation of the social order on the basis of certain principles: 'primacy of the *person* – (hence justice, liberty, against slavery, peace, control of technology etc.). Primacy of *wisdom and love* (hence against materialism, hedonism, pragmatism etc.).'[42]

Merton knew there were people who would listen to what he had to say. He was mindful of wanting to say something about everything. He knew his voice would frequently be dismissed as an empty protest; but he was convinced that 'there is a need in the world for something I can provide and ... [that God] is asking me to provide it'.[43] His caricature of the world as 'one immense and idiotic fiction'[44] might suggest a throwback to the disdain for the world he had felt in earlier years, but the 'primacy of the person' and the 'primacy of wisdom and love' provided the imperative which would direct his thinking and his writing. He could no longer stand aside: 'An idea, an inspiration, to him was not an idle matter, something to toy with. He saw response and action as necessarily called for ... He took a stand. He had a point of view. He took sides.'[45]

Power and the abuses of power

It was the corrupting influence of power to which Merton returned time and
again: the military power of the United States; the totalitarian ideology of
Soviet Russia; the arrogance of new technologies; the all-pervading influence
of the mass media, of advertising, of entertainment. He had taken American
citizenship in the summer of 1951, but he feared the combination of power,
decadence and naivety that he found in his adopted country.

His love–hate relationship with the United States contained the familiar
ingredients of anxiety, despair and foreboding. The triumphalism of American
patriotism was to be resisted as fiercely as the triumphalism of medieval
Catholicism. He challenged the myth-dream of a global power which invested
in under-developed countries in order to secure an economic, cultural and
political supremacy. His accusation was that the United States, government and
people alike, had believed its own propaganda about the American dream, the
unlimited resources at its disposal, and the rightness of its kind of democracy.
One issue after another – civil rights, the arms race, and especially the Vietnam
War – represented for him lost opportunities in showing the world how power
might be properly used. This is a judgement which begs many questions, but it is
one which subsequent generations would have little difficulty in understanding.
His complaint about the prevailing culture of the United States – 'mindless,
obtuse, self-deluded, self-complacent – destructive'[46] – led inevitably to his
continuing anxiety that internal tensions made it impossible for the United
States to exercise serious democratic leadership.

Merton's critique of the global scene was not confined to the failings of the
United States. He was no less strident in his denunciation of 'the degenerate
fascist Marxism of Stalin'.[47] Taking his characterization from Albert Camus, the
French existentialist philosopher, he likened the two great powers to sorcerer's
apprentices, expending vast sums of money on the arms race and the exploration of space, while ignoring the needs of two-thirds of the world's population
for the basic necessities of life. Like Gog and Magog, in their representation of
the lust for power and the love of money, the Soviet Union and the United States
were set fair to tear each other apart. Their societies – totalitarian or liberal as
the case may be – were 'becoming anthills, without purpose, without meaning'.[48]

The Marxist interpretation of history, on which the Bolshevik Revolution had
theoretically been based, was seriously flawed in Merton's judgement because
Marx in his analysis had made the capitalist the scapegoat for his discontents.

Merton was even-handed in his criticism when it came to the abuses of power. One of his charges against Marxist thought was that, in spite of its many protestations concerning the rights of the proletariat, it actually denied the rights of the individual. Something of what Merton meant was demonstrated by the treatment Boris Pasternak received at the hands of the Soviet authorities when he was required to refuse the Nobel Prize for Literature in 1958. But the Soviet Union, the United States and – increasingly – China were bracketed together in Merton's mind as global powers whose 'greatest sin' was not greed, or cruelty, or infidelity to the truth, but an *unmitigated arrogance toward the rest of the human race*.[49]

Behind the tyranny of the world powers lay the arrogance of technology. For one who was alert to all that was happening in the world, Merton's frequently negative approach to technology is somewhat surprising. He feared the consequences that flowed or might flow from a technological mind which had lost its grounding in the intuitive wisdom that only a profoundly religious understanding of life could give. Merton mocked the popular conception that 'science can do everything, science must be permitted to do everything it likes, science is infallible and impeccable, all that is done by science is right'.[50] It was an idea that would establish itself even more securely in the public mind over the coming decades; but it was for him a mind-set that was flawed and potentially destructive. Technology could only serve humankind's proper interests if it remembered that the ground of all being, the ground of all true wisdom, is God.

But nearer home, and impinging more directly on the lives of ordinary people every day, lay the highly seductive and deeply intrusive tyrannies of the mass media, advertising and popular entertainment. These were the activities which in Merton's judgement were responsible in large measure for creating a moral climate characterized increasingly by a resigned compliance. Words were in danger of losing their meaning: they had become too cheap. Political activity was increasingly suspect: programmes grew on every tree. One of the unhappy consequences was a frenetic desire to stay abreast of ever-changing orthodoxies which required individuals to re-define themselves in the light of all that was happening around them.

Merton drew attention to the myths and the illusions with which men and women comforted themselves. He acknowledged all that had been achieved by the American dream, but he could not fail to reflect upon 'a huge sense of desperation running through the whole society, with its bombs and its money and its death wish!'[51] For Merton, the violence that found expression in the racial crisis, in the possibility of a nuclear war, and in due course in Vietnam, had its roots both in the psychology of the American people and in the prevailing culture. 'It is a great, rich, blind, absurd nation, stiffnecked with pride in its own money and accomplishments, vulgar in its assumed simplicity, complacent in its imagined innocence.'[52]

Merton looked out not only upon his adopted country but upon a world which seemed to be dominated by 'totalitarian and passive conformities'.[53] He reckoned that it was not an age in which 'great things are to be done by brilliant men', and he feared that it might prove to be 'one in which blind forces work in and through men who are in many ways stupid, blind, yet terribly shrewd in their opportunism – and, above all, *tireless in working* for what they want'.[54]

Merton's reflections on the society in which he lived could be apposite, prescient, but they could also be too sweeping, too dismissive. It was for him an age of 'materialism, collectivism and power politics'.[55] He bemoaned the 'trivialities and illusions' of contemporary life.[56] He saw the potential for good, but he had an increasing sense of 'impending cosmic disaster'.[57] He identified the experience of alienation which necessarily had its roots for him, at least in so far as the Western world was concerned, in the loss of the religious dimension. The abandonment of a fundamentally religious understanding of reality had compromised men and women's integrity as persons and diminished their capacity to apprehend the meaning of truth and love.[58]

Oppression and discrimination

Merton's trenchant criticisms of the corrupting influence of power were fully matched by his compassion for the victims of all abuses of power. From the late 1950s onwards, one of the issues that dominated his thinking was the question of racial justice in the United States, as he turned his attention to the racial tensions in the South, and especially in Alabama. What was happening spoke to him of the nihilism, the confusion, of the American nation. He observed the valiant efforts of Martin Luther King Jr. and others to eschew violence as they argued their case by petitions, marches and peaceful demonstrations. The black-led, non-violent, civil rights movement was hailed by Merton as 'the greatest example of Christian faith in action in the social history of the United States',[59] but he denounced the inhumanity of those who were determined to keep black people down at all costs and feared for the violence that would inevitably follow.

It was for Merton 'a question of conscience for the entire nation'.[60] The everyday experience of discrimination, the instances of personal abuse and violence, the question of voter registration, the displays of police brutality through the use of truncheons, of dogs, of fire hoses, the burning of a church, the inevitable deaths of adults and children: all these were 'a judgement of our public daydream'.[61]

The circumstances surrounding the assassination of President John F. Kennedy continue to intrigue. It may not be the case that racial tensions provided the primary motive, but Merton made connections between what had happened in the South and the death of the President. So far as he was concerned, 'before the President was killed by the assassin's bullet, he had been assassinated a thousand times and more by Southern tongues and Southern newspapers'.[62] Merton understood the degree to which large public events are shaped by the small private events in which large numbers of people are caught up day by day. It may not be accurate to lay Kennedy's death at the door of the violent, at times murderous, white oppression in the South, but there is justice in the charge that 'the President's assassination was simply one in a series of murders which had recently taken place in the South and which were all manifestations of the same confusion, irresponsibility, malice, lawlessness and hatred'.[63]

Merton was fully persuaded that the churches had failed to give adequate support, colluding far too often with the practice of segregation in the South. He bemoaned the benign liberalism displayed by bishops, priests and ministers, questioning whether it amounted to anything more than 'a spiritual luxury, to calm the conscience of those who cultivate it'.[64] His complaint went beyond the complacency of Christians to accommodate all white liberals, including legislators in Washington, who on the grounds of self-interest sought to advance the rights of black people but none the less supported discrimination in their own cities. He feared for an uncertain future: 'Many chickens are coming home to roost in the white man's parlor. Some of them are going to be pretty large chickens, and some of them are going to have the manners of vultures. Too bad. The white man thinks himself sincere and honest, but he will gradually begin to find out what a con man he has been.'[65]

The questions raised in Merton's mind by racial tensions in the United States had wider connotations. It was self-evident to him that 'The problem of racial conflict is part and parcel of the whole problem of human violence ... The problem is in ourselves ... The racial conflict is only *one* symptom.'[66] His identification with the struggles of black people led him to look beyond the United

States to South Africa, and any initial thought that the policy of apartheid was merely an extension of the racial prejudice that could be found in the southern states of America had to be radically revised in the light of the massacre at Sharpeville in March 1960. He could not then fail to see the plight of the black South African as 'a completely degraded, concentration camp existence, not in misery only but in squalor, degradation, and suffering'.[67]

Merton's holistic approach to life enabled him to put both the civil rights movement in the United States and the fight against apartheid in South Africa in a global context, but everything had also to be put in a theological frame. He feared that the spiritual crisis which lay at the heart of these grotesque abuses of power might soon reach apocalyptic dimensions and had already shown the capacity to do so:

> … in Auschwitz, and in Babi-Yar. In Dachau, and also in Norilsk. In Birmingham and Johannesburg, but also in Chicago, Paris, New York, and London. In the bombing of Coventry and Rotterdam, yes: but also in the bombing of Hamburg, Dresden and Berlin. And, as with everything else in our time, all moral roads lead us eventually to Hiroshima and Nagasaki.[68]

The profound sense of the inter-connectedness of all life, which is found repeatedly in Merton's understanding of the relation of human beings both to the natural world and to one another, was to be found here also in his diagnosis of the human psyche which, alienated from its proper rootedness in God, allowed men and women to abuse, oppress and destroy one another.

Merton took encouragement from the way in which the forces of life assert themselves whenever violence has its way. He wrote as one who was deeply committed to policies of non-violence, but as he reflected on the scene in Latin America he saw the inevitability of revolution. His fellow countrymen failed to understand the grievances of Latin America and to see how the involvement of the United States in that sub-continent would be interpreted. Reading, poetry, correspondence and discussion came together to impress upon Merton how often poverty and exploitation went hand in hand. The Cold War offered a stark choice for the people of Latin America between the United States and Soviet Russia – 'the two giants that stand over all of us'[69] – both of whom represented for Merton exploitation in one form or another.

The whole American continent – North and South – mattered enormously to Merton. He found in the South elements of stability and permanence that were not necessarily present in the North, or in the North as Merton perceived and portrayed it. He hoped for sweeping social reforms in Latin America, and he found through his correspondence with Latin American poets a new spiritual awareness to which he attached great importance. It may be that his reaching out, if only in his writing, to South America, and in due course through his ecumenism to the Far East, represented an implicit rejection of the West: both Western Europe and the United States. He wrote somewhat grandiloquently: 'My vocation is American – *to see and to understand and to have in myself the life and the roots and the belief and the destiny and the Orientation of the whole hemisphere*.'[70] It is difficult to know what meaning to place upon these words, but there was undoubtedly a sincere desire to identify himself with the poor, the oppressed and the exploited.

What Merton found in the United States as the non-violent civil rights movement was increasingly called in question by the activities of Black Power, and what he discerned in Latin America as the demand for reform, if not revolution, gathered pace, spoke to him of a comprehensive rejection of colonial oppression in whatever form it might appear throughout the world. Nationalist uprisings and guerrilla warfare, which might be judged by the Western world to be threats to the established order, were seen by Merton as 'messianic, quasi-political, eschatological movements'.[71] He had little doubt that the whole world was in the throes of a vast upheaval, and with the United States and the Soviet Union locked in a life and death struggle for global supremacy, Merton looked increasingly to Latin America, to Asia and to Africa for signs of new life.

War and peace: Violence and non-violence

Overarching all social issues were the perennial questions of war and peace, the entirely new problems posed by the existence of atomic and nuclear weapons, and traditions of non-violence. Merton's protests against the corruptions of power led him to believe that 'Power has nothing to do with peace. The more men build up military power, the more they violate peace and destroy it.'[72] His starting point was the evil of war, and one of the touchstones of prophetic Christian discipleship was the decision as to where any individual might stand on this particular issue. He attempted to address the climate of opinion – the mental climate, the moral climate – in which lives are lived, judgements are formed and decisions are taken. He saw very clearly the impossibility of withdrawing from the struggle, but he came to feel increasingly a sense of great foreboding.

Merton was returning in these later years to concerns that had preoccupied him as a student in the late 1930s. He had not been a pacifist in those years, but he had come close to that position, believing that there were few wars that could be justified. Questions of international law, of just and unjust wars, of the rights of conscientious objectors had loomed large in discussions with friends. The German occupation of Czechoslovakia in 1938 had depressed him, and he knew that a situation would soon arise in which personal beliefs or disbeliefs would count for nothing and he would simply be caught up in the long list of those to be drafted. His emphasis upon the integrity and the freedom of every person, his critical questioning of the authority of established hierarchies, his empathy with those who found themselves oppressed: all these things, which became so prominent in the years at Gethsemani, were to be found there at the beginning as he struggled to make sense of his burgeoning vocations against the backcloth of a world that was being drawn into war.

What had changed in the post-war years was the awareness that the threat of war was now not merely the threat of global war but of nuclear war. What Merton most feared was the destruction of entire populations in a nuclear war whose consequences for people and for the land would be felt for generations to come. It was not that atomic and nuclear weapons were more immoral than conventional weapons, but that policies which might lead to total annihilation were necessarily and inherently evil. The nature of war had changed, and Merton found it easy to imagine a situation in which world leaders, encouraged and endorsed by the mass media and carried forward by a great outpouring of popular support, would be powerless to stand against a tide that would draw them inexorably into a war of vast proportions. It was a situation in which the idea of a just war would be utterly irrelevant. Traditional distinctions between combatants and civilians no longer applied, and he therefore doubted the wisdom of a strategy that placed such emphasis upon the balance of power, nuclear deterrence, the threat of retaliation, and (in the wings but scarcely out of sight) the possibility of a pre-emptive strike.

Merton saw himself over the years as a man whose task was to work for the abolition of war. As early as the late 1940s, he was increasingly persuaded that 'a Christian ought to be something very close to an *absolute pacifist*'.[73] He deplored the failure of Catholic theologians to speak out against the inhumanity of war, and presumed to ask: 'How many Christians have taken a serious and effective stand against atomic warfare? How many theologians have striven to *justify* it?'[74] The possibility of nuclear war was for him a threat to the survival of the human race, and he made few concessions to those who wrestled with the realities of power politics. His position was unambiguous: 'Even though one may not be able to halt the race toward death, one must nevertheless *choose life*, and the things that favour life.'[75]

The qualifications, even the contradictions, in his position remained unresolved. He would not call himself a total pacifist. Indeed, he conceded the need in some circumstances and when everything else had failed to use violence in the struggle against dictatorships; but because it seemed to him to be inevitable that any outbreak of war, however limited in scope, might lead to nuclear war, he came to believe that war must be eliminated as a means of settling international disagreements. In the early 1960s, Merton was writing at a time of heightened international tension and before the Test Ban Treaty of 1963. He might speak of a nuclear war as absurd, unjust, suicidal, immoral, but he rejected as inadequate both the tradition of total pacifism and unrealistic proposals for unilateral disarmament. He could even contemplate – surprisingly, in the light of his many strictures and forebodings – 'a very limited use of atomic weapons in a clearly defensive situation.'[76] In fact, he came to see the importance of unilateral initiatives in a step-by-step progress towards disarmament and argued the case for an international authority which could monitor and hold in check the manufacturing and stockpiling of nuclear weapons.

Merton recognized that any commitment to the abolition of war required a willingness to look first at 'the psychological forces at work in ourselves and in society'.[77] He identified the fear that lies at the root of all war and the ease with which the claims of conscience are abandoned. He feared a public mind-set which, given the choice between the survival of communism and the destruction of the entire human race, might actually choose death and destruction. He looked with abhorrence and despair upon a scene in which the chances of survival were being weighed against an immense and inconceivable loss of life.

Merton had welcomed the Christmas messages of Pope Pius XII and Pope John XXIII with their condemnation of the immorality of total war, but in general he was frustrated and angered by what he saw as the apparent indifference and incomprehension with which most Christian people watched the pressures that accumulate until a nuclear war becomes inevitable. Merton's response was to unleash a flood-tide of books, articles and poems which, from the autumn of 1961, placed him in the forefront of the debate. It was the period when he declared 'war on war'.[78] Articles appeared in a variety of journals – *Commonweal*, *Jubilee*, *Fellowship*, *Blackfriars*, *Catholic Worker*, *Peace News*, *Saturday Review*, *Pax Bulletin* and *Peace*; and a handful of titles indicate the focus of his concerns – 'The Root of War is Fear' (*Catholic Worker*, October 1961), 'Religion and the Bomb' (*Jubilee*, March 1962), 'Ethics and War' (*Catholic Worker*, April 1962), 'Red or Dead: The Anatomy of a Cliché' (*Pax Bulletin*, May 1962) and 'We Have to Make Ourselves Heard' (*Catholic Worker*, June 1962).

The threat of censorship was never far away, and Merton had already decided to circulate privately to a small group of contacts a series of mimeographed letters, which reached a wide circle of readers. *The Cold War Letters*, which were written and circulated between October 1961 and October 1962, were written in haste and in the heat of the moment. They spoke passionately of his concern that men and women were unwilling to contemplate 'the total immorality and absurdity of total war'.[79] He made little of the threat posed by the Soviet Union, but protested against what he saw in the United States: 'a warfare state built on affluence, a power structure in which the interests of big business, the obsessions of the military, and the phobias of political extremists both dominate and dictate our national policy'.[80] Meanwhile, articles which were only published under the title of *Peace and the Post-Christian Era* in 2004 were simultaneously circulated in a mimeographed form in some 500 or 600 hundred copies.

It was the hope that some of these items might be published that finally drew down the formal inhibition that Merton must have anticipated. It was inevitable, given the times and the traditions of the Order, that Merton should have been required to keep silent on questions of war and peace. A letter from the Abbot General categorically refused permission for the publication of *Peace and the Post-Christian Era* on the grounds that Pope John's encyclical *Pacem in Terris* had already said what Merton was wanting to say. Merton rejected the argument that contemplatives should remain silent. He acknowledged the right of his Superiors to require his obedience, but it did not therefore follow that he would be 'interiorly servile'.[81]

It was none the less a matter of deep concern for Merton that the silence imposed on him was tantamount to 'a silence which is deeply and completely in complicity with all the forces that carry out oppression, injustice, aggression, exploitation, war'.[82] The inhibition touched a raw nerve where Merton's understanding of the monastic and the contemplative vocations were concerned. It was not merely that the freedom he sought for himself was being denied, but rather that what he judged to be near the heart of the monastic life – the opportunity to be 'attuned to the inner spiritual dimension of things' – required for him a high degree of free and spontaneous expression.[83] Censorship in the Order was relaxed over the next year or two and Merton was then permitted to write about peace but not about war. 'This seems to mean that I can radiate sweetness and light but not condemn the bomb. How much sweetness and light can you stand?'[84] Meanwhile he continued his literary activity, his links with the Peace Movement and his growing involvement in ecumenical dialogue, securing for himself along the way a position of privileged detachment at Gethsemani.

What lay increasingly at the heart of Merton's writing about war and peace was a firm commitment to non-violence. He saw very clearly the limitations of violence which could do little more than 'transfer power from one set of bull-headed authorities to another'.[85] He sought a new way of resolving conflict and one which sought a change of mind on the part of the oppressor. Non-violence represented an entirely new way of looking at life, of being, of living. It was tanta-mount to conversion, representing for Merton a form of religious humanism, but it attempted to address the political implications of the Gospel and sought 'a *more Christian and more humane notion of what is possible*'.[86] The theological foundations were contained within the Beatitudes, and Merton wrote as one for whom non-violence came close to the heart of the Gospel.

Martin Luther King and Mahatma Gandhi impressed Merton deeply as men who in their political struggles embodied the principle of non-violence. Gandhi, whom Merton had defended in a school debate at Oakham, exercised the greater influence, representing for Merton one of the outstanding person-alities of the first half of the twentieth century. He had identified himself with the dispossessed in his struggle for the liberation of India from Imperial rule, and yet, drawing his inspiration from both Hindu mysticism and the Christian Gospel, he understood something of the two worlds, the East and the West, that had come to mean so much to Merton. He was utterly persuaded of the sacredness of all life and believed that religious faith and political action are ultimately inseparable. He spoke of *satyagraha*, the power of truth and love, and held that a free and just society could only be established on the basis of non-violence. *Ahimsa*, or non-violence, was for Gandhi 'the basic law of our being'.[87] It was a principle, a way of living, that was to be found supremely in the Christ of the Gospels, who remained for Gandhi a supreme model of non-violent resistance. Merton acknowledged his indebtedness to Gandhi, even though he struggled with transposing Gandhi's principles so that he might make sense of his own situation. But he needed no persuading that 'The way of peace is the way of truth'[88] and he found in Gandhi's writings a message not just for India but for the whole world.

Merton was well aware that he was one of the few Catholic priests in the United States who had declared his hand unequivocally for a fight, an uncompromising fight, for the abolition of war and for the adoption of non-violent means in order to settle international conflict. It was no longer a protest against the bomb, against nuclear testing, against the Polaris submarines, against the whole policy of deterrence, but against *all violence*. He feared the outcome of the policies being pursued by the great powers: 'How long can the menace of war grow and grow, and still not end in war?'[89]

It was a commitment that brought him into contact with different people within the broad umbrella of the peace movement – Joan Baez, Dorothy Day, Dan Berrigan, Jim Forest and others – together with the more formal groupings represented by the *Catholic Worker*, the Catholic Peace Fellowship and the Fellowship of Reconciliation. He welcomed 'patriotic dissent and argument'[90] and he responded warmly to the social awareness and the generosity of spirit that he found among the young people who identified themselves with the peace movement. It was easy for Merton to align himself intellectually with 'the pacifists, the "non-violent", the radicals, the "outsiders"',[91] but he became increasingly aware of things that were 'morally sloppy and irresponsible'.[92] He compared the activities of some people in the peace movement unfavourably with the work of Martin Luther King and Mahatma Gandhi, sensing that 'there is something radically wrong somewhere, something that is un-Christian'.[93]

The burning of draft cards and, even more, the isolated instances of self-immolation at the time of the protests against the Vietnam War confirmed his worst fears. He applauded the idealism, but he could not endorse actions which were being used to gain publicity, to create an image, and he deplored what he identified as 'a spirit of madness and fanaticism'.[94] There were significant differences of opinion, hasty responses on Merton's part, fractured relationships, and he found himself obliged more and more to confine himself to a non-participative role, while reserving the right to make his own protest from time to time as he might see fit. But nothing would qualify in any way Merton's conviction that non-violence remained a 'witness to living alternatives ... *essential* for the survival of a society'.[95]

So many things came together as the Vietnam War unfolded: Merton's growing disenchantment with the United States, his opposition to the corruptions of power, his increasingly global perspective, his commitment to non-violence. He wrote of 'the agony of the Vietnamese conflict'. It was for him 'an unjust war, a war of tragic stupidity'.[96] His savage criticism of American policy, and of President Lyndon B. Johnson in particular, led him to denounce the way in which the United States exercised its power in the world. He made connections between the attitudes of mind that had surfaced in the racial conflicts in the Southern states of America and the military action that was taking place in Vietnam: 'We have decided that we will police the world – by the same tactics as used by the police in Alabama: beating "colored people" over the head because we believe they are "inferior".' [97] But behind this tendentious statement lay something of greater moment: Merton had come to believe that 'the real problem is with the delusory character of American thinking about life, reality, what the world is all about'.[98] He saw a generation of people and their leaders 'lost in abstractions, sentimentalities, myths, delusions',[99] and – to compound the folly – he saw them not merely defending their own understanding of reality but actually setting out to impose it forcefully on the rest of the world.

Merton's tirade of accusations was not confined to the United States. If – in his judgement – the Pentagon did not want peace, he was equally clear that Red China was no less guilty. He abhorred the cynicism and the indifference to basic human rights that seemed to characterize whatever strategy the Chinese might have, and he judged that Peking would be content to see the war continue indefinitely. Meanwhile he feared the consequences of developments in China itself as a new cultural revolution was being staged: 'A tightening of the same screws by a lot of kids who are just being given their first taste of power.'[100]

One of Merton's greatest concerns was the way in which modern warfare, even in a relatively confined area, inflicted the greatest loss of life upon the civilian population. His reckoning suggested that in the Korean War (1950–3) 84 per cent of the fatalities had been civilian deaths. And so in Vietnam, as he read of guerrilla attacks by the Viet Cong on American bases in South Vietnam, he knew that retaliatory attacks in North Vietnam, including the use of napalm, would inevitably mean the systematic destruction of towns and villages and vast swathes of jungle in the hope that a handful of guerrillas would be killed.

Merton reflected upon a scene in which the Vietnamese people were the victims of the atrocities committed by both sides. It was they who were 'being burnt, cut to pieces, tortured, held as hostages, gassed, ruined, destroyed'.[101] He lamented the impersonality of what warfare had become – 'modern techno-logical mass murder'.[102] Merton, even as he condemned the Vietnam War as 'a piece of irreparable folly',[103] was brought back to his primary emphasis upon the integrity of the person, whose value could only be discerned by an empathy, an identification, that proceeded from love. Technology, uninformed by the wisdom of the Gospel, could not begin to understand. It was a theological perspective that underscored his conviction that 'the Vietnam War is more fantastically inhuman and absurd than ever'.[104]

The social critic: Strengths and weaknesses

It is in Merton's work as a social critic that the element of divine discontent – in his passion for justice, freedom and humanity – can be seen most clearly. He brought to this work the perspectives of his vocations as a monk and a contemplative, but his openness to all that was happening in the world, his critical and enquiring mind, his passion for truth and for life ensured that in all his chosen areas of engagement what he sought was a God-centred humanism. Just as he battled for a greater degree of freedom in the interpre-tation of his monastic calling, so he called for the freedom which enabled men and women to respond to life. But freedom implied responsibility, and no one could be properly understood outside the network of social relationships and social obligations. It followed, therefore, that the Christian vocation can only be explored in the modern world if there is a desire to build a society set free from war, oppression, poverty and discrimination. For Merton, 'To build the Kingdom of God is to build a society that is based entirely on freedom and love.'[105]

Merton understood the need to interpret the human scene. Reading, writing, correspondence and the exchange of ideas at his Sunday Conferences and with individuals and groups who came to see him at the hermitage gave him the opportunity to modify and to enlarge his judgements. Many of his opinions were pertinent, some were prescient, even perhaps prophetic, but there was always the tendency to over-simplify, to dramatize. A reading of his *Journals* often suggests that he thought as he wrote, that he wrote as he felt. He was not always able to develop a coherent critique, and he was mindful of serious limita-tions in his writing.

I am disturbed at my combativeness ... It comes out most when I think I have a just cause ... I come out for 'justice' and 'truth', but I come out swinging at everything ... Often I am premature, my opinions are ill-considered and undocumented, and on the strength of a couple of fairly good intuitions I may end up by a useless and harmful blast that takes in the good with the bad in the general explosion.[106]

It was an honest self-assessment.

Merton wrote of the contemplative's need to have a sense of history, but the ease with which he resorted to 'instant value-judgements' betrayed for some his lack of any thoroughgoing historical discipline.[107] Certainly he failed to show any proper awareness of the limitations of power experienced by those who hold high office, of the difficulties of making decisions, of the hard slog of achieving desired ends. One of Merton's great strengths as a social critic was his capacity to direct attention to the root causes of specific problems in society and in ourselves. It was in that spirit that he asked for 'a realistic acceptance of the fact that our political ideals are perhaps to a great extent illusions and fictions to which we cling out of motives that are not always perfectly honest'.[108]

Merton's social criticism, especially on questions of war and peace, were challenged at one point by Czesław Miłosz. Merton had already acknowledged in an earlier exchange of letters that he was often far too indignant about 'something vague and abstract', but then – in words so characteristic of a radical student in the 1930s – he spoke of the guilt he felt by virtue of his background: 'I am after all the prisoner of my class ... But the fact remains that I hate being bourgeois, and hate the fact that my reaction against it is not a success: simply the bohemian reaction ... with a new twist, a religious modality.'[109]

But Merton's self-criticism is not necessarily more accurate than his social criticism. What is so remarkable is the degree to which he combined his vocations as monk, as writer, as contemplative, as social critic. He carried his passions in his heart, and he used every opportunity he could find to bring them into the light of day. He was willing to concede that his writing could be 'too loud, too sweeping, too excited, too preachy'.[110] He knew that he was often misunderstood – and not only by his Superiors – but even as he took a stand, recognizing the limitations of all judgements, he continued to deploy his greatest strengths, wrestling with a global perspective, a theological interpretation.

The present world crisis is not merely a political and economic conflict ... It is a crisis of man's spirit. It is a great religious and moral upheaval of the human race, and we do not really know half the cause of this upheaval … That is why our desperate hunger for clear and definite solutions sometimes leads us into temptation. We oversimplify. We seek the cause of evil and find it here or there in a particular nation, class, race, ideology, system. And we discharge upon this scapegoat all the virulent forces of our hatred, compounded with fear and anguish.[111]

Merton wrote, as a social critic, with a good deal of self-knowledge. But Czesław Miłosz had one pertinent question to ask of him. What was he doing *as a contemplative* engaging so wholeheartedly with these matters of political and social concern? 'I ask myself why you feel such an itch for activity?'[112] Was Merton trying to compensate for the years he had spent as a Trappist monk? Were questions of war and peace a means whereby he could establish links with young American intellectuals? Was it appropriate for Merton to become 'a belated rebel out of solidarity with rebels without a cause'?[113] Merton had long since found his justification in the conviction that God is active in history, and that the contemplative cannot be fully true to his vocation unless he confronts 'the Lord of History … in the awful paradoxes of our day'.[114] It was certainly an argument that served to justify the several vocations that he was determined to pursue simultaneously.

Merton knew the limitations of his vocation as a contemplative, but he remained confident in what he was attempting to do. The questions raised by Miłosz were entirely pertinent, but Merton continued to insist that only contemplation enabled men and women to see their world aright. 'Without contemplation we remain small, limited, partial: we adhere to the insufficient, permanently united to our narrow group and its interests, losing sight of justice and charity, seized by the passions of the moment.'[115] It is a passionate *raison d'être* of the life to which he had been called and of the distinctive interpretation he placed upon it. What he sought in all his vocations (and not least of all in his work as a social critic) was nothing less than '*a conscious confrontation* with Christ' both in himself and in others.[116]

The Ecumenist

I will be a better Catholic, not if I can refute every shade of Protestantism, but if I can confirm the truth in it and still go further.

So, too, with the Muslims, the Hindus, the Buddhists, etc. This does not mean syncretism, indifferentism, the vapid and careless friendliness that accepts everything by thinking of nothing. There is much that one cannot 'affirm' and 'accept', but first one must say 'yes' where one really can.

If I affirm myself as a Catholic merely by denying all that is Muslim, Jewish, Protestant, Hindu, Buddhist, etc., in the end I will find there is not much left for me to affirm as a Catholic: and certainly no breath of the Spirit with which to affirm it.[1]

One of Thomas Merton's insights concerning contemplative prayer was that beyond the darkness in which familiar words and images are abandoned, there lies a new awareness of God which – because it leads back into the life of the world – has a prophetic dimension. If the Christian understanding of incarnation and eschatology provided the theological springboard for Merton's work as a social critic, it was his experience of contemplative prayer that opened the way for an ecumenical vision that went far beyond anything he could have foreseen at the outset.

Merton set his face firmly against any kind of religious syncretism, but he believed that contemplatives had a major contribution to make to the peace of the world and the unity of humankind. They might be isolated and misunderstood, but they could still hold in their individual lives whatever is most valuable in all the great traditions of faith. Indeed, he believed that the Christian faith, significantly different in important respects from other world faiths, might none the less realize its full potential only through a serious encounter with the religions of the East. It was the measure of his openness that he looked for the things that are held in common, pleading for a contemplative ecumenism which could witness to the shared experience of the divine presence.

Merton's understanding of his monastic calling, with its emphasis upon the role of the religious as a marginal person, enabled him not merely to see himself as a pilgrim and an exile, but to find a sense of solidarity as 'the friend and brother of people everywhere, especially those who are exiles and pilgrims like myself'.[2] In his Preface to the Japanese edition of *Seeds of Contemplation*, published in 1965, Merton reflected upon the meaning of the contemplative life. He described a 'journey without maps', leading into 'rugged mountainous country' where the one who travels is increasingly required to travel alone, but where 'he meets at times other travellers on the way'.[3] And so, distancing himself from the men and women of his own tradition of faith, caught up in all the preoccupations of the Western world, he identified himself in spite of all the differences with those who, like the Zen monks of ancient Japan, represented an ancient tradition of intuitive wisdom.

Merton tried to get beyond the cultural and institutional trappings that obscured the life of the church. For him, the activist stance, which the church invariably presented, was worthless without 'the secret, interior, lowly, obscure knowledge of God in contemplation'.[4] He was identifying by contrast a way of living, a way of being, that was both possible and necessary. Such a way did not represent a diversion from the hard realities of life. It was an austere, costly vocation, and its defining characteristics were solitude, emptiness, identification, suffering. It proposed to the world an entirely different viewpoint that went beyond doctrinal definitions and ethical codes. For Merton, the Catholic Trappist monk, it was rooted in the fundamental mysteries of Christian faith – death and resurrection, liberation and transformation – but its goal was 'a living contact with the Infinite Source of all being'.[5]

Inextricably bound up in Merton's mind with the practice of contemplative prayer was the God-given freedom which he sought for himself and for all people. His incarnational faith required him to speak of the presence of Christ in the unbeliever as *'perhaps the deepest most cogent mystery of our time'*.[6] It was, therefore, axiomatic for him that 'The Lord who speaks of freedom in the ground of our being still continues to speak to every man.'[7] But the solitude which leads to interior freedom must give rise to 'the independent voices' which cannot fail to cry out against every devaluation of humanity, and for Merton it did not matter if the voices that spoke were those of Christian saints, Oriental sages, Zen Masters or Jewish philosophers. 'God speaks, and God is to be heard,

not only on Sinai, not only in my own heart, but in the *voice of the stranger* …
We must, then, see the truth in the stranger, and the truth we see must be a
newly living truth, not just a projection … of our own self upon the stranger.'[8]

A wider ecumenism

Even in his years as a student at Columbia in the late 1930s, as Merton was
moving towards Catholicism and beginning to find his vocations, there are
hints of a wider frame of reference. One of his closest friends, Robert Lax, had
studied Jewish mysticism. Another friend, Sy Freedgood, was instrumental
in introducing him to Bramachari, a Hindu monk, who directed Merton's
attention to the spiritual writings in the Christian tradition: the *Confessions*
of St Augustine and *The Imitation of Christ*. Merton's notebooks suggest early
forays into the writings of Chuang Tzu and Zen Buddhism, together with
an awareness of the ascetical and contemplative traditions of Hinduism. The
Catholicism that Merton embraced with such fervour at that time did not afford
much scope for a burgeoning ecumenism and the years of monastic formation
at Gethsemani, together with the increasingly heavy burden of writing, gave
him little time or space in which to take forward some of the elements in his
earlier thinking. But by the late 1950s, important developments were taking
place, influenced as always by his monastic calling, by reading, correspondence
and conversation, and by the way in which his several vocations stimulated
each other.

Merton's awareness of the traditions of scholarship to be found in
Protestantism owed much to his reading of Karl Barth and Dietrich Bonhoeffer.
'There is so much truth there, he wrote of Barth, 'so much of the Gospel,'[9] and
by the same token he endorsed much of Bonhoeffer's thinking in his *Ethics* and
his *Letters and Papers from Prison*. He distanced himself from those whom he
called Bonhoeffer's followers with their notions of 'religionless religion', but
he was entirely in sympathy with Bonhoeffer's understanding of 'Christian
worldliness', judging him to be much closer to Catholicism in that respect than
Barth. It is fascinating to see how easily Barth and Bonhoeffer were absorbed
by Merton into his own theological world-view. Indeed, Merton linked Luther,
Kierkegaard, Barth, Bonhoeffer and the Protestant existentialists in his brief
acknowledgement of those whose writings are faithful to what he called 'the
original grace of Protestantism'.[10]

Ecumenism was given its greatest fillip in the Catholic Church by the work of the Second Vatican Council, but for several years prior to the Council groups of Protestant clergy, ministers and seminarians had met regularly at Gethsemani. Baptists, Disciples of Christ, Episcopalians and Methodists came at different times from Kentucky, Indiana and Tennessee, together with universities from the Midwest, and Merton was a key player in initiating and managing these informal dialogues. He had little time for 'official' ecumenism and dismissed out of hand what he disparagingly described as 'formalized and stereotyped gatherings for the celebration of clichés'.[11] He delighted in the fact that the conversations at Gethsemani brought together groups of Christian people who could meet and talk in charity with one another. He might reflect with a certain sardonic humour on 'the sweet earnestness of Methodists', on 'the polish and sophistication of Episcopalians', and on 'the sometimes rather taut fervor of the Baptists';[12] but his primary concern was always for the good that might be achieved by ordinary conversation, and he came more and more to see 'the validity of Protestantism and its spirit'.[13]

The wider ecumenism that Merton sought received quiet encouragement in the Council's *Declaration on the Relationship of the Church to Non-Christian Religions (Nostra Aetate)* in October 1965. Merton was able to quote with approval the statement that 'the Catholic Church rejects nothing which is true and holy' in the other great traditions of faith, acknowledging that they might 'often reflect a ray of that Truth which enlightens all men'.[14] It gave Merton whatever endorsement he might require. A global consciousness required a global vision. A global vision demanded a global ecumenism. And ecumenism – as a word – had come to represent for Merton the universality which historically had been implicit in Catholicism. Any failure on the part of the church to enter into dialogue with non-Christian faiths would, therefore, be for him a denial of her much vaunted Catholicism.

By the early 1960s, Merton's horizons had extended far beyond his early literary preoccupations. His work as a social critic was paralleled by an ecumenical vision. His concern in both spheres was to discern the truth of the situation, to relate to those who shared his priorities, to speak (so far as he was permitted) without fear or favour, to get beyond the lines of demarcation, and to embody – above all to embody in his calling as monk, as priest, as hermit – the hopes of a tormented and divided world. His starting point was faith, Christian faith; and his hope – earnest, symbolic, even somewhat pretentious in the words he used – was that he might make some contribution to a greater understanding between the churches. 'If I can unite *in myself* the thought and the devotion of Eastern and Western Christendom, the Greek and the Latin Fathers, the Russians with the Spanish mystics, I can prepare in myself the reunion of divided Christians.'[15]

Friendship was an important catalyst in the development of Merton's thought, and the men and women who became friends exercised a significant influence. Merton was consistently open to new ideas, new influences. He was aware of new attitudes in ecumenism, and he was at pains to insist that there must be an entirely new awareness of the Church's task. So it was that alongside his reading of Protestant theologians and Russian mystics, together with his informal discussions at Gethsemani, he set out consciously to embrace a wider ecumenism. He had come to feel that the contemporary scene called for a dialogue between East and West, in religion as well as in politics, and he was more and more convinced that the tradition of wisdom to be found in Western Christendom could be seen in Orthodoxy, and also in Islam and in the religious traditions of Asia.

It was the judgement of several friends that the depth of Merton's Christian commitment made it possible for him to engage with other traditions of faith. His prophetic awareness enabled him to look beyond the existing world order and to plead for new perspectives, believing that the mind-set he sought would lead to 'a recovery of ancient and original wisdom'.[16] He attempted to build upon a foundation of Christian mystical theology and Christian contemplative prayer as he established a dialogue with like-minded persons of other faiths, attempting to discern a common tradition of contemplative experience. The necessary qualifications for such an exploration were a sincere desire for truth, serious goodwill and a genuine love for one another. Men and women of different traditions had lived in different circumstances and their faith had been shaped accordingly; but – Christian, Buddhist, Muslim or Jew as the case may be – their common ground was 'direct confrontation with Absolute Being, Absolute Love, Absolute Mercy or Absolute Void, by an immediate and fully awakened engagement in the living of everyday life'.[17] Contemplative prayer and contemplative action continued to go hand in hand.

The theocratic humanism that was so conspicuous in his social criticism was also to be found in his ecumenical encounters. Merton's incarnational faith enabled him to see every person as being in Christ, or being Christ, and it therefore followed that ecumenism could no longer be confined to dialogue between the churches. His aspiration – 'we must contain all divided worlds in ourselves and transcend them in Christ'[18] – had been written with regard to relations between the separated Christian traditions, but his vocation as an ecumenist was assuming a far wider interpretation.

The Abrahamic faiths

It was through his extensive correspondence with Abraham Heschel, a Jewish rabbi and teacher, with Zalman Schachter, an Hasidic scholar, and with Erich Fromm, a writer and a psychoanalyst, that Merton deepened his appreciation of Judaism and of his earlier insights into the Jewish mystical tradition. Merton had great reverence for the Jewish scriptures, and especially for the psalms and the prophets. He identified himself with the 'experience of bafflement, compunction and wonder' that he found in the psalms[19]; and he recounted with delight the times he had sat on the porch of his hermitage and sung in the Latin translation chapter after chapter of the prophetic writings, allowing his rendering to ring out over the valley. For Merton, the Bible – the Christian Bible in its entirety – was not a denial but an affirmation of Judaism. What he found in the prophets was not merely the prophets themselves but the ever-challenging word of God; and the discovery of that word – and of its power to speak today – required of Jew and Christian an attitude of mind that was humble, receptive and reflective.

Merton wrote out of a sense of belonging to the people of Judaism through a shared experience of the desert tradition. Repentance, magnanimity and truth were his carefully chosen words when he intervened on behalf of the Jewish people in a plea to Cardinal Bea, who presided over the Secretariat for Christian Unity, in the course of the deliberations of the Second Vatican Council. An early draft on the Catholic Church's relations with the Jews, greeted by some as a prophetic statement, had been withdrawn; and Merton, responding to pressure from Abraham Heschel, urged that political considerations such as the concern of bishops in Arab countries should not be decisive, and that, at the very least, there should be some acknowledgement of the degree to which anti-Semitism had informed Catholic thought and feeling down the centuries.[20]

The sensitivity of Merton's approach to Judaism was undoubtedly coloured by his abhorrence of all that the holocaust represented for his generation. It was a sign of everything that Christians had lost sight of over the centuries: namely, that – for the Christian – Israel and Christ cannot be separated. The Suffering

Servant of the Songs of Isaiah is both Israel and Christ: 'There is one wedding and one wedding feast ... There is one bride. There is one mystery, and the mystery of Israel and the Church is ultimately to be revealed as One.'[21] Merton's expressed wish was that he might be 'a true Jew under my Catholic skin',[22] and nothing conveyed that desire more completely than his conviction that 'the Christian needs to wait with the longing and anguish of the Jew for the Messiah, not with our foregone-conclusion, accomplished-fact-that-justifies-all-our-nonsense attitude'.[23] It was the word of a true, if somewhat impatient, ecumenist.

It was the uncertain relations between Christians, Jews and Muslims that had threatened to be so contentious in discussions at the Vatican Council. Merton was alert to the political sensitivities and greatly regretted that any mutual understanding was hard to find, but the common inheritance of faith weighed heavily with him. He wrote of reading the Quran with reverence and serious attention, and delighted in 'its spirit of loneliness, independence of men, dependence on God, emptiness, trust'.[24] His discovery of the mystical writings of the Sufis was an important breakthrough for Merton and he was able to jest that 'I am the biggest Sufi in Kentucky though I admit there is not much competition.'[25]

Merton's study of Islam, the third of the Abrahamic faiths, was influenced at the outset by Louis Massignon, a Catholic priest in the Melkite rite and one of the twentieth century's most distinguished scholars of Islam. Massignon's studies had led him to the story and the writings of Akhbar al-Hallaj, a ninth-century Sufi mystic, and it was there, guided no doubt by Massignon, that Merton began to see the importance of Islam. As early as March 1960, Merton wrote of finding in al-Hallaj 'the inexorable face of sanctity', and he went on to ask 'Where has it gone, this sense of the sacred, this awareness of the Holy?'[26]

Massignon had also encouraged Abdul Aziz, a student of Sufism living in Pakistan, to write to Merton. Aziz had been deeply moved by Merton's study of St John of the Cross in *The Ascent to Truth*. The correspondence between Merton and Aziz, including the exchange of books, continued throughout the last eight years of Merton's life, and by May 1961 Merton was writing of 'the solidity and intellectual sureness of Sufism', confident that it provided 'a deep mystical experience of the mystery of God our Creator'.[27] Both men, Merton and Aziz, were making connections with each other's traditions of mystical theology and contemplative prayer; and something of what they had in common is represented by Merton's translation of lines from Ibn Abbad, a fourteenth-century Islamic mystic.

To belong to Allah
Is to see in your own existence
And in all that pertains to it
Something that is neither yours
Nor from yourself,
Something you have on loan;
To see your being in His Being,
Your subsistence in His Subsistence,
Your strength in His Strength:
Thus you will recognize in yourself
His title to possession of you
As Lord,
And your own title as servant:
Which is Nothingness.[28]

Like St John of the Cross and the dark night of unknowing, Merton found in Ibn Abbad that only in the emptiness, in the desolation, could the possibility of mystical union arise.

Eastern traditions

Something of the tolerance and the inclusivity that he sought was found by Merton in Hinduism which, in spite of a great diversity of practice, represented for him 'a devotional and philosophical polytheism'.[29] Merton had probably received his first introduction to the contemplative traditions of Hinduism through his reading of A. K. Coomaraswamy's book *Transformation of Nature in Art* while he was a student at Columbia. It had shown him the necessity of asceticism and contemplation in the work of the Hindu artist. Twenty-three years later, Merton wrote to Coomaraswamy's widow that her late husband had been for him the model of one who had completely united within himself the insights and the traditions of East and West. For Merton, the importance of such people lay in the fact that they could be sacraments or signs, preparing the ground in the minds of their contemporaries for the reception of new ideas.

No person fulfilled that particular role more cogently for Merton than the Mahatma Gandhi. It was the contemplative tradition of Hinduism that informed so much of Gandhi's life and teaching, enabling him to respond as a devout Hindu to the Person of Jesus and to the teaching of the Sermon on the Mount. Gandhi's claims upon Merton were strengthened by his commitment to non-violence, and Merton's anthology of Gandhi's writings enabled him to draw out Gandhi's emphasis upon an entirely new way of living – *satyagraha* – which might lead to the transformation of all persons, of all situations, by love. It was, therefore, 'a *universally valid* spiritual tradition' that Merton found in Gandhi,[30] a way of being that looked not merely to the liberation of India but to 'the awakening of a new world'.[31]

Merton spoke of Hinduism as 'the oldest surviving culture in the world' and he discovered its insights and its traditions in the *Vedas*, the *Upanishads* and the *Gita*.[32] It was especially in the *Bhagavad Gita* that he found the ideal of a life in which worship, action and contemplation are drawn together. Merton feared that the activism that had so shaped Western culture would prove to be self-destructive, and he looked increasingly for an experience rather than an idea of God as the 'ultimate ground of reality and meaning'.[33] That was the common ground that Merton sought and in which he rejoiced when he found in any correspondent, such as Amiya Chakravarty, the Indian poet, philosopher and scholar, a shared experience of the Divine Life and Light.

Merton remained earthed in his Christian faith, although his discovery of the *Brihad-Aranyaka Upanishad* in 1961 led him to exclaim '*Kairos*! Everything for a long time has been leading up to this, and with this reading – sudden convergence of roads, tendencies, lights, in unity!'[34] But the convergence was not taking place at the expense of his own tradition of thought and prayer, and the entry in his journal for that day concluded: 'Scriptures. Greek patrology. Oriental thought. This enough to fill every free corner of the day not given to prayer, meditation, duties.'[35] It was his rootedness in his Christian tradition that was to be of particular importance as he came to explore the religious dimensions of Tao, Zen and Buddhism.

Tao means quite simply *the way*, and Merton's exposition led him to speak of 'the inscrutable way of God'.[36] Taoism has much in common with Confucianism, but whereas the latter places a greater emphasis upon formation in external forms of behaviour, the former is focused entirely upon the source of all being which cannot be named or known. There are hints as early as his student days when he worked on his master's thesis that Merton had taken note of some of the masters of Taoist and Zen thought.

Paul K. T. Sih, of the Institute of Asian Studies at St John's University in Jamaica, Daisetz Suzuki, a Zen scholar and university teacher, and John Wu, who was both a scholar and a diplomat, were deeply influential in guiding Merton towards some of the classic Taoist texts and in enabling him to delight especially in the writings of Chuang Tzu, the Chinese Taoist master of the fourth century BC.

Merton responded with great eagerness to Chuang Tzu, whom he regarded as the most impressive and the most eloquent representative of Chinese Taoist thought. His translations of Chuang Tzu's poetry[37] make it possible to see the connections that Merton was making. There is an obvious parallel, for example, between the Taoist sense of no-being and the Christian apophatic tradition, exemplified by St John of the Cross.

> To name Tao
> Is to name no-thing.

> Tao is beyond words
> And beyond things.
> It is not expressed
> Either in word or in silence.
> Where there is no longer word or silence
> Tao is apprehended.[38]

But there was something more: Merton's monastic perspective put him increasingly at variance with the aggressive self-assertion of Western culture. What Merton found in the writings of Chuang Tzu was a tranquillity which goes beyond any distinction between action and contemplation, drawing all things into a living, dynamic whole.[39] Mystical thought and mystical experience were never far from Merton's mind and undoubtedly assisted his exploration of Taoism. He was also looking, in step with a Taoist approach, for the transformation of everyday life and for an awareness of the cosmic unity which underlay all things. John Wu described Merton as 'a true man of Tao,'[40] but the man who was both social critic and ecumenist could never retreat into a philosophical position which set him apart from the world.

> Can a man cling only to heaven
> And know nothing of earth?

They are correlative: to know one
Is to know the other.

To refuse one
Is to refuse both.[41]

It is perhaps here that Merton's innate strength as a Christian exponent of Eastern thought is to be found. As he considered Taoist texts in the course of a discussion of the Christian scriptures, he wrote of finding in Taoism 'a full awareness of the transcendent dimensions of everyday life in its very ordinariness'.[42]

In correspondence with his friend and guide, Daisetz Suzuki, Merton came to see the early Chinese Zen Masters as the true heirs of Chuang Tzu. If Tao can be conveniently described as *the way*, then Zen must be seen primarily as *awareness*, but it is an awareness, immediate and intuitive, of the ground of being. Zen is not a religion or an ideology, nor is it to be confused with techniques of meditation. It is a type of spirituality which is at variance with the rationality and self-consciousness of men and women in the Western world. 'Zen teaches nothing; it merely enables us to wake up and become awake. It does not teach, it points.'[43] Zen is realization not revelation, experience not explanation. It represents a liberation from all ideas of subject and object, of the individual in relation to God and to others. It is an awareness of the dynamism of life itself living in us, but being at one and the same time the one life that lives in all.[44]

There is little evidence of any wide-ranging study of Eastern thought on Merton's part before the mid-1950s, but from that time he was drawn increasingly in that direction. The previously unpublished manuscript 'The Inner Experience' (1959) and *New Seeds of Contemplation* (1962) both indicate the influence of Zen on Merton; and from the early 1960s a large number of essays appeared which focused in one way or another on the religious experience of East and West, leading in the last two years of Merton's life to the appearance of two books – *Mystics and Zen Masters* (1967) and *Zen and the Birds of Appetite* (1968) – where the substance of his thought in this area is to be found.

Paul Sih, Daisetz Suzuki and John Wu continued as correspondents to influence the development of Merton's thinking, and Merton was also greatly assisted by the visit to Gethsemani in May 1966 of Thich Nhat Hanh, a Vietnamese Buddhist monk. Wu, who was a Chinese convert to Catholicism, was unapologetic about the fact that he had brought Confucianism, Taoism and Zen with him into his Christian faith, and Merton's conversation with Nhat Hanh led him to observe:

> He is more my brother than many who are nearer to me by race and nationality, because he and I see things exactly the same way ... It is vitally important that such bonds be admitted. They are the bonds of a new solidarity and a new brotherhood which is beginning to be evident on all the five continents and which cut across all political, religious and cultural lines to unite young men and women in every country in something that is more concrete than an ideal and more alive than a program.[45]

Merton was sceptical of the superficial response to Zen in the West. The new solidarity that he was identifying was located for him in the ancient mystical wisdom of the East and in its many correspondences with the contemplative and mystical traditions of Christianity. There were connections to be made in Merton's mind between the writings of Zen Masters and the sayings of the Desert Fathers and the tradition of prayer associated with Meister Eckhart and the Rhenish mystics. The Zen Buddhist emphasis on *sunyata* (or emptiness) had resonances with the understanding in Christology of *kenosis* (or self-emptying) and the experience in Christian ascesis of the dark night of the soul beyond which illumination is to be found in God Alone. And so Merton, reading Suzuki's books, could write that 'Time after time ... something in me says, "That's it!" Don't ask me what. I have no desire to explain it to anybody, or to justify it to anybody, or to analyze it for myself. I have my own way to walk, and for some reason or other Zen is right in the middle of it wherever I go ... I'll say simply that it seems to me that Zen is the very atmosphere of the Gospels, and the Gospels are bursting with it.'[46]

There is also in Zen – and this would have mattered a great deal to Merton – a refusal to separate matter and spirit. Enlightenment is to be found in the ordinary, the pedestrian, the everyday experiences that life presents. There is, therefore, no question of passivity, of withdrawal. Being and seeing and doing are synonymous and interchangeable, and so the Zen experience, which is neither more nor less than an awareness of the unity of things visible and invisible, could be seen as 'an Asian form of religious existentialism',[47] and John Wu could pass on the comment that Merton's writings were 'full of Zen even when they were not about Zen'.[48]

The sheer volume of Merton's literary output might suggest a preoccupation with words, but Zen Buddhist meditation commended itself to Merton because it required the practitioner 'not to *explain*, but to *pay attention*, to *become aware*, to *be mindful*, in other words to develop a certain *kind of consciousness that is above and beyond deception* by verbal formulas'.[49] But Merton went on to insist that at the heart of the Christian tradition is 'a *living experience* of unity in Christ' which goes beyond all doctrinal statements.[50] For Merton, Christian experience could not be detached from the Person of Christ and the corporate life of the church as His mystical body; but nor could revelation be confined to 'a system of truths *about* God', nor to 'a moral discipline', nor to 'a feeling of confidence that one has been saved'.[51] It is rather 'a living theological experience of the presence of God in the world and in mankind through the mystery of Christ'.[52] Faith does not merely provide access to authoritative teaching but to 'a deep personal experience which is at once unique and yet shared by the whole Body of Christ, in the Spirit of Christ'.[53] There is a freedom in Zen in its refusal to be enclosed within institutions and formulas that would have spoken to Merton's restless spirit, and for him Zen was entirely compatible with Christian belief and Christian mysticism if by Zen what is meant is 'the quest for direct and pure experience on a metaphysical level'.[54]

It was Merton's interest in Zen that led him eventually to a deep affinity with Buddhism. The Zen approach to life is essentially contemplative, and for Merton the importance of Buddhism lay in the fact that it is at heart not a religion or a philosophy but a way of being in the world. Merton rejected all caricatures of Buddhism, and especially the charge that it is life-denying, and he found in its many variations – in Burma, in Ceylon, in Japan, in Thailand, in Tibet – a view of reality, a way of looking at life, which is in no sense hostile to the spirit of Christianity.

The ideal to which the Buddhist aspires is one in which 'the individual ego is completely emptied and becomes identified with the enlightened Buddha, or rather finds itself to be in reality the enlightened Buddhist mind'.[55] It is a process of self-abandonment, of identification, of transformation, which is to be paralleled in the Christian experience of death and resurrection and transfiguration. And so it is that nirvana speaks of an understanding of life which is to be found 'in openness to being and "being present" in full awareness'.[56] It is not an escape from life, but it is to be found in the midst of life and suffering and death.

Merton's monastic life gave him a good deal of insight, and he warmed to the idea of Zen monks placing direct experience over and above the theoretical knowledge that comes through study. He understood the Buddhist monastic life as a life of pilgrimage in which the training, the disciplines, the teaching and the observances are not allowed to become ends in themselves. Perhaps there was the merest hint of monastic jealousy as he reflected on Buddhist practice in giving the monk a high degree of spiritual freedom to pursue *on his own*, in the light of Buddhist precepts and meditation, the path to enlightenment. This was something he struggled to secure for himself at Gethsemani.

Merton's ecumenism had strong Christian foundations. He might plead that he was doing nothing more than exploring the truth of Christ as it might be found in other faith traditions, but he realized that the church was required – perhaps for the first time – to take note of non-Christian religions and to do so *in their own terms*. It was for him a matter of deep concern that he should be part of that early dialogue. What mattered was his commitment to 'a wider *oikoumene*', an ecumenism that extends beyond the bounds of Christianity to all those seeking the ultimate meaning and purpose of life.[57] But something else was being identified. Merton had acknowledged with Suzuki that love – rather than enlightenment – was what mattered most in both Buddhism and Christianity. Openness, awareness – yes; but more than anything else, nirvana spoke to Merton of 'the wisdom of perfect love grounded in itself and shining through everything'.[58] Merton had identified the only ground on which dialogue could proceed.

The basis of dialogue

Merton consistently set his face against ecumenical endeavours, especially between the Christian churches, which were inherently bureaucratic. Friendship, spiritual freedom and spontaneity were the things that mattered. He protested instinctively against the individualism, the activism, of a Western Christian culture and he despaired of any suggestion of superiority: churches in relation to other churches, churches in relation to other world religions, churches in relation to the world.

Merton deplored the failure of the church in its missionary work over the centuries to encounter the Christ who was already present – implicitly present – with the result that it had become, in consequence, an agent for disseminating European culture and Western power. It was not that Christianity needed the insights of non-Christian religions to complete the revelation it had received, but rather that the Western philosophical and mystical tradition would have

been greatly enriched if the church had been open to the religious thought
and the philosophy of the East. The church had all too often displayed in its
relation to the indigenous cultures where it had attempted to take forward its
missionary endeavours the same arrogance that the West repeatedly demonstrated in the political sphere. His judgement was a clear indication of the basic
stance that he would adopt in any wider ecumenical dialogue: 'If I insist on
giving you my truth, and never stop to receive your truth in return, then there
can be no truth between us.'[59]

There was a global dimension in Merton's thinking that took him far beyond
the constraints of the Western Christian tradition. He discerned the growth of
a universal consciousness, and although he could not see what it might mean in
practice, he was absolutely clear about the need to find new perspectives in a fast
changing world. Confident in his own faith, it was none the less as though he
needed to cross the boundaries of faith in order to find with those in other traditions the full meaning of faith for himself. The differences between the world's
great religions might be substantial, but the analogies that were to be found in
the realm of religious experience were too important to be disregarded. What
he sought was the free exchange of ideas, of experience. It would be a dialogue
in which the key characteristics would be compassion and identification.

There was for Merton at the heart of all the world's great religions an original
unity 'beyond words ... beyond speech ... beyond concept'[60] which can only be
located in religious experience. He was feeling after a wider frame of reference:
'The more I am able to affirm others, to say "yes" to them in myself, by discovering them in myself and myself in them, the more real I am. I am fully real if
my own heart says *yes* to *everyone*.'[61] These are slippery words, but it is impossible to sustain the charge of doctrinal indifference. For Merton, Christianity
was first and foremost a way of life rather than a system of thought. New birth
in Christ required 'a continuous dynamic of inner renewal';[62] and, feeling his
way against a background of monastic vocation and contemplative prayer, it
was in the solitude of a life hidden with Christ in God that the true wisdom of
the Spirit would be apprehended.

Merton knew that his approach was too intuitive, but what he found in
his Christian tradition of faith and in the ancient religions of the East was
'a principle of liberty',[63] which sets men and women free from the deceptions of the ego and enables them to engage with the world. It was part of the
attraction of Zen Buddhism for Merton that 'It is nondoctrinal, concrete, direct,
existential, and seeks above all to come to grips with life itself, not with ideas

about life, still less with party platforms in politics, religion, science or anything else.'[64] Merton was especially alert to people in the Western world who did not profess any Christian faith but who, like men and women in the East, were none the less alert to silence and solitude. It was a constituency which enabled Merton to justify his experiential approach and to persevere in the work of exploring new depths of awareness in human existence. What he sought was a life-affirming spirituality which might hold in tension contemplative prayer, the fullest development of the human person, a critical solidarity with the world, and – beyond all faith and prayer – union with God who, unseen and unknown, is yet to be encountered as the ground of all being.

Everything was used by Merton to inform his monastic vocation, but it was a two-way street. Merton was no less mindful of the unique insights that monastic life might bring to ecumenism. The perception of truth, which lay at the heart of all serious religious experience, was directly related – certainly in Merton's judgement – to the distinctive contribution which men and women of prayer, and especially religious, might bring to any dialogue between the various Christian traditions but also with other communities of faith.

It may be that Merton was seeking a far wider interpretation of mystical theology, of contemplative prayer, than had previously been attempted. Eastern thought and Eastern monasticism became significant elements in his writing. He was a self-appointed go-between, enabling men and women of faith across the religious divides to learn something of each other's traditions. He had come to see that Christian mysticism has no monopoly when it comes to the deepest promptings of the human spirit. He had found too much in the mystical traditions of Judaism, of Islam, of Hinduism, of Zen Buddhism, to confine himself exclusively to Christian insights. His approach to the East might have lacked the necessary rigour, but he brought an open mind and an open heart to his encounters. Jean Leclercq, with whom Merton corresponded over so many years, identified the one other all-important quality that was increasingly important in Merton's ecumenical endeavours: 'there was growing in him, more and more, a search for the essential which is love.'[65]

The Asian journey

It was the Asian journey, Merton's final journey, in the autumn of 1968 that enabled him to take forward his exploration of the shared wisdom of East and

West. What he sought was an exchange of ideas, a greater understanding of the religious experience of the East, and a personal encounter with Buddhist monasticism. He set out with commitments to give lectures to conferences in Calcutta and Bangkok, to spend Christmas with the community at Rawa Seneng in Indonesia, and tentatively to give some talks at the Trappist monastery on Lantau Island, Hong Kong. He expected to receive invitations along the way to give retreats and conferences in other Asian monasteries and he hoped that he might see some Zen monasteries in Japan. But his first concern was to meet with Buddhists, and the conversations he hoped to have in different places, and especially with the Dalai Lama, constituted a vital ingredient in the projected itinerary. At a time when he believed Western monasticism to be in a state of crisis, he hoped that he might bring back something that would be useful, but he went to listen, to experience, to interpret and to share.

The circular letter that he sent to friends prior to his leaving Gethsemani spoke of the urgency of the times, the need for monastic renewal, and the isolation of Christian religious communities in Asia, but these considerations would not divert Merton from his desire to explore something of the meaning of Asia. 'I do not know if I have anything to offer Asians, but I am convinced I have an immense amount to learn from Asia. One of the things I would like to share with Asians is not only Christ, but Asia itself.'[66]

Merton brought a keen eye as he travelled to Bangkok, Calcutta, New Delhi, the Himalayas, Madras, Ceylon, Singapore, and finally back to Bangkok where his journey was cut short by his tragic death on 10 December. His *Asian Journal*, which was drawn together from different notebooks by editors after his death, is a wide-ranging kaleidoscope of impressions: the sights and sounds, the fast-changing human scene, the people whom he met, conversations, ideas, notes from books, reflections, flashes of humour. The immensely rich experiences the journey afforded were stepping stones along the way of understanding for a man who was marvellously open to everything around him.

The journey enabled Merton to meet with monks, lamas, scholars, poets and artists. His visits took him to a Mission Ashram in Calcutta, which served also as an agricultural college, a school for the blind and an orphanage. His talk on the theology of prayer at a Jesuit Scholasticate in Darjeeling included the reflection that the West desperately needed the religious genius of Asia if it was to find a new depth of understanding.[67] He considered the possibility of editing in due course a collection of extracts from the writings of Buddhists on meditation. He explored with others the question that arose on several occasions concerning the possibility of establishing a contemplative Christian monastery with a strong commitment to dialogue with Buddhists.

There are references in passing to discussions with Hindu scholars and with Sufis, but Merton's primary preoccupation was with Tibetan Buddhists. His discussion with Buddhist monks in Thailand, or with a small community of Tibetan lamas in the Himalayas, or with individuals, and most notably with Chatral Rimpoche, explored methods of meditation, transcendental awareness, *sunyata* (the void or ground of being), and – beyond all traditions of mysticism and asceticism – the goal of enlightenment.

It was, however, Merton's three discussions with the Dalai Lama which represented for him the most significant encounter of the whole journey. He described the approach to the Dalai Lama's encampment: 'What was for me on Friday a rugged, nondescript mountain with a lot of miscellaneous dwellings, rocks, woods, farms, flocks, gulfs, falls, and heights, is now spiritually ordered by permanent seated presences, bearing with a lamplike continuity and significance, centers of awareness and reminders of dharma (that is, the way).'[68] The conversations were lively and congenial. Merton found the Dalai Lama 'a very solid, energetic, generous and warm person'[69] and he responded to his mind: 'He is a very consecutive thinker and moves from step to step.'[70]

Their conversation was confined to religion and philosophy. The Dalai Lama expressed some concern about distorted views of Tibetan mysticism in the West. They talked about methods of meditation, and Merton shared his belief in the need for monks in the world to demonstrate in their lives both the freedom and the transformation of consciousness that meditation can give.[71] The Dalai Lama placed great emphasis on detachment, on the living of an 'unworldly life', and yet acknowledged it was also for him the way of understanding and participation in the problems of the world.[72] The Dalai Lama asked questions about monasticism in the West: the meaning of monastic vows, the rule of silence, the ascetic way. But the conversation returned at the end to *sunyata*, the ultimate void or emptiness – not an object to be acquired (a state of mind), or a concept to be achieved (wisdom), but the ground of being in which all things find their identity, their reality.[73] It ought not to pass unnoticed, however, that in spite of the restlessness Merton had displayed over so many years, the Dalai Lama commented that 'This was the first time I had been struck by such a feeling of spirituality in anyone who professed Christianity.'[74]

For Merton, the conversations with the Dalai Lama and with many other Tibetan Buddhists constituted an experience of Buddhism which was entirely in harmony with his Christian faith. He continued to read widely and to make notes throughout the journey, but with his premature death there was no opportunity to go back over the material and give it any kind of coherence. His account of discussions with those whom he met, his quotations from the various writers he read, his reflections as he pursued his journey merely follow upon one another, but they are none the less helpful as markers along the way as he tried to understand and interpret.

Quotations and reflections to be found in his journal touch upon *the abandonment of the ego* ('Cease to identify yourself with race, clan, name, form and walk of life. These belong to the body, the garment of decay');[75] *the rigour required in the contemplative or mystical life* ('It is the tradition of the fortunate seekers never to be content with partial practice');[76] *the significance of suffering* ('Only when a person was fully convinced of the immensity of suffering and its complete universality and saw the need of deliverance from it, and sought deliverance for *all* beings, could he begin to understand *sunyata*');[77] the centrality of solitude, truth and love ('Truth must be found in solitude. The ability to bear solitude … is therefore one of the more elementary qualifications for those who aspire towards selfless love');[78] and *the goal to which all must lead* ('One is to attain enlightenment and become a Buddha only for the sake of others').[79]

The centrality of contemplative prayer, the renewal of monasticism and the dialogue between East and West were the dominant themes in Merton's lectures in Calcutta and Bangkok. *The Asian Journal* preserves the informal talk he gave in Calcutta when he returned to the familiar theme of the monk as a marginal person, who accepts the basic irrelevance of the human condition but who, in daring 'to go beyond death even in this life', might therefore be a witness to life. It is a life of faith, but faith involves doubt, and the monk who is called by the voice of God seeks in solitude a new dimension in human experience.[80] But Merton appends a warning to his remarks. He speaks of the upheaval that is taking place in monasticism in the West, despairing that things of great value are being discarded. And so, speaking as one religious to others, he urges his audience to keep faith with their ancient tradition. The journey of discovery is all-important, and Merton's approach to monasticism can no longer exclude the possibility of meaningful contacts, not at an institutional level but among those who are seeking. What Merton is sketching is not a blueprint for ecumenical dialogue, but a depth of communion in which there is the possibility of discovering an older unity. 'My dear Brothers, we are already one. But we imagine that we are not. And what we have to recover is our original unity. What we have to be is what we are.'[81]

Merton's address to the Temple of Understanding Conference at Calcutta was given to a diverse group of representatives of many of the world's religions. He did not follow his prepared text, but the Notes contained in *The Asian Journal* suggest that he returned with renewed emphasis to the theme of dialogue. His title was *Monastic Experience and East–West Dialogue*. He provided a comprehensive definition of monasticism, but spoke of discerning 'a transcendent dimension of life beyond that of the ordinary empirical self'.[82] Such a dimension possesses a universal quality to which the world's great religions bear their complementary testimonies. It was, however, between the contemplative and monastic tradition in the West and the various contemplative traditions in the East that Merton hoped to make serious connections. He suggested that even where there are irreconcilable differences in doctrine there might still be 'great similarities and analogies in the realm of religious experience'.[83] What he sought was 'dialogue in depth' at an 'existential level of experience and spiritual maturity'.[84]

He was persuaded that the point had been reached when it was possible for someone to remain faithful to a Christian and Western monastic commitment, and yet learn in depth from the experience of Buddhists or Hindus. For Merton, such a process could only assist the task of monastic renewal in the West. But true communication at the deepest level – what Merton called 'a communion in authentic experience' – required both discipline (monastic formation) and freedom (openness to new possibilities). Merton might well have been reflecting upon his own monastic journey as he spoke of what would be required.

> The monk who is to communicate on the level that interests us here must be not merely a punctilious observer of external traditions, but a living example of traditional and interior realization. He must be wide open to life and to new experience because he has fully utilized his own tradition and gone beyond it.[85]

Merton was alert to the dangers – endless talk, a facile syncretism, a sitting lightly to doctrinal differences, a preoccupation with secondary matters – but there was a compulsion about the task. A world that was witnessing 'the growth of a truly universal consciousness' required for the sake of its own survival the element of 'inner transcendent freedom'. It was 'the peculiar office of the monk in the modern world to keep alive the contemplative experience and to keep the way open for modern technological man to recover the integrity of his own inner depths'.[86]

The connections that Merton made between the contemplative tradition, the monastic calling and the needs of the modern world, brought together his work as a social critic and an ecumenist. It was, therefore, entirely appropriate that his final lecture in Bangkok, delivered on the day of his death to a conference of religious in the Far East, should have been entitled *Marxism and Monastic Perspectives*.[87] Merton recognized at the outset the need for the monk to engage in 'a dialectic between world refusal and world acceptance', but – for the monk – implicit in world refusal would be a desire for change. It might therefore be thought that the monk and the Marxist would have much in common since both speak of alienation, but for the monk alienation derives not from economic circumstances but from estrangement from God and from the truth of who we are as human persons.[88]

Merton proceeded to suggest that Christianity and Buddhism share a common concern 'to transform and liberate the truth in each person, with the idea that it will then communicate itself to others'. The monk takes his place in the world as one who has come 'to experience the ground of his own being in such a way that he knows the secret of liberation and can somehow or other communicate this to others'.[89] It was at this point that Merton moved on to the insights of his own mystical theology. He insisted that 'The whole purpose of the monastic life is to teach man to live by love' and drew upon the Augustinian formula, which tells of 'the translation of *cupiditas* into *caritas*, of self-centered love into an outgoing other-centered love', but then, in a sentence which summarized his deepest convictions, he added: 'So in each one of us the Christian person is that which is fully open to all other persons, because ultimately all other persons are Christ.'[90]

It is, therefore, purity or single-mindedness of heart to which the monastic life must lead. Everything must serve that end. The structures that had secured the place of monasticism in society in earlier centuries could no longer be taken for granted. 'The monk belongs to the world, but the world belongs to him insofar as he has dedicated himself totally to liberation from it in order to liberate it.'[91] For Merton, there lay beyond monasticism – Christian and Buddhist monasticism – a freedom and a transcendence that rejoice in the interdependence of all living things. It followed, therefore, that monastic renewal must involve a deepening of such an awareness, and so Merton concluded:

I believe that by openness to Buddhism, to Hinduism, and to these great Asian traditions, we stand a wonderful chance of learning more about the potentiality of our own traditions, because they have gone, from the natural point of view, so much deeper into this than we have. The combination of the natural techniques and the graces and the other things that have been manifested in Asia and the Christian liberty of the gospel should bring us all at last to that full and transcendent liberty which is beyond mere cultural differences and mere externals.[92]

The priority of love, purity of heart, contemplation, a relation to the world that is passionate but critical, an affirmation of the interdependence of all life, monastic renewal, ecumenical encounter, and freedom – full and transcendent freedom in God: these did not merely constitute a collection of appropriate themes for a last lecture, they could have served as a confession of faith, an *apologia pro vita sua*.

A Study in Divine Discontent

... the unanswerable question: 'What on earth am I doing here?' I have answered it a million times. 'I belong here' and that is no answer. In the end, there is no answer like that. Any vocation is a mystery and juggling with words does not make it any clearer.

It is a contradiction and must remain a contradiction.

I think the only hope for me is to pile contradiction upon contradiction and push myself into the middle of all contradictions.[1]

Something of the secret of Thomas Merton's fascination is to be found in the vocations that he pursued over the years. The vocations are clearly identifiable and yet they were deeply interdependent, even as they competed for space, bringing Merton into conflict with his Superiors and with himself, and calling into question in the minds of some the priority of his monastic calling. They have much to say about the man – the range of his concerns, the imagination, the passion, the restlessness. But they also speak of contradiction, of ambiguity, of paradox; and the discontents that Merton displayed throughout his adult life owed something to the contradictions with which he lived.

The contradictions are numerous. His primary vocation was to the religious life, and it is in the working out of that particular vocation – and of the ones that impinged most directly upon it – that the contradictions are most apparent. He comes down as:

a monk who chose a life of withdrawal, silence and solitude, but who continued to enjoy so far as he could the company of friends, of women, and for whom conversation, books, ideas, drink, jazz were so important, especially in his later years;

a monk who, living in community and carrying substantial responsibilities, nevertheless distanced himself emotionally from the life of the community in so many ways, negotiating for himself a position of some detachment;

a monk whose primary vow of stability did not prevent him from exploring times without number the possibility of moving to another Order, another place, a new foundation;

a monk whose vow of obedience was observed scrupulously, but whose relationship with Abbot James Fox over a period of 20 years was a continuing tussle;

a monk who embraced the life of a contemplative, but who found that his vocation as a writer condemned him to a maelstrom of activity – deadlines to be met, proofs to be checked, and the endless round of correspondence with agents, publishers, superiors, censors, critics, fans;

a monk whose journey into God as a contemplative, as a mystic, required him to lose himself in the dark cloud of unknowing, but who wrote so extensively and so compulsively about himself;

a monk who aspired to live the life of a hermit, but whose time at the hermitage accommodated in the space of three years the visits of large numbers of people who came to see him at Gethsemani, the affair with a student nurse, the social round in Louisville under the guise of keeping medical appointments, and the continuing concern to speak with a prophetic voice to the torments of the world;

a monk whose Trappist vocation had represented – at least at the beginning – a renunciation of the world, but who came in due course to stand in critical and passionate solidarity with the world, addressing so many of the political and social concerns of his day;

a monk who had embraced so wholeheartedly as a young man the orthodox pieties of a pre-Conciliar Catholicism, but who found himself increasingly at variance with the institutional life of the church – its triumphalism, its bureaucracy, its disengagement from the world;

a monk whose rootedness in God and in the Catholic faith was never called in question, but who embarked upon a wide-ranging ecumenical endeavour, turning to the East to find in the other great world religions the complementary insights on which he might feed.

It is no small part of Merton's fascination that he embodied so many contradictions. The perennial tug of war between the *ideal* and what is actually *real* is one that is all too familiar. There are contradictions, or apparent contradictions, in his story which amount to little more than legitimate developments in the life of any person over a period of 30 years. But there are some contradictions which cannot be so easily explained and which proved to be the cause of a good deal of anguish. Timothy Kelly, who had been a novice under Merton in the late 1950s and who was subsequently elected Abbot of Gethsemani in 1973, wrote of 'the contradictions, ambiguities, inconsistencies, misplaced enthusiasms' which obscured the depth of the man and yet revealed 'the reality of the very human person'.[2]

Merton, Gethsemani and the Cistercians

One of the problems in exploring the truth about Thomas Merton is the degree to which judgements are informed by what he wrote in his *Journals*. His letters and his articles display a fair degree of informed restraint; his books were subject to revision and amendment; his poems were often exercises in quiet reflection; but in his journals, although he undoubtedly had an eye to publication, he wrote as he felt at the time. They tell so much of the story, but it cannot be assumed that everything he wrote enables the reader to see the whole truth. It is not a question of wilful distortion; rather that, in pouring himself into his journals, what is presented cannot always stand critical scrutiny. The truth is sometimes less dramatic, more nuanced.

It was with a fair degree of insight that Merton confided in his journal two months after Solemn Profession that the religious life, even though it was not necessarily the life best adapted to his needs, none the less represented the place where God wanted him to be.[3] Even at that relatively early stage in his life as a religious, Merton had a sense of being somewhat isolated from his brothers at Gethsemani, writing of himself as 'a step-child in the Order'; yet he knew himself sufficiently well to add, 'But the truth is I would feel like an orphan, a step-child, an exile anywhere.'[4]

Merton struggled with the irritations of community life, but his vocations as monk, contemplative and writer had pulled at each other from the beginning, and he recognized the contradiction of making his vows in a contemplative Order only then to go on and live an active life.[5] He was aware that conflicts within himself were being laid at the door of the community, but he became increasingly dismissive of the life that was lived at Gethsemani and of what he called 'active contemplation'.[6] His repeated attempts to consider pursuing his monastic vocation in a different Order or in a different community were constantly rebuffed, and it has to be asked what was driving Merton as he returned to the question, albeit in many different forms, over the years. Was it a genuine desire for greater solitude, for contemplative prayer? Was it an indication of his frustration with Gethsemani? Or was it – as he himself suggested in the year of Solemn Profession – something deep within himself, a 'private poisonous urge to change everything, to act without reason, to move for movement's sake'?[7]

His problems with the community were exacerbated by his relationship with Abbot James Fox, whom he found in many respects to be 'a depressing and deadening force in my life'.[8] What Merton could not fully acknowledge, however, was all that his Abbot had done in setting him free in the later years to pursue his own path and in saving him from himself. It has to be asked from what interior depths he summoned up his recriminations against Abbot James, but Merton was bound to concede that he was equally well able to be less than honest – duplicity was the word he used against himself on one occasion – in his dealings with his Abbot.[9]

It is possible to take too seriously some of the dismissive comments that Merton made about Gethsemani and Dom James. The community and the abbot gave Merton the stability and the discipline that he undoubtedly required. The two men had, in spite of many appearances to the contrary, a shrewd if somewhat grudging awareness of what the other one was contributing; and Merton undoubtedly needed an abbot who would say 'No' to him at regular intervals.

Merton's discontents were frequently focused on Abbot James, but his frustrations went far beyond Gethsemani. 'I do not think I am bound to narrow my spiritual life (if any) and my ideals (if any) down to the narrow, rather rigid concepts of this Order of Strict Observance with which, as ideals go, I agree less and less.'[10] The Trappist life had represented for Merton at the outset the ideal of total self-abandonment in his search for God, but he came to abhor even at an early stage what he caricatured as 'that old Trappist business of trying to starve and beat your way to sanctity'.[11] It was for him a negative ideal and, writing at a far later date, he questioned if the strict Trappist interpretation of the rule had done anything to deepen the spiritual life of the monks: 'It keeps them in line, but there is *no development*.'[12]

Merton's influence in enabling the Order to move forward in new directions was considerable, and yet it was only to be expected that Merton's free spirit would rebel against the heavy-handedness with which his Superiors exercised their authority. What it raised for him, however, were searching questions about the understanding of the Order regarding vocation, obedience, discernment and – dare it be said? – the possibility of change.

The Order is always right, the individual is always wrong, whenever there is question whether or not the Order is the proper place for him and whether he could do better, for God and for his own soul, elsewhere. Always a prevarication! Change out of the question. The situation you are in is always the best for you ... the status quo is purely and simply the will of God.[13]

It is scarcely surprising that one who placed so much emphasis upon the freedom of the individual in relation to institutions and structures should have found himself in an uncomfortable situation with the community and the Order. Merton took his vow of obedience very seriously, but he could not be constrained by it. He came increasingly to feel that he was 'a prisoner of *vanitas monastica* (monastic pride) and its crudities, incomprehensions, and falsities!'[14] He was seeking a fair degree of personal autonomy in his interpretation of the monastic rule: the freedom to explore solitude in greater depth; the freedom to write and publish without unacceptable inhibitions; the freedom to engage wholeheartedly with the world and its contemporary concerns. He could no longer accept that solitude should mean *for him* a position of indifference to, or separation from, what was happening to everyone else in the world. The vow of obedience remained a matter of primary importance, but that could not include a denial of conscience, the acceptance of things that (at least in his eyes) were abhorrent to God.

Merton acknowledged that the monastic life secured for him the necessary space and perspective, but there was still a weariness of spirit that overtook him at regular intervals. How could there fail to be? He cherished the periods of solitude – in the fields, in the woods, at the hermitage. They were his happiest times, and they were also the ones when he felt closest to God. But he drove himself relentlessly in his writing, and even his teaching – informed, lively, good humoured – led to occasional bouts of self-questioning, of self-doubt.

He returned frequently to the ambiguity of his position in the community. He recognized that the problems were at least in part of his own making, that he was unwilling or unable to accept the limitations of Cistercian life, and that he had been given opportunities to move forward in ways that the community would not (at least at that time) choose for itself.[15] The diversions that had attracted him at different times – the possibility of temporary travel, contacts with other like-minded people, his writing, special adjustments within the framework of the community – were no longer seen to provide any solution. Merton accepted that Gethsemani represented the best compromise he could hope for: 'This kind of place is where I am finally reduced to my nothingness and have to depend upon God'; and yet he could insist with more than a touch of bravado that after 25 years 'I am in a position where I am practically laicized and de-institutionalized.'[16]

But Merton had too much self-knowledge, too much honesty, to jump at the deceptively easy solution. He might reflect that 'life here is too much of a lie', but the possibility of leaving raised other questions. 'Perhaps it is I who am the liar and perhaps leaving it would be the greater lie.'[17] The nature of his relationship with the community continued to puzzle him. It could not be easily put into words, but there were times when he wrote quizzically, poignantly, and with affection. 'The community to me is a curious, sometimes funny, sometimes crazy phenomenon which does not even understand itself. It bewilders me, and yet I am so much part of it.'[18]

The interior wounds

The contradictions that dominated Merton's life are not sufficient in themselves to account for the discontents that he displayed. What hidden depths within himself nurtured the frustrations? What was he tapping into, at least from time to time, in being so badly thrown? His *Notes for a Philosophy of Solitude*, which appeared in *Disputed Questions* in 1960, included a pertinent sentence when he wrote of 'the anguish of realizing that underneath the apparently logical pattern of a more or less "well organized" and rational life, there lies an abyss of irrationality, confusion, pointlessness, and indeed of apparent chaos'.[19] Is it the nature of the human condition that he is exposing, or is it something of the truth about himself? Is it a mirror that he is holding up before the reader, or is it a light that he is shining into the depths of his own psyche?

Merton spoke at different times of the tidal wave that overwhelmed him, of an abyss of self-hatred;[20] and again of upheavals of resentment, disgust and depression;[21] and yet again of the neurosis that ran like a sore about which he was entirely helpless.[22] He could justly say, 'And yet I am joyful. I like life, I am happy with it, I have really nothing to complain of', but the journal entry goes on to speak of 'a little of the chill, a little of the darkness, the sense of void in the midst of myself'.[23] Matthew Kelty, one of Merton's contemporaries at Gethsemani, wrote an affectionate tribute the day after Merton's funeral. He had no hesitation in describing Merton as the merriest of men, and yet he added that there were within him 'depths of sadness it were best not to mention'.[24]

How did it come about that Merton exhibited throughout his life as a religious the insecurity and the neuroses of which he was fully aware? Was it a throwback to the bittersweet experiences of his earliest years: the death of his mother before his seventh birthday; the somewhat rackety life as he lived with or without his father and his younger brother in Bermuda, in the United States, in France; the very different character of educational establishments in France and England; the death of his father as he approached his 16th birthday; the self-destructive hedonism of his year at Cambridge; the rejection by his guardian at the end of that year and his subsequent departure for his grand-parents' home in Douglaston, Long Island? Were the wounds so deep that more than 16 years after going to Gethsemani he could write in a moment of quiet reflection of his 'despair of ever being truly able to love, because I despair of ever being worthy of love'?[25] And was his sense of self-worth so stunted that when he eventually found a romantic and erotic love, albeit one which flew in the face of his vocation, he could none the less bring against himself the charge of using that love 'to give my life "*value*" – as if my worth consisted in loving ['M'] and being loved by her?'[26]

Was there perhaps something that required him to move from one challenge or crisis to another, erecting only in order to surmount them barriers that appeared to call everything in question?[27] Did he fail to find his true vocation at the beginning? Had he embraced an ideal only to find that the reality was very different? Or was it merely a struggle to the end between the true self and the false self, the inner self and the external self? Should he have been a Carthusian, or should he have sought from the outset the life of a hermit? Had he been closest to the truth when, reflecting on the things that tempted him to leave Gethsemani, he acknowledged 'the old story of "something missing". What? Is it something essential? Won't there always be "something missing"?'[28]

Had Merton inherited from his parents an artistic temperament which made him unable to conform? Or did he go through life, shaped no doubt by early influences, in a stage of arrested adolescence: kicking over the traces, pushing at the boundaries, asserting his autonomy? He came to see himself as a non-conformist and a non-participant where the community was concerned. He knew that he could be a disruptive influence and seemed to delight in raising dangerous questions. Could it be that Merton was a person who could not be at peace – either with himself or with those around him – wherever he might happen to be?

Reading and writing informed his understanding of himself, and his respon-sibilities as Master of the Novices strengthened his determination to become familiar with the insights of psychology and psychoanalysis. There are allusions in successive letters to Naomi Burton Stone in the spring and summer of 1956 to 'the brat experiences of my childhood',[29] to the neurotic needs which compelled him to indulge in childish behaviour,[30] and to the discontents which he projected on to his mother, his country, his monastery and the church.[31] He acknowledged that he was in rebellion, that he carried hostilities and resistance within himself, and yet he remained persuaded that he was pursuing the right path: 'not just the institutional Cistercian path – [but] *my* path'.[32]

In an essay entitled *'Neurosis in the Monastic Life'*, circulated privately to friends at the time of writing these letters, Merton identified some of the manifestations of neurotic anxiety.

> [If] a would-be ascetic is not mature and well-balanced ... His emotional reactions and his judgements and desires are, without his knowing it, fundamentally infantile ... He is not moved by the Holy Spirit so much as by the energy generated by deep subconscious anxieties and fears.
>
> Life is not something that he is content to live: he wrestles with it, never at peace with himself or with others, because he is not at peace with reality.
>
> Anxiety is not always felt. Sometimes, beneath the apparently calm surface of the soul, there is severe anxiety at work, but the subject is not conscious of it. This anxiety may leave its mark not on his soul but on his physical organism. It may be taking effect in a stomach ulcer, colitis, or other psychosomatic sicknesses.
>
> ... a subject feels in part the anxiety which troubles him about himself, but he projects a large part of his anxiety on to his brothers, the superiors and the community.[33]

In spite of the caveats that might properly be made, there is much here that could easily serve as a commentary upon Merton as he presents himself in his journals and as he was undoubtedly seen from time to time by others.

A traumatic encounter with Dr. Gregory Zilboorg in July 1956 introduced a significant diagnosis into any discussion of Merton's mental and emotional stability. He had gone, together with Fr. John Eudes Bamberger and (for part of the time) with Abbot James Fox, to a conference at St. John's University, Collegeville, Minnesota, which was to be addressed by Zilboorg, who was both an established and well-regarded Freudian psychiatrist and a Catholic convert. The conference consisted in large part of a workshop on psychiatry and its application to the religious life. It was envisaged that the conference might assist

Merton, in common with other religious, in developing his psychological skills and especially with regard to his work as Master of the Novices. Merton was already struggling to come to terms with himself, but Zilboorg's confrontation, although it raised necessary and pertinent questions, was seriously flawed by the heavy-handedness with which he approached Merton.

Zilboorg had persuaded himself that he could analyse Merton merely on the basis of his writings. He was dismissive of Merton's unpublished article on 'Neurosis in the Monastic Life'. He judged it right (if Merton's account is to be taken at face value) to be brutally outspoken in his one private meeting with Merton;[34] but then, in violation of all professional disciplines, he shared his assessment with Dom James at a subsequent meeting, in which Merton was reduced to furious rage and tears, thereby confirming – at least in Merton's opinion – his Abbot's anxieties concerning him and strengthening any resolve to contravene over the years ahead the questions that Merton would raise concerning the development of his monastic vocation.[35]

The substance of Zilboorg's 'analysis' was that Merton was narcissistic: that is to say, that he was influenced by self-love to the point where his behaviour was persistently attention-seeking and his primary concern one of self-aggrandizement. Merton's summary of Zilboorg's charges against him reads as follows:

> You are a gadfly to your superiors … Very stubborn – you keep coming back until you get what you want … You are afraid to be an ordinary monk in the community … You like to be famous, you want to be a big shot, you keep pushing your way out – to publicity – Megalomania and narcissism are your big trends … Your hermit trend is pathological.[36]

Merton does not appear to have dissented from this assessment or to have been unduly hurt by what was said to him in private. Indeed, he wrote to Naomi Burton Stone two days later that 'Zilboorg is the first one who has really shown conclusively that he knows exactly what is cooking.'[37] There was undoubtedly some truth in Zilboorg's assessment. Quite apart from the numerous attempts to renegotiate the basic ground rules of his monastic life, it provides an explanation of Merton's prolific writing about himself, sparing no effort along the way to secure the safe-keeping and the survival of all that he ever wrote. The inexcusable sadness is that Zilboorg's assessment was not grounded in an understanding that was both better informed and more compassionate. What is most telling, however, apart from the suggestion of narcissism, is the judgement (if the words that Merton attributed to Zilboorg are accurate) that there was an inevitability about the self-made traps into which Merton so often fell. 'These are not things you can foresee. They are traps you fall into as you go along and you don't realize until you are hurt.'[38]

It was Bamberger's judgement that Zilboorg was given to making rash statements on the spur of the moment which he would subsequently change.[39] Whatever the truth of the matter, Merton was familiar with the language and all that it might represent in relation to his monastic vocation. Zilboorg subsequently dismissed any suggestion that Merton should be in analysis, but he put him in touch with Dr. James Wygal, a psychiatrist in Louisville whom Zilboorg had already commended for work with the novices, and with whom Merton met from time to time in later years. His dealings with Wygal were far more congenial – pleasant talks rather than counselling – although yet again professional boundaries were crossed as discussion gave way to a good deal of socializing. Wygal's assessment was that Merton's problems did not derive from any neurosis but were an entirely natural reaction to the situation in which he found himself at Gethsemani, and that Merton would be assisted by getting away from the monastery as circumstances permitted in order to restore his perspective.[40] It was a task which Wygal was only too happy to facilitate. But the sense of 'something missing', or of depths within himself which easily disturbed the rhythm of his life, continued to be present, as references appear in journal entries and in letters to his need for acceptance, to hierarchical conspiracies, to self-pity, to the search for the feminine and for the intimacies of human love, and to masochism, insecurity and self-defeat.

Human and divine discontents

And yet this man – wounded, flawed – none the less brought to his life a deep love of the natural world, an enquiring mind, a delight in books, ideas, conversation, a capacity for friendship and for inspiring deep affection. He brought also, although he was inhibited in so many ways by the inflexibility of the Cistercian tradition, a creativity of mind, an openness to new possibilities, which enabled him to ask serious questions about the renewal of monasticism, the contemporary world and its presenting problems, and the insights of the other great world traditions of faith.

But the inadequacies he brought with him to Gethsemani – and which he would undoubtedly have taken with him wherever he had gone – constituted a substantial wound. It may well be that there were questions to be asked, protests to be lodged, about the life to which he had freely committed himself, but the wisest of Superiors would not have found it easy to contain Merton, who was unable to settle comfortably for the concessions, the compromises, that living in community – or, living in that particular community at that particular time – required.

It must be asked, however, if the discontents that Merton displayed were anything more than the all too familiar *human* discontents that might be exhibited by any person at any time. In spite of the undoubted priority of God, Merton is a man of changing moods. There are times of deep frustration, self-pity, disgust, anger, contempt. He has a feeling of not always belonging: of being different from, distanced from, those to whom he is bound by the common life of his monastic calling. He experiences a great sense of power-lessness, and he is quick to select others as the focus of his discontents. There are touches – and more than touches – of self-deception, of self-righteousness, of wilfulness. These various aspects of his temperament and personality are more than mitigated by great intellectual curiosity, by a strong pastoral instinct, by an infectious good humour; and, running through it all, there is his unequivocal commitment to God, to solitude, to contemplative prayer. He remains throughout his life a man who is journeying, searching, questioning, willing to take risks, open to all that might come his way.

But in what sense could it be argued that Merton is a study in *divine* discontent? What do the words mean? When do the discontents that are inextricably bound up with being human become something more or something different? And is there a hard and fast distinction to be drawn between the two, or is it rather a question of how the discontents are used? Could it be that the thing that makes the difference in any understanding of human and divine discontent is the theological framework within which lives are lived and interpreted? If the distinction between the secular and the sacred is fundamentally false because all life is in God, does it therefore follow that the things that are unmistakeably human are seen in an entirely different light because of the perspective, the direction, the sense of destiny, the meaning that individuals bring to bear upon them?

The gospel narratives suggest at times how easily words such as *human* and *divine* might be transposed. It might be pertinent, for example, to consider the Christ who speaks not of bringing peace on the earth, but a sword;[41] or the Christ who asks James and John if they can drink of the cup that He must drink;[42] or the Christ who weeps over the city;[43] or the Christ who cleanses the temple.[44] A reading of the narrative that has removed any theological dimension would merely take note of *human* foreboding, anguish, compassion, anger; whereas a theological reading would find depths of meaning in the light of a *divine* purpose which makes it necessary to speak of symbolic words and symbolic actions which tell of the holiness of God, the priority of the Kingdom, an inclusive compassion, the suffering that is inseparable from the call to discipleship, and the impending hour of judgement.

Merton was content to describe himself as 'a self-questioning human person who ... struggles to cope with turbulent, mysterious, demanding, exciting, frustrating, confused existence'.[45] He came to see that 'our first task is to be fully human';[46] and for him, speaking with a prophetic understanding, the *divine* as it is to be found in biblical theology does not concern 'the explication of a "divine nature" but of God's acts in the world'.[47] Many of these acts, especially in the Old Testament, are 'perfectly ordinary and seemingly trivial',[48] and yet there is still to be discerned a transcendence, which defies all definition, in the revelation of the One who can say 'I am who I am.'[49] It does not follow that the two words *divine* and *human* are interchangeable; rather that, at the heart of biblical faith, of Christian faith, there is the conviction that what are called *divine* and *human* can so penetrate each other that it is possible at one and the same time to see something of the truth about God and something of the truth about humanity. It is in this sense that Merton, drawing upon a long-established mystical tradition, could say that in finding God he had found himself, and in finding his true self he had found God.[50]

Human and divine: where does one stop and the other begin? Human and divine discontents: is it possible to see the divine purpose, the divine grace, at work in a flawed and wounded humanity to the point where what is unquestionably human is also seen to be something more? For Merton, the presence of the divine is to be found in 'radical being, actuality, aliveness, power, love, concern'.[51] The elements of transcendence and immanence are never lost: 'Beyond all and in all is God.'[52] But the truth of all that the divine represents is the promise that is waiting to be claimed: 'Eternity is in the present. Eternity is in the palm of the hand. Eternity is a seed of fire, whose sudden roots break barriers that keep my heart from being an abyss.'[53]

The desert tradition

As he wrestled with himself and with the meaning of his vocations, Merton came to accept Gethsemani as the place where he was bound to remain, and yet he was quick to add that he had 'never felt so strongly that I have "no place" ... since becoming fully reconciled to this as "my place".'[54] It followed, therefore, that 'My place is in reality no place ... I am an alien and a transient.'[55] What emerged was an understanding of the monastic vocation – repeated time and again in his writings – which placed great emphasis upon the religious as an exile, a stranger, a marginal man or woman, a wanderer. It was for Merton only in such a role that the religious could find the detachment and the perspective with which to engage with the world.

For reasons that had much to do with his deepest needs as a person, Merton could justly speak of his vocation as that of 'a pilgrim and an exile in life'.[56] He was someone for whom it was necessary to walk in darkness, to travel in silence, to fly by night.[57] His conviction that the monastic calling required the freedom and the courage and the cross of the alien and the exile was entirely appropriate for him. It was an interpretation of the task of the religious that played to his strengths and to his needs, but it took him right back into the desert tradition, the desert experience, that had been the bedrock of monasticism from the beginning.

Monasticism provided the framework – theological, vocational, ascetical – within which Merton was able to locate himself and search the depths of meaning within and beyond himself. The calling, the rule, the life and the community constituted a desert experience, and there is so much in Merton's story and in his several vocations which only makes sense when it is seen in the light of the desert tradition. The desert is not merely a place. It is a *type* of Christian experience. The emptiness and the silence of the desert stand as symbols of the isolation and the desolation to which some are condemned at particular times. The desert, both the physical desert and the spiritual desert, tells of a day-by-day struggle to survive. It provides its own predicaments and temptations. It involves a confrontation with the 'devils' within. And yet those who can face the truth of their condition become for others signs of hope. It is not the least of their achievements that, isolated and incomplete, they stand none the less with 'their raw edges reaching always towards the heavens'.[58]

Few people in the twentieth century have represented this tradition more completely than Thomas Merton. Few of his literary activities gave him greater pleasure than his collection of the stories and sayings of the Desert Fathers, published in 1960 under the title *The Wisdom of the Desert*. Any study of the desert – and not least of all Merton's own contribution to the subject – suggests several connected themes: withdrawal, solitude, testing, self-emptying, encounter. Merton, as a Trappist monk, was heir to that tradition, and in his parallel but deeply connected lives it is these themes that dominate the story.

Merton had discerned with remarkable foresight what the actual experience of his austere vocation would entail. On his first visit to Gethsemani as a private retreatant in Holy Week 1941, he had reflected on the difference between seeing 'a kind of truth all at once, in a flash, in a whole', and then exploring it, drawing out its full meaning – perhaps over many years – by 'a series of minute, difficult, toilsome steps'. He went on to speak of 'a long desert of difficulties' through which it was necessary to pass if the idea that had been grasped at the outset is to be lived and worked out 'in the manner appropriate to our own sad contingent and temporal state where nothing is possessed but in scraps and pieces, imperfectly, successively'.[59] It was a moment of profound insight, and it captured at the very beginning what the desert experience would mean *for him* as a member of the Order of Cistercians of the Strict Observance. Withdrawal, solitude, testing, self-emptying, encounter – yes; but with the advantage of hindsight it is possible to trace in this journal entry another theme which is inseparable from the desert tradition – *transfiguration*. This is the additional and all-important dimension which time and again in Merton's story transforms the apparent barrenness of the scene with its contradictions, its ambiguities, its wounds. It is the element of transfiguration that makes it possible to speak of *divine* discontent.

Transfiguration

It is a commonplace that only those who have nothing can accept everything, but *everything* in the context of the desert tradition is nothing less than the totality of God. The desert represents a descent into nothingness, but it speaks unequivocally of the divine mystery of life and death and life. The desert is all too often presented in the literature of the Christian church as the place of the cross, the place of sacrifice, but it is also the place of revelation, of vocation. It is supremely the place of transfiguration, which is participation in the life of God.

Merton had instinctively grasped the meaning of the desert experience. He knew that 'Though we may run in the dark, our destiny is full of glory',[60] but he also understood that to participate in the life of God is to share actively in His continuing work of transfiguration. There is a prophetic tradition which speaks of the day when the desert shall become like the garden of the Lord, a place of thanksgiving and the voice of song.[61] Transfiguration has far wider connotations than personal sanctification. The breaking in of God's Kingdom must encompass a transfiguration of the whole created order. The desert was Merton's training ground not merely as a monk and a contemplative, but also as a writer, a social critic and an ecumenist.

The solitary life, which lay at the heart of Merton's understanding of monasticism, was a call into the desert. It represented a kind of unknowing, a kind of doubt, about the very roots of his own existence; and yet it was only there, in the midst of uncertainty and nothingness, that Merton could find an awareness of the presence of God. He saw the need for 'a dialectic between community and solitude' and he wrote of 'the fruitful antagonism' that must subsist between them,[62] even though his actual relationship with the community meant that the antagonism might sometimes appear to be more apparent than the fruitfulness. The element of ambivalence remained until the end as he struggled with himself and with what he judged to be the inadequacies of community life as it was practised at Gethsemani. His pondering of the question, 'What am I here for?', led him to propose an answer that offered little comfort. 'The only satisfying answer is "for nothing". I am here *gratis*, without a special purpose, without a special plan ... I am not here because of some elaborate monastic ideal ... but simply this is where "God has put me".' [63] And yet the element of transfiguration is to be seen in the gradual realization of what he called 'The mystery of my monastic community as my place of salvation and encounter with God.'[64] He had discovered that the desert – *when it is accepted as a desert* – can become a paradise.[65]

Merton's monastic life was his primary vocation, and it is there that the element of transfiguration must first be sought. Something of the meaning of the desert is to be found in Merton's initial act of unqualified commitment, but this did not provide any protection against the discontents that welled up within him. He knew the folly of building a life '*merely* on a feeling of interior peace, or a vague sense of oneness with God'.[66] Faith, the desert faith, was nothing less than 'a clear penetration into the heart of darkness where God is found'.[67] The freedom that he sought in interpreting his monastic calling, although it brought him into conflict with his Superiors, enabled him to speak for others. He was mindful of the questions that a younger generation of postulants was bringing into monastic orders. He was far from persuaded that adjustments to the religious life, prompted in large measure by a response to the Second Vatican Council, constituted responsible developments. He continued to plead for a rediscovery of the things that went to the heart of the monastic life – silence, solitude, penance – and he believed it was an important part of his vocation to secure wherever possible 'a living continuity with the past and with what is good in the past'.[68]

But did it really add up to transfiguration? It would be absurd to over-emphasize Merton's influence upon changes that have taken place in religious communities over the last 50 years, but many have found even in the face of serious numerical decline a greater freedom for personal development, a greater emphasis upon contemplative prayer, a greater commitment to dialogue with the world. Merton knew the importance of the questions that had to be asked, and time and again he articulated the concerns, the frustrations, even the aspirations of a generation of religious who left their Orders in such large numbers in the 1960s and the 1970s and, indeed, of those who, in an earlier generation, would have made their way into the religious life. Merton saw very clearly that the questions people were asking had moved on from what they had been in an earlier generation, and that the answers which remained unchanged were not, therefore, necessarily apposite. It may be that the questions were never articulated with sufficient clarity, and that the guidelines for new directions were never spelt out with anything like sufficient detail; and yet the representative role that Merton fulfilled enabled him to straddle the generations and to give voice to the questions that remain unanswered, and to which monasticism has always returned in changed and changing circumstances. But the questions that Merton asked took him back into the experience of the desert, in so far as they proceeded from his understanding of fidelity – not to inherited structures and established patterns, but fidelity in openness and risk to the unpredictable word of God.

Merton's writing about solitude and contemplative prayer captured something of the terror of the desert experience. 'Solitude means being lonely not in a way that pleases you but in a way that frightens and empties you to the extent that it means being exiled even from yourself'.[69] It was, however, through the experience of these things that Merton realized a far deeper understanding of the world, and it is here also that the element of transfiguration is to be found as his monastic life informed his other vocations. 'Solitude has its own special work: a deepening of awareness that the world needs. A struggle against alienation. True solitude is deeply aware of the world's needs'.[70] Merton had come to see that the contemplative is one who so enters into the pain of the world that he cannot fail to take to himself something of the torments of humankind.

Merton knew that the contemplative life entailed for him suffering and self-denial, loneliness and frustration, confusion and absurdity.[71] But the life story, the wounds, the psychology, the special needs that influenced Merton's experience of the contemplative life as a testing to the point of utter self-abandonment do not have the last word. His enquiring mind, his imagination, his ability to make unlikely connections, his need to get to the heart of the matter, his empathy, his sense of solidarity with the dispossessed: all these connected with each other and assisted the developments of his later years. Solitude and contemplative prayer were the barren and apparently unpro-ductive soil with which he worked, but the harvest was a critical and passionate engagement with the world through his work as a writer, a social critic and (in the widest possible sense) an ecumenist.

The discontents, human or divine, with which Merton wrestled throughout his life were the subject of a somewhat tortured self-examination in February 1964 as he reflected on 'years of relative confusion, often coming close to doubt and infidelity, agonized aspirations for "something better", criticism of what I have, inexplicable inner suffering that is largely my own fault, insufficient efforts to overcome myself, inability to find my way'.[72] It may be that Merton is 'the lost soul of the twentieth century, looking for redemption, looking for recovery, looking for God;'[73] but could it also be that there is a significant element of transfigu-ration in what he represents, displaying discontents that are inseparable from the human story and serving, therefore, as a role model for all who are caught up in the pain and the contradictions of the world? In his refusal to conform, to give way, to settle for a quiet life, Merton continues to encourage those who go beyond the conventions and the superficialities of life and dare to claim for themselves and for others something of the freedom of the sons and daughters of God.

In his contribution to the *Letter of Contemplatives to the World*, written at the request of Pope Paul VI in August 1967, Merton wrote of the work of the contemplative in exploring 'a desert area of man's heart'.[74] He had known long since that the contemplative cannot separate himself from the men and women of his day and that any participation in their struggles would involve, at least for him, 'a cloud of darkness far more terrible than the innocent night of unknowing'.[75] What is being hinted at is an identification with a world in which men and women are disconnected from each other and from God. But his response was to argue fiercely for the freedom that he judged to be the hallmark of a person's integrity: 'freedom from domination, freedom to live one's own spiritual life, freedom to seek the highest truth'.[76]

Merton insisted that his monastic calling, in spite of innumerable complaints, had enabled him to live in the most meaningful way, although he readily conceded that it had meant 'a lot of conflict, questioning, searching'.[77] The discontents undoubtedly spoke of conflicts within himself, and yet he hinted at something more. The solitude he sought could only be described at times as 'an abyss opening up in the center of your own soul'.[78] But as he alluded to the desolation of the abyss, was he merely trying to make sense of the darkness that overtook him from time to time? Or was he speaking yet again of the inevitable conflicts as his vocations struggled with one another in their desire to secure some wider recognition? Or was it a cry of pain from one who went out on a limb in his work as social critic and ecumenist, challenging received orthodoxies, charting new courses? Or did it speak also of an identification with the pain of the world and, even if that is only partially true, could it be that the going down into the darkness was also the ground of the hope of which he wrote with so much discernment?

Merton understood that 'hope is a gift … total, unexpected, incomprehensible, undeserved', but he knew that it can only be received by those who 'descend into nothingness … into death'.[79] But hope in the biblical tradition is 'the primary prophetic idiom', it is 'the refusal to accept the reading of reality which is the majority opinion'.[80] Could it be that the discontents that Merton endured and with which he wrestled for so long constituted the crucible in which his prophetic consciousness took shape? Could it be that the element of transfiguration is to be found supremely in the prophetic awareness, the prophetic voice, which can be seen and heard in so much of his work and which represents no small part of his continuing fascination?

Merton, writing in the Prologue to *The Sign of Jonas*, spoke of himself as one who, like Jonas, was 'travelling toward [his] destiny in the belly of a paradox'.[81] It is an image which speaks of the darkness of the deep, of the hidden life, of the call to obedience that has yet to be fully realized. It speaks of the paradoxes, the apparent contradictions, of any prophetic calling. But paradoxes, like contradictions, pile upon one another in any reading of Merton's story. He recognized in due course that a life that had been 'almost totally paradoxical' had none the less enabled him to find 'the greatest security'. Indeed, he went on to acknowledge that the occasions of depression and despair had often turned out to be times of renewal, of new beginnings.[82]

There are paradoxes – apparent contradictions – throughout the story: the dialectic between community *and* solitude; his call for a rediscovery of the fundamentals of the monastic tradition *and* the ability to voice the questions of a generation who left their monasteries because they had ceased to have meaning; the burden of his discontents *and* yet the cry for an authentic freedom and the resolve to ask, to seek, to press forward; the encounter with the mystery of God *and* therefore with the truth about himself; solitude, contemplative prayer *and* a passionate engagement with the world; the darkness of the abyss *and* the development of a prophetic awareness, a prophetic voice. In all these areas it is possible to trace the dominant marks of the desert tradition – withdrawal, solitude, testing, self-emptying, encounter *and transfiguration*.

There is, however, something more as Merton identifies the primacy of love as the utterly indispensable and irreplaceable element that transfigures and transforms:

> What is my new desert? The name of it is *compassion*. There is no wilderness so terrible, so beautiful, so arid and so fruitful as the wilderness of compassion. It is the only desert that shall truly flourish like the lily. It shall become a pool, it shall bud forth and blossom and rejoice with joy. It is the desert of compassion that the thirsty land turns into springs of water, that the poor possess all things.[83]

The full meaning of a person's life can only be discerned when that life has run its course. Merton remains immensely fascinating and deeply influential because he continues to represent for large numbers of people not merely the unpredict-ability of life with all its contradictions, but also the enduring vitality of a faith that is open to all possibilities. What is to be found throughout his story is a desire for God, which alone could withstand the confusions and finally enable him to make 'the leap into pure faith, pure prayer'.[84] 'On the surface I have my confusion. On a deeper level, desire and conflict. In the greatest depths, like a spring of pure water rising up in the flames of hell, is the smallness, the frailty of a hope that is, yet, never overwhelmed but continues strangely and inexplicably to nourish in the midst of apparent despair.'[85]

Merton's Funeral Mass and Burial Service began with the words from *The Sign of Jonas*: 'I have always overshadowed Jonas with My mercy ... Have you had sight of me, Jonas My Child? Mercy within mercy within mercy.'[86] They are words that tell of the longing that had penetrated his monastic life, his writing, his prayer, his encounter with the world, his dialogue with people of other faiths. Merton had concluded *The Seven Storey Mountain* with a reflection that included the words 'You will have gifts, and they will break you with their burden.'[87] Merton had not been broken either by his gifts or by the pain that he had carried. On the contrary, it was other characteristics that were far more likely to be recalled: the twinkling eye, the ready riposte, the lightness of touch, the good humour, the laughter; but, then, he had learned in the hardest of all schools that 'love laughs at the end of the world because love is the door to eternity, and he who loves is playing on the doorstep of eternity'.[88]

A Prophetic Voice

He was a sort of question demanding an answer ... He was unsettling, disturbing, not comfortable to live with ... There was a kind of truth about him that got under your skin, into your heart. He belonged to nobody, free as a bird. He could not be categorized, labelled, pigeonholed. And he had vision ... [and] a sort of prophetic fire, the fire Christ came to cast on the earth, and called on this man to cast ... He was a great gift of God.[1]

The desert experience is ultimately inseparable – certainly in the biblical tradition – from a prophetic consciousness, a prophetic voice. Scholarly studies identify the primary threads in prophetic ministry, and Merton was indebted to the writings of Abraham Heschel, the Jewish scholar with whom he corresponded on various matters over many years. He was familiar with Heschel's work, and his book *The Prophets* was welcomed by Merton as something that he might use in his conferences with the novices.

Prophecy speaks of experience and interpretation. It goes far beyond social criticism and social action. It does not concern itself with predicting future events, although there might be some intuitive awareness of how events will unfold. The focus of the prophet's concern is the contemporary scene and the burden of the prophet's message is nothing less than a declaration of the word of God. The thrust of Heschel's exposition of the biblical prophetic tradition is set out in his Preface to *The Prophets*: 'Prophecy is an interpretation of a particular moment in history, a divine understanding of a human situation. Prophecy may be described as exegesis of existence from a divine perspective.'[2]

There is, therefore, a corporate dimension to the prophetic task: it concerns the whole life of a community. The distinctive characteristic of what such a vocation might mean is something that was explored for a later generation by Walter Brueggemann, whose seminal book *The Prophetic Imagination* was published in 1978. Brueggemann wrote of the dominant culture to be found at any time in human society and argued that prophetic ministry must be concerned to nurture an alternative consciousness,[3] but such an end is not achieved simply by addressing one issue after another as though every presenting problem had an independent life of its own. What is required is an identification of the dominant crisis – enduring and resilient – which makes itself known in specific ways.[4] His argument assumes that the prophetic voice will address this crisis in such a way that people, seeing life in an entirely new light, might claim this alternative consciousness for themselves.[5] Prophetic ministry is concerned, therefore, with the empowerment of people, individuals and communities, 'to engage in history' so that the community of faith might then be equipped to move forward.[6]

Heschel writes of prophecy as the voice that God gives to the silent pain of all who are troubled and tormented. The prophetic word is compared to 'a scream in the night'[7] and it is through the prophetic voice that 'the invisible God becomes audible'.[8] It does not follow, however, that the prophet will command a hearing. His perceptions might well have been shaped by a deep identification with his people's story; his watchwords might be freedom, justice, compassion; but the prophetic voice can be too incisive, too austere. Heschel writes of the prophet employing notes 'one octave too high for our ears'.[9] If – in Heschel's terms – the prophet is one who says 'No to his society',[10] if – in Brueggemann's terms – the prophet is looking for an entirely new reading of reality, a counter consciousness; then the response that is required is unlikely to be forthcoming. It can all too easily become a step too far.

It is a necessary part of the prophetic task to point beyond established ortho-doxies, to challenge the complacency of a shallow optimism, to spell out the difference between substance and illusion. Everything will turn, however, on a correct identification of the *kairos*: the acceptable time, the day of decision. Prophetic ministry will be deeply disturbing, and yet there is an awareness of direction, of meaning. Something of what these things might mean in practice is to be found in the hope expressed by Thomas Merton in his Prologue to *Raids on the Unspeakable* that the book might 'enable a rare person here and there to come alive and be awake at a moment … of ultimate choice, in which he finds himself challenged in the roots of his own existence'.[11] *Kairos*: the time of deliverance!

The desert tradition encompasses monasticism and prophecy. Merton was mindful of the changed circumstances in which monastic houses found themselves in the middle years of the twentieth century and judged that the wilderness perspective was, therefore, all-important, ensuring that the monk – *some* monks – might find the necessary insight. The monk was called, then, to be an exile, a pilgrim; and from that distinctive vantage point he could plunge deep into the heart of the world, taking to himself the torments of humankind.

The monastic vocation, like the contemplative vocation, does not necessarily lead to a prophetic ministry, and yet Merton remained convinced that the monastic life has 'a certain prophetic character about it'.[12] The monk must at the very least know the folly of embracing the spirit of the world, but even more the monk, nurtured by traditions of solitude and contemplative prayer, is well placed to find 'a special awareness and perspective, an authentic understanding of God's presence in the world and His intentions for man'.[13]

Jean Leclercq had no hesitation in seeing Merton as a man with a message, and for him it was a message with a prophetic dimension, timely and apposite, in a world that was moving beyond the traumas of the Second World War. Other colleagues, friends and interpreters have spoken of him as someone who was 'just too far in front of the pack on social issues',[14] someone who could 'read the signs of the times better and more closely than others'.[15] He was for many a man with 'a prophetic religious sensibility',[16] a man with 'a prophetic voice for our times'.[17]

Merton brought to his work the Cistercian traditions of withdrawal, solitude and silence. These were the inescapable disciplines in the formation of any prophetic consciousness. But he brought also an identification with the world and with a troubled and wounded humanity, together with the hope, rooted in an eschatological faith, which looked for the breaking in of God's Kingdom. He saw himself increasingly as a solitary explorer who, like the poet of whom he wrote, was alert to 'awakening voices that are not yet audible to the rest of men'.[18]

For Merton, prophetic living was not an optional extra. Christians were required to choose: *either* to 'face the anguish of being a true prophet', *or* to 'enjoy the carrion comfort of acceptance in the society of the deluded by being a false prophet and participating in their delusions'.[19] It may well be that living the life of the Kingdom as though the Kingdom has already come is an adequate definition of prophetic living, of prophetic witness, but speaking with a prophetic voice requires something more. Merton's several vocations shaped his prophetic consciousness, but his voice was so much more than the voice of a monk, a writer, a contemplative, a social critic or an ecumenist.

There is no doubt about Merton's poetic awareness, but is it possible in going beyond poetry to prophecy to speak not only of prophetic sensitivity but of prophetic voice? Bishop Jean Jadot saw Merton 'not as a great thinker or philosopher, but more as somebody who had intuitions, feelings, the ability to see in what direction to go during a very troubled era'.[20] Merton undoubtedly embodied something of the spirit of a generation which in the 1960s, the last decade of his life, was eager to kick over the traces, to establish a world made new. But Merton's continuing fascination turns on his abiding appeal, on his capacity to speak today to a very different generation. Can it be justly claimed that he speaks with a prophetic voice, and in what sense can those words be used?

It is only in relation to the various strands that have been identified in the prophetic tradition that any claim to have spoken – *and to continue to speak* – with a prophetic voice might be made on Merton's behalf. It must, therefore be asked:

Was the contemporary scene the focus of his concern?

Did he speak the word of God to the here and now?

Did he bring a divine perspective to his interpretation of events?

Did he call in question established orthodoxies, challenging the prevailing consciousness and arguing for an alternative consciousness?

Did he identify the dominant and enduring crisis in the light of which judgements are made, and policies are formed, and the minds and hearts of men and women are shaped?

Did he enter into the pain of the world?

Did he fail to secure a hearing? Was his word too incisive, too austere?

Did he attempt to identify the *kairos*, the day of decision, the time of deliverance?

Did he enable people to come alive and be awake at a moment of ultimate choice?

Did he attempt to equip the community of faith, enabling the people of God to move on to a new understanding of their task?

Merton's voice is heard in large measure through his writing, but everything that is known about the man comes together to inform, to engage and to challenge.

Identifying the dominant crisis

Merton understood the meaning of prophecy. He knew that it involved seeing life as it really is, and his experience of contemplative prayer enabled him to insist that 'God works in history'.[21] It followed for him that there must, therefore, be a Christian understanding of society and of 'the providential events of the day'.[22] But the prophet, as he emphasized in his study of William Blake, is not one 'who exactly predicts future events but ... who "utters" and "announces" news about man's own deepest trouble – news that emerges from the very ground of that trouble in man himself'.[23]

It is implicit in such an understanding of the prophetic task that the prophet is one who can identify the *kairos*, which is nothing less than the breaking in of God's Kingdom. Merton's prophetic consciousness enabled him to look beyond the existing world order and to plead for new perspectives. In many respects, he straddled the divide between the past, the present and the future, but he was aware of the dangers of being obsessed by both the past and the future. His instinct was always to cast his lot with the future, but this required that nothing could be allowed to get in the way of the 'obscure but dynamic possibilities' represented by the present.[24]

But there is no prophetic consciousness, no prophetic voice, without the pain that is inseparable from a deep identification with the pain of the world. It may be that the discontents that plagued Merton throughout his years at Gethsemani served none the less as a framework – perhaps, even, as a field of energy – within which one who was separated from the world could find an openness, a heightened sensitivity, which enabled him to enter into the universal anguish.

Merton knew that for those who enter the world's pain 'there are no easy answers, no pat solutions to anything'.[25] There are times when his voice was too strident, when it might be inferred that he had a firmer grasp on the answers than was actually the case. But he knew that 'To live prophetically, you've got to be questioning and looking at factors behind the facts'.[26] He understood with a prophet's intuition that it was not carefully formulated responses that were required but 'difficult insights at a moment of human crisis'.[27] Could it be that this is the authentic form of the prophetic voice in today's world?

A prophetic vocation cannot fail to be shaped by the raw material – intellectual, emotional, psychological – that a person brings to life. But no overview of Merton's prophetic ministry can ignore the degree to which it was underscored by the life-long search for God in which he was engaged. It was buttressed by an incarnational faith which, in the light of a mystical theology, found the presence of Christ in every person, and by an eschatological hope which saw God's purposes being worked out in history. It was informed also by a contemplative tradition which brought the whole world within the parameters of the contemplative life. These were the presuppositions – personal, theological, experiential – that determined the direction in which Merton moved forward, as he learned to embrace the world and to give voice to his prophetic understanding.

But to what purpose? What difference did it make? There was certainly no ready response to the things that Merton had to say – within monasticism, or within the wider church, or within the world at large. But the word of the prophet, like the seed that is buried in the ground, will not bear fruit immediately. The perspective of a subsequent generation is required before a word can be seen to have been truly prophetic. For Walter Brueggemann, prophetic ministry involves radical criticism, but he recognizes that the prophet is all too often condemned to live with 'the hope that the *ache* of God could penetrate the *numbness* of history'.[28] It is a sentence that captures the situation in which Merton repeatedly found himself as he pursued what many regarded as nothing more than the inconvenient questions of a radical social criticism.

Brueggemann's interpretation of prophetic ministry is helpful in several respects in coming to some appreciation of what it means to speak with a prophetic voice. Merton's continuing fascination for large numbers of people throughout the world two generations after his death is not sufficient in itself to justify the extravagant claims that might be made on his behalf; but it does mean at the very least that he meets the requirement that the prophet is one who sparks the imagination of the people. He stands, if Brueggemann is right, within a tradition of prophetic witness which places a strong emphasis upon energizing people. 'If the task of prophecy is to empower people to engage in history, then it means evoking cries that expect answers, learning to address them where they will be taken seriously, and ceasing to look to the numbed and dull empires that never intended to answer in the first place.'[29]

It is, however, Brueggemann's primary hypothesis that '*The task of prophetic ministry is to nurture, nourish and evoke a consciousness and perception alternative to the consciousness and perception of the dominant culture around us.*'[30] Merton addressed a succession of issues, but can it also be argued that he identified the dominant crisis? and did he suggest that such a crisis manifested itself as one problem after another presented itself? and did he have an entirely new way of looking at life, an alternative consciousness, to propose?

The dominant crisis which shapes the public consciousness and influences private perceptions is bound to be subject to critical dispute. Denials of the freedom and the integrity of the individual; the subordination of the person to public institutions; power and the violence[31] which is implicit in every abuse of power – these are all bound to be strong contenders. All featured prominently in Merton's social criticism, but the evidence of his vocations and his writings, of his private convictions and his public profile, is that *for him* the dominant and enduring crisis is encapsulated by the idea of *alienation*. For Merton, alienation is an experience of disconnectedness, of fragmentation, of despair. It is persistent because it is to be seen in every relationship, every circumstance. It is enduring because it is a universal phenomenon which passes in its varying forms from one generation to another. It is not merely a question of politics or economics. It is related far more to the loss of the religious dimension. It is, in short, 'a crisis of man's spirit' with global dimensions that are religious and moral.[32]

It was the monastic perspective that enabled Merton to have some understanding of the human predicament in what he called 'an age of alienation'.[33] He took note of the tell-tale signs: the perceived absence of God; the decline into a new barbarism in which the freedom of the individual loses all meaning; the claims for personal autonomy that are deceptive and ultimately self-destructive; the emergence of a culture which is acquisitive, aggressive; the obsession with money and power; the preoccupation with clichés, with intellectual abstractions, with sensual fantasies;[34] and the myth – the idolatrous myth – that 'we are of all generations the most enlightened, the most objective, the most scientific, the most progressive and the most humane'.[35] The alienation of which Merton spoke was not determined by economic circumstances but – as he argued in his final lecture at Bangkok on the day of his death – by men and women's estrangement from God and from their deepest selves as human beings.

It was the inherent falsehood of what he observed as he looked out upon the world, and especially the Western world, that preoccupied Merton.

The things that we do, the things that make our news, the things that are contemporary, are abominations of superstition, of idolatry, proceeding from minds that are full of myths, distortions, half-truths, prejudices, evasions, illusions, lies … Ideals that claim to be humane and prove themselves, in their effects, to be callous, cruel, cynical, sometimes even criminal.[36]

Christian elements might still be found, but the culture is profoundly atheis-
tical. God and religion might be tolerated, but the prevailing world-view
excludes God.

Merton did not pretend to understand all that was happening. He did
not stop to ask if life had been different at any other time in history. But his
experience told him that life is all too often 'a continual series of moments
of untruth', and he was aware of the desire on the part of people for solutions
which would conveniently locate the source of all problems in other nations,
races, ideologies.[37] What Merton sought, however, was a deeper awareness,
new perspectives, an entirely different viewpoint. Without the contemplative
dimension, he feared that men and women would continue to be possessed
by 'the passions of the moment', imprisoned by the self-interests of the narrow
group to which they belonged.[38]

It was the urgency of the present moment that compelled Merton to embrace
the possibilities and the challenges. He had welcomed the recognition in the
Second Vatican Council's *Constitution on the Church in the Modern World* that
the world was entering upon an entirely new age in human history. It was for
him a time of crisis, of struggle. What he saw could only be likened to 'a deep
elemental boiling over of all the inner contradictions that have ever been in
man, a revelation of the chaotic forces inside everybody'.[39] It was a revolution
without parallel in human history and its dimensions were political, economic,
scientific, technological, demographic, cultural and spiritual. It could only
be interpreted in the light of his reading of New Testament eschatology as a
'decisive and critical breakthrough in man's destiny'.[40]

Merton was feeling after the alternative consciousness that his experience of
alienation required. If alienation tells of a universal condition, the alternative or
counter consciousness that Merton proposed was the realization of a universal
consciousness. He had come to see the world as a single organism and spoke
of 'one human family, one world'.[41] What was required was 'a transformation of
man's consciousness'.[42] Political and economic considerations, the movement
of peoples, trade, cultural ties: all these made it necessary for men and women
to recognize their responsibility for one another. The presenting problems
in society could only be understood and resolved in a global context. It is a
world-view for which Merton argued: a global context, a global awareness, a
global ethic.

Merton does not offer a prophetic programme, but he speaks with a
prophetic voice. He is clear about the part to be played by those who stand in a

contemplative tradition, realizing a universal consciousness within themselves and taking it back, so far as they can, into the communal consciousness. But he does not believe that those who are equipped to interpret ancient religious traditions are able *on their own* to make the necessary breakthrough. The recovery of sanity and of spiritual balance will require dialogue and trust between 'the traditional, contemplative disciplines and those of science, between the poet and the physicist, the priest and the depth psychologist, the monk and the politician'.[43]

What Merton demonstrates is a broad, humane and compassionate vision. Christianity, because it is a religion of love, must therefore also be 'a religion of dynamic change'.[44] The emphasis in Merton's writings falls at one and the same time upon the individual and the world in its entirety. 'Everything that God wills in my life is directed to this double end: my perfection as part of a universal whole, and my perfection in myself as an individual person, made in God's image and likeness'.[45] Merton was able to hold within one vision, within one perception of reality, the idea of alienation with its experience of death and destruction, of fragmentation and decay; the aspirations of different races, cultures, religions; and the feeling after a deeper unity, harmony, wholeness.

The environment

One large area where alienation cast a dark shadow was the natural world in which Merton found so great a delight. As he wrestled in his mind with the devastation that would be inflicted upon the earth by a nuclear war and with the far more modest but none the less serious consequences of intensive farming, technology, the use of chemicals, and the movement of people from the country to the town, he wrote fearfully of 'the destructive unbalance of nature, poisoned and unsettled by bombs, by fallout, by exploitation: the land ruined, the waters contaminated, the soil charged with chemicals, ravaged with machinery, the houses of farmers falling apart because everybody goes to the city and stays there'.[46]

It was for Merton a matter of deepening concern over the years that, although humankind had the choice to survive or not to survive, the 'titanic power' that was now possessed included the possibility that not only civilization but life itself might be destroyed.[47] He was greatly moved by Rachel Carson's book *Silent Spring*, where the threat to the environment is explored in some depth, and he wrote to the author immediately on reading the book, identifying men and women's capacity for self-destruction as 'a *consistent pattern* running through everything we do, through every aspect of our culture, our thought, our economy, our whole way of life'.[48]

Military, commercial and technological considerations were predictably easy targets for Merton, who feared that they would inevitably lead to an irreparable loss of the earth's natural resources and of the living species – the plants, the birds, the insects – on which the balance of the whole ecological system depended. But Merton also bemoaned the ease with which, even when men and women believe they respect the natural world, it is possible 'to deal death all around us *simply by the way we live*'.[49] For himself, and for those who would read his *Journals* in due course, he confided that 'Perhaps the most crucial aspect of Christian obedience to God today concerns the responsibility of the Christian in technological society toward God's creation'.[50]

Many individuals and traditions of thought shaped the ecological consciousness of Merton's later years. The undoubted influence of his father, who was a landscape painter; the physical location of Gethsemani and the Benedictine tradition which, understanding the fragility of life in the desert, had given to monasticism an abiding respect for the natural world; the influence of an Eastern tradition of theology and spirituality, which is to be seen – at least in part – in his prose poem *Hagia Sophia*; William Blake's much-quoted comment that 'Everything that is, is holy';[51] Gandhi's affirmation of the Hindu teaching 'that ALL life (not only human beings but all sentient beings) is one';[52] Teilhard de Chardin's emphasis upon the 'holiness of matter';[53] and from Zen Buddhism an insight into 'the one life that lives in all':[54] all these and many others exercised an influence which can be traced in Merton's journals, letters, poetry and books, and which became especially pronounced in the last years of his life.

Merton's response to the alienation that was represented by the wilful or careless exploitation of the natural world was to rejoice in the wonder and the diversity of nature. The whole world was 'a transparent manifestation of the love of God', characterized – even down to the smallest of God's creatures – by 'the most wonderful interrelationship between them'.[55] The created order was nothing less than 'a living and self-creating mystery',[56] and men and women, while transcending nature, are at the same time part of nature. Creation is 'a clean window through which the light of God could shine … Sun and moon, night and day, rain, the sea, the crops, the flowering tree, all these things were transparent.'[57] They are 'sacraments of God's presence,'[58] and all living creatures are 'syllables in a song which God is singing'.[59]

There is a great simplicity in Merton's approach to nature. His one requirement was that all living things might delight, quite unselfconsciously, in the freedom that God has given them. So it is that for Merton 'a tree gives glory to God first of all by being a tree,'[60] birds are encouraged to 'be what you are: be *birds*',[61] and as for the rabbits, wreaking havoc as they overran the fields surrounding Gethsemani, Merton's only advice to his novices is 'to love the rabbits for what they are, rabbits; and if you just see that they are rabbits you suddenly see that … the *rabbitness* of God is shining through all these darn rabbits'.[62]

Merton delighted in the colours, the sounds, the rhythms of the natural world, and yet there was a fair degree of romanticism in his approach. *Fire Watch*, the glorious prose poem with which he concluded *The Sign of Jonas*, finds him looking out late at night over the valleys and the hills that surround the monastery, but Czesław Miłosz, the poet and writer and Nobel Prize winner, found it less than adequate. For him, Merton's way of looking at nature as it was presented in *The Sign of Jonas* was too 'soothing', serving as 'a veil or a curtain', and failing to pay attention to 'torture and suffering in Nature'.[63]

The charge was justly made, but Merton continued to rejoice in the kinship that he felt with all living things. He lamented the fact that the church – in common with government, with business, with the armed services, and with the world at large – was indifferent to environmental concerns. He was increasingly persuaded that every human being is deeply bound up with the whole creation, intimately and profoundly connected with 'this world of matter and of men'.[64] The integrity of the whole creation, solidarity, mutual interdependence and justice: these were the watchwords of an environmental awareness, an ecological commitment, that were pleading for an entirely new way of looking at the world around us.

There can be little doubt that if Merton had lived for another 10 or 15 years he would have been at the forefront of discussions about the environment, but it would have been a theological perspective that he brought to bear. He has been identified with a 'creation spirituality', but what he offered as a counter-consciousness to the alienation which he so feared has a far greater theological depth than such a title might suggest. In the silence of the dawn, of the woods, of the hermitage, he found the necessary perspective. It was for him 'the stillness, the silence, the poverty, the virginal point of pure nothingness which is at the center of all other loves'.[65] It was there that he found the global, even the cosmic, dimension that was so important in his search for God and for his understanding of the inherent unity of all things.

What is to be found throughout the years at Gethsemani in all his writings is an affirmation of the created order as something that has its own integrity and freedom. It is not provided for convenience, or pleasure, or exploitation. Merton rejects any pagan view that the natural world is merely there to be used. On the contrary, he insists that 'If you love God, you will respect His creatures, and respect all life because it comes from Him.'[66] And again: 'Nothing that is important to [God] can be treated by us without the greatest respect.'[67]

One of the developments in Merton's thinking over the years concerned his understanding of the world which represented no longer only the totality of human concerns but the whole environment, human and non-human, within which men and women take their place and with which they must establish a proper relationship. The creation speaks of God, because the Triune God has planted 'His undivided power / In seed and root and blade and flower',[68] and God's purposes of redemption and transformation encompass the whole created order. Merton's understanding of hope includes 'the pledge of a new heaven and a new earth, in which all things will be what they were meant to be ... The beasts and the trees will one day share with us a new creation and we will see them as God sees them and know that they are very good.'[69]

Women and men

The idea that all things in the created order will be what they were meant to be serves also to inform Merton's approach to a somewhat different situation: the subordination of women to men. His comments are largely confined to retreat addresses he gave during the last year of his life to the prioresses and sisters of contemplative communities for women at Gethsemani in December 1967 and May 1968 and to the Cistercian nuns of Our Lady of Redwood Abbey at Whitehorn, California, in May 1968. His challenges were directed to the experience of women in the church, and especially in religious houses, but he was concerned no less with the oppression of women in society. His far more general concern that the church was still in thrall to a medieval world view led him to complain that such a view was based on an idealization which enabled society to use women for its own purposes, and for him that was alienation.[70]

Merton's views on a subject which was to assume a huge significance in the years after his death were largely undeveloped, although he had been feeling his way theologically during the previous decade. A triptych, which he had identified as Hagia Sophia, prompted a letter to the artist in May 1959 in which he explored his understanding of Holy Wisdom: 'God is not only a Father but a Mother. He is both at the same time, and it is the "feminine aspect" or "feminine principle" in the divinity that is the Hagia Sophia.'[71] It followed, therefore, that the masculine–feminine relationship reflected – or is required to reflect – something of the truth about God.[72] God is 'at once Father and Mother';[73] the birth of the Christ Child is 'a revelation of the infinitely motherly compassion of God' for humankind;[74] and Merton applauds the late medieval English mystics who 'spoke in their hearts to "Jesus our Mother"'.[75]

But Merton's theology was always informed by his experience of life. His Trappist vocation could not inhibit his delight in the company of women, in the dream figures who came from time to time to intrigue and entice, and in the intense experience of loving and being loved in the summer months of 1966. There is an entry in his journal in September 1966 as he struggled to release himself from any commitment to 'M': 'Strange connection in my deepest heart – between M and the "Wisdom" figure – and Mary – and the Feminine in the Bible – Eve etc. – Paradise – wisdom. Most mysterious, haunting, deep, lovely, moving, transforming!'[76] He could not be indifferent to the claims of the feminine and, therefore, to the implications of a theology which acknowledged an equality of purpose within the divine economy.

Merton had been aware at the time of the Second Vatican Council of the reluctance of members of the curia to take seriously the experience of American women. He was critical of the formation that Catholic priests received in their seminaries and believed that clergy and religious had an entirely unrealistic idea of women.[77] He abhorred the caricatures which any idealization of women encouraged and with which women, lay and religious, were only too willing to collude. He challenged the idea of a 'feminine mystique', believing that women were both idealized and humiliated by it.[78] It was 'an instrument of oppression'.[79]

One of his addresses to the contemplative religious at Gethsemani in May 1968, entitled 'The Feminine Mystique', spoke of the way in which certain qualities – judged to be inherently feminine – are idealized. He derided any suggestion that women alone are necessarily passive and mysterious, or that women cannot be rational in the way that men are rational but possess instead 'a particular kind of intuitive wisdom'. He rejected the idea that 'women and men are two specifically different kinds of beings, as if they each had a different nature' and urged the women 'to rebel for the good of the church itself', defying 'this image of the mysterious, veiled, hidden woman who is an "enclosed garden"'. For Merton, prevailing attitudes represented nothing less than a humiliation, and his concern was to encourage the women with whom he was talking to claim their individuality like everyone else.[80]

Drawing upon insights from modern psychology, he wrote in a different context of the limitations of 'a theology built exclusively on an authoritarian father-figure'.[81] He recognized that many of the presenting problems in this area had something to do with men's psychology. He talked of the American male being just 'half a human being', at times destructive and insensitive, repressing instincts and feelings which he believed to be feminine, unable to engage with women in a relationship of equality, and revealing all too often 'a guilty, sick and ambivalent attitude towards women'. The rehabilitation that Merton sought would be to the advantage of men and women: 'men will be more whole when women are'.[82]

Merton was not sure where his thoughts might lead. He knew that changes had to take place in the church and in society, and believed that women were capable of making a far larger contribution. Sister Jane Marie Richardson, one of the Sisters of Loretto, who had worked with Merton on various matters in the mid-1960s and who had been present at the Gethsemani conferences in 1967 and 1968, saw him as someone who 'was ahead of almost all others, including women religious, in this recognition of a growing feminine consciousness and its meaning for our whole society, as well as for women's religious communities'. She acknowledged none the less that Merton was still struggling with what it might all mean.[83]

Merton was alert to questions that would loom increasingly large over the years, although he had no easy answers. He saw the problems posed by the vow of celibacy in enabling religious to come to terms with their masculine and feminine sides. He was open to the possibility that Catholic priests might be allowed to marry, although he doubted if many would choose to do so. He was not sure if questions about the masculine and the feminine in the life of the church would be usefully addressed by the ordination of women to the priesthood, but he left the question open for the women contemplatives: 'I don't know. I leave that to you to figure out.'[84] But he knew that the culture had to change, and he was outspoken in encouraging these women religious 'to develop their vocations with a new maturity within a patriarchal system".[85]

If there is an alternative consciousness in these matters, it is to be found in Merton's determination to point to the possibilities that are locked up within men and women. He might insist that everyone is both masculine and feminine, and that what is required is 'a whole new understanding of what a human being is, what a woman is, what a man is'.[86] But Merton goes deeper and, drawing upon insights afforded by the Jewish Hasidic tradition, speaks of God and the glory of creation and the divine spark in all created things. It is the human task to see these things; but women, by virtue of the feminine principle of which he wrote in *Hagia Sophia*, have a distinctive vocation. The whole creation is waiting for women to set free the divine element within it so that 'everything becomes one great blaze of glory to God'.[87]

The contemporary scene

It is in his critique of the contemporary scene – the world in the more restricted sense of human activity and human folly – that Merton's understanding of alienation is so pertinent. His rediscovery of the world and his delight in people, sustained and informed by a tradition of contemplative prayer, could not conceal the bleakness of his judgement concerning the situation in which men and women lived their lives, both individually and corporately as members of interest groups, of societies, of nation states, of power blocs. He despaired of the preoccupation with materialism, with collectivism, and with power politics, and feared that civilization contained within itself the seeds of its own destruction.

Merton took note of the degree to which life was determined for people by influences over which they had little control. Mindful of the struggle to achieve what he judged to be a necessary degree of freedom in his own monastic vocation, he set his face against situations in which men and women were bullied into submission, seduced by technology, by the mass media, by mindless violence. He was alert to the totalitarian pressures that were all too readily brought to bear upon individuals by institutions. Power and the corruptions of power were a constant concern in his social criticism, and he looked towards a world in which collective pressures ceased to determine the response of individuals. Authentic religion included 'the ability to say one's own "yes" and one's own "no" and not merely to echo the "yes" and "no" of state, party, corporation, army or system'.[88]

It was inevitable that Merton should turn in the first instance to the United States. He knew what the American dream represented, and yet he perceived that 'We are living in a society which for all its unquestionable advantages and all its fantastic ingenuity just does not seem to be able to provide people with lives that are fully human and fully real.'[89] He deplored the cult of celebrity and the emptiness that lay just beneath the surface. He saw too much evidence of power, money, complacency and a great capacity for self-deception. He could say without any equivocation that 'There are wonderful people' in the United States and yet he required his readers 'to face the fact that we live in a pretty sick culture.'[90]

Merton observed a society in which life must be filled 'with movement and activity, with speech, news, communication, recreation, distraction.'[91] He might be anxious about the consequences of modern technology, but his primary complaint concerned the loss of the wisdom that is informed by a religious understanding of life. All that would be left would be 'an empty shell of technology, scientific vanities, urban conglomerations of impersonal persons.'[92] The abandonment of a spiritual awareness would inevitably mean the progressive loss of the values on which society had been established.

But what was the prevailing consciousness against which Merton protested? What was the meaning of alienation as he reflected upon the American scene and offered his partial but persistent critique? And what was the alternative perception of reality, the alternative consciousness, that he proposed?

Merton's exposition of the end-time in *Raids on the Unspeakable* has a global reference, but the signs of which he speaks are to be seen most obviously in the Western world and, therefore, in the United States. He describes a situation in which 'the technological furies of size, volume, quantity, speed, number, price, power and acceleration' take precedence. People are 'numbered in billions, and massed together ... taxed, drilled, armed, worked to the point of insensibility, dazed by information, drugged by entertainment, surfeited with everything, nauseated with the human race and with ourselves, nauseated with life.'[93] When every allowance has been made for the way in which he writes – melodramatic, apocalyptic – what Merton depicts is a state of alienation in which men and women, lacking all awareness of the truth of their situation, are estranged from their true selves.

He acknowledged the ease with which men and women identify themselves with a secular culture, but he rejected the security, the comfort and the illusory freedom which it offers.[94] His approach to the prophetic task, as he addressed the dilemma confronting people, could therefore be expressed with great simplicity: 'before we can become prophetic we have to be authentic human beings'.[95] The burden of his counter-consciousness is, then, a profound emphasis upon authenticity: the integrity of the individual, freedom, mutual responsibility, justice.

But the authenticity of which he spoke was grounded in the freedom of the individual, while simultaneously calling in question any unqualified commitment to complete personal autonomy. It was for Merton the claim to complete autonomy, presented in different guises, which lay at the heart of attempts by men and women to explain their existence and justify their actions. Such a claim was entirely fallacious. Freedom is God's gift to His creation and to those who, in the light of the cross, reject notions of individual fulfilment and satisfaction. It is the prophetic task of the church to interpret contemporary events in the light of this conviction.

The exercise of power, both by commercial interests and by nation states, was central to so much that Merton had to say in the 1960s. His observations concerning the role of the United States throughout the world reflected anxieties that have become better understood and far more widely shared with the passing years. It is easy to forget the burden carried by the United States on behalf of the 'free world' in the years that followed the Second World War. Strident comments concerning the way in which America conducted itself on the world stage would not easily commend themselves to his fellow countrypeople, although later generations might hesitate before condemning out of hand suggestions that the United States failed to pay sufficient attention to the way in which other nations might see the world;[96] or that investment in under-developed countries was far too often determined by political, economic and cultural considerations;[97] or that many activities would be seen by others as an attempt to police the world, determining for other countries how they should live;[98] or that efforts to contain by violence revolutionary activities in different parts of the world were ultimately self-defeating.[99] Merton's melancholy reflection was that 'there is now in the world an anti-americanism which is a hatred comparable to anti-semitism'.[100]

In all situations – at home and overseas – Merton understood the need for diagnosis and criticism: 'the prophetic task of finding and identifying the injustice which is the cause of *all* the violence'.[101] He was writing with particular reference to the struggle for civil rights in the United States, the tradition of non-violence represented by Martin Luther King, and the rise of Black Power. He put the activities of Black Power in a wider frame, judging it to be 'part of a world movement of refusal and rejection of the value system we call western culture.[102] The struggle for racial justice, punctuated by repeated acts of violence against the most vulnerable, was for Merton a judgement of the illusions with which the nation had consoled itself. His sympathies were entirely on the side of the dispossessed. His strongest criticism was often reserved for the cautious liberalism which concealed a good deal of complacency. He pleaded for a recognition that the present crisis might be *for black and white alike* a time of promise and not merely an hour of judgement.

Merton's critique of power and the abuses of power were not confined to the United States but embraced both Soviet Russia and China. He had little time for totalitarian ideologies, but he was no less critical of any alternative that the free world might offer, informed by the myth-dreams of his adopted country. For Merton, the greatest sin of the great powers was the arrogance that they displayed in their dealings with the rest of the world.[103]

Few events encapsulated such arrogance more completely in Merton's judgement than the Vietnam War. He was highly critical of the part played by China and the United States, although his most trenchant criticism was reserved – somewhat unjustly – for President Lyndon B. Johnson and the political–military establishment that determined the course of events. He was troubled by the political and the moral problems raised by the intervention of the United States in different parts of the Third World, and he related with some feeling the comment of a Catholic Youth Leader in Saigon. 'We are caught in a struggle between two power blocs ... Many people told me you cannot trust Americans, but I never accepted it. Now I am beginning to believe it. You come to help my people, but they will hate you for it.'[104]

Merton saw the extent to which the world was changing. It was no longer sufficient for the nations of the West to lead under-developed nations towards the cultural agenda that they, the Western powers, had set for themselves. He was mindful of the importance of China, India and Japan, but he recognized that Asian and African countries would demand an active role in directing the fortunes of their own peoples. Pragmatic considerations, quite apart from any theological understanding, required a global consciousness. Interconnectedness and interdependence might well be the watchwords of a new order in which everyone carried some responsibility for what happened on the other side of the world. The survival of the world, quite apart from the survival of anything that might be called civilization, would require 'a new world-culture that embraces all civilized philosophies'.[105] But Merton – the experiential theologian, the

Christian hermit, the contemplative – was bound to add that 'Ultimately there is no humanism without God.'[106]

War and the violence of war

The exercise of power leads invariably to the abuse of power, and no abuse is more prevalent than the violence with which it is all too often associated. Merton spoke of humankind's 'fatal addiction to war',[107] but he also noted how easily injustice, and fear, and fantasies, and obsessions, and indiscriminate acts of violence feed off one another, until – when the claims of conscience are finally abandoned – they escalate out of control. Violence has become the universal currency of choice, and Merton feared for a world in which 'slaughter, violence, revolution, the annihilation of enemies, the extermination of entire populations and even genocide *have become a way of life*'.[108] The law of cause and effect could be seen as outwardly well-ordered social structures, established upon varying degrees of social injustice, attempted to manage and control the resentments to be found beneath the surface. Merton's anxiety was that violence would become increasingly 'aimless, nihilistic, arbitrary, destructive and non-amenable to reasonable control'.[109] What violence therefore makes explicit is the enduring crisis of alienation when constraints are abandoned, value systems lose all meaning, and life itself is held to be of little or no account.

It was the arrogance and the brutality of power against which Merton railed: the oppression of colonial powers; the Nazi concentration camps and the Soviet labour camps; persecution on the grounds of race, colour, ethnicity, religion; the influence of money and power, the influence of the military in shaping public perceptions; the indiscriminate application of technology; the rhetoric of the Cold War; and – above all for Merton – the fearsome events of Hiroshima and Nagasaki.

What connects all these grotesque instances of violence is nothing less than the inhumanity of humankind, and Merton's sombre conclusion is that 'There is hardly a nation on earth today that is not to some extent committed to a philosophy or to a mystique of violence.'[110] Merton did not attend to the constraints experienced by those who are required to exercise power, nor did he attempt to understand the circumstances in which compromise becomes an unavoidable act of policy, but the stark realities – as he understood them – led only to the melancholy questions 'Will there never be any peace on earth in our lifetime? Will they never do anything but kill, and then kill some more?'[111]

It was the nightmare scenario of a nuclear holocaust that dominated so much of Merton's thinking during the last ten years of his life. He feared that a large-scale war in any part of the world could easily turn into a world-wide nuclear catastrophe. He was utterly persuaded that 'the *massive and uninhibited use of nuclear weapons*, either in attack or in retaliation, was contrary to Christian morality',[112] but he recognized that in East and West nuclear weapons were now taken for granted, that nuclear deterrence was accepted as a responsible way of maintaining peace, and that nuclear war was reckoned to be 'a rational option'.[113] But he also knew how easily things could go wrong through accident, miscalculation, technical failure or mental breakdown; and he pleaded for an awareness of how the good that has been intended can be overtaken by the evil that is permitted.

Merton recognized that decisions concerning military strategy were being made in a post-Christian world in which Christian ethics were all too easily marginalized, but he pleaded that 'every sane and serious moral code' must cry out not only against nuclear weapons but also against the 'massive destruction of cities, populations, nations and cultures by any means whatever'.[114] He knew that moral thinking, if it is only guided by pragmatic considerations, tends 'to be very vague, very fluid';[115] and he was compelled to acknowledge that what is often referred to as 'Christian society' amounts to little more than 'a materialistic neopaganism with a Christian veneer'. Behind that, when the veneer has been stripped away, nothing is to be found but 'the awful vacuity of the mass-mind, without morality, without identity, without compassion, without sense, and rapidly reverting to tribalism and superstition'.[116]

Through his correspondence, through his published writings, through the circulation of mimeographed copies of both his *Cold War Letters* and the unpublished manuscript of *Peace in the Post-Christian Era,* through his active engagement in the peace movement, Merton became an important voice of protest during the 1960s. He challenged the ignorance, the passivity, the complacency and the confusion of clergy and laity alike. He called in question a situation in which – from his perspective – national policy was being deter-mined by the interests of big business, the obsessions of the military and the phobias of political extremists. He rejected what he saw as the prevailing consensus of opinion within the United States – 'a highly over-simplified and mythical view of the world divided into two camps: that of darkness (our enemies) and that of light (ourselves).[117]

What Merton sought was the abolition of war as a means of solving problems, although he held back from embracing a position of unqualified and unequivocal pacifism. He saw the inability of the United Nations, frustrated so often by the nuclear powers, to be an effective arbiter in international disputes, and he was sufficiently in touch with the unavoidable obligations of *realpolitik* to recognize that unilateral disarmament was not going to happen. In political, tactical terms, he accepted that the only responsible way forward was to align himself with those who looked for multilateral disarmament, but he identified some of the atrocities of war – the use of torture, the killing of hostages, genocide – with which later generations are still all too familiar.

Merton's book *Peace in the Post-Christian Era* was eventually published in 2004, and Jim Forest, who had worked alongside Merton in the peace movement in the 1960s, commended it in a Foreword as a book that remains relevant and timely. A world that has lived with the nuclear threat for seven decades, surviving the Cold War and the uneasy balance of power, might easily become indifferent to the threat that is posed by weapons of mass destruction. But Merton's strictures and questions remain. Nations and peoples are no less gripped by fears and fantasies in the early decades of the twenty-first century. A new world order continues to take shape, but there is ample scope for unease: the proliferation of nuclear weapons, the ambitions of international terrorism, the emergence of 'rogue states', and the fear that one day another lunatic leader will arise for whom death and destruction on a massive scale might represent nothing more than the last throw of the dice.

Merton's exposition of non-violence might appear at first sight to represent the alternative consciousness that he was proposing. He found its theological foundations in the Beatitudes, but it took its place for him within a spiritual tradition that transcended the boundaries of faith communities, possessing an inherently global validity. It was a form of religious humanism and it repre-sented a substantial power for change. He believed that it had been consistently misunderstood and misrepresented, and he challenged a new generation to consider the claims of non-violence afresh.

Merton's concluding remarks in his submission on *Civil Disobedience and Non-Violent Revolution* to the National Commission on the Causes and Prevention of Violence in 1968 encapsulate the unavoidable limitations imposed upon non-violence as a strategy for moving forward.

If we live in what is essentially a culture of overkill, how can we be surprised at finding violence in it? Can we get to the root of the trouble? In my opinion, the best way to do it would have been the classic way of religious humanism and non-violence exemplified by Gandhi. That way seems now to have been closed. I do not find the future reassuring.[118]

Merton remained committed, intellectually and emotionally, to a tradition of non-violence. It was for him a 'witness to living alternatives ... *essential* for the survival of a society'.[119] He stood four-square with Gandhi in the conviction that 'Mankind is at the crossroads. It has to make a choice between the law of the jungle and the law of humanity'.[120] But in so far as he held back from a position of unqualified pacifism, accepting that in some circumstances it may be necessary to use violence in the fight against dictatorships,[121] and even – perhaps most surprisingly – being open to the possibility of a very limited use of atomic weapons in self-defence,[122] it is impossible to see non-violence as Merton's distinctive understanding of the counter-consciousness.

War and the violence of war speak of the tragedy of the human condition. The message that they conveyed could be summed up for Merton in the one word, *alienation*: the alienation of men and women from each other and their inability to come to terms with life. If alienation is the persistent and enduring crisis, then violence constitutes one of its most visible manifestations. If the acceptance of war as an inescapable fact of life is one of the many presenting crises, then Merton's response is to turn again to the human condition and look for any explanation in the psychology of individuals and nations.

It was not non-violence that Merton was offering as a new way of looking at life, a new strategy for dealing with war, but a fundamental change in the hearts and minds of men and women. He took full account of 'the constant deluge of irresponsible opinions, criminal half-truths and murderous images' disseminated by the mass media, but for him the problem would only be solved '*in our thoughts, in our spirit*'.[123] He wrote of the ease with which we 'go through life without seeing that our own violence is a disaster and that the overwhelming force by which we seek to assert ourselves and our own self interest may well be our ruin'.[124] It was not a question of men and women loving war for its own sake, but rather one of being 'blindly and hopelessly involved in needs and attitudes that make war inevitable'.[125]

The prophetic voice is not to be found in the prediction of events which are only now unfolding, but in the awareness of a situation which continues to exist and in which truths – deeply disturbing and unpalatable truths – are to be found by those who have eyes to see and ears to hear.

> Let us for the love of heaven wake up to the fact that our own minds are just as filled with dangerous power today as the nuclear bombs themselves. And let us be very careful how we unleash the pent-up forces in the minds of others. The hour is extremely grave … It is because the minds of men have become what they have become that the world is poised on the brink of total disaster.[126]

The prophetic word is not always heard, but there was for Merton in his prophetic awareness the possibility that the word of judgement, if only it could be received, might be the word of promise. 'What if we awaken to discover that *we* are the robbers, and our destruction comes from the root of hate in ourselves?'[127]

The church in a post-Christian world

But what did all these things have to say to the predicament in which the church found itself in the middle years of the twentieth century? Merton was unsparing in his criticism as he surveyed a church which had lost its bearings in a post-Christian world. Christendom had been so identified with the structures that had dominated European and Western life for over fifteen hundred years that fantasies of triumphalism, of superiority, were still to be found, together with the idea – perhaps even more seductive – that churchmen might continue to act 'as if we are still running things, still in a position to solve all the world's problems and tell everybody what to do next'.[128]

Merton's consistent complaint throughout the 1950s and 1960s was that the institutional life of the church had led to a situation in which the church was increasingly disengaged from the life of the world. He lamented 'the *absolute need for external control* over souls in order to save them'[129] and wanted the church to find the institutional humility which might enable it to break the habit of 'handing down categorical answers, in terms of absolutes, right from the word go'.[130] Personal and group psychologies, institutional demands and expectations, social conventions and pious customs worked together to establish and maintain traditions of conformity and security, but it was for Merton these very things that were inhibiting the work of the gospel.

Merton pays little regard to patterns of personal piety, experiments at parochial or diocesan levels in pastoral care and missionary endeavour, traditions of public or civil religion. His reading of the situation was that the church was now compelled to live in a post-Christian age; that another critical juncture had been reached – as in the time of Galileo – when entirely new thinking was required; that religion was being weighed in the balance; and that the church would no longer have an accepted place in society. He never doubted the survival of the church, but he believed that Christians would become increasingly marginal: 'Diaspora Christians in a frankly secular and non-believing society.'[131] But the diaspora was not the ghetto, and Merton wanted the church to face its responsibilities to the future, urging that it might move forward in a spirit of open dialogue.

Alienation does not speak, therefore, merely of the church's detachment from the world, but even more of its estrangement from its own true vocation. 'We have taken Christianity for granted for hundreds of years and now all of a sudden I think some of us are beginning to wake up to the fact that we have almost forgotten what it means, and that our ideas of God and His ways are far from corresponding to the actuality.'[132] Whatever crisis of identity Christianity might face, the church would be judged by the willingness of Christians to let go of anachronistic images, of false securities, making a new evaluation of the world and finding a new commitment to their place within it. Merton had no illusions about the magnitude of the task and he identified fully with the judgement that 'It was doubtless easier to make the conversion from pre-Christian to Christian than it is from post-Christian to Christian.'[133] But his perception of reality, his counter-consciousness, left him in no doubt that the church's prophetic vocation was to be 'a stumbling block to the world, a sign of contradiction'.[134]

It was yet again a desert perspective that Merton brought to his reflections on the church and there was an overlap where his observations about the church and monasticism were concerned. He was well aware of the large numbers of younger religious who had left their monasteries in recent years, unable to find in the traditional framework the necessary freedom to grow as they believed God was calling them to grow. His anxiety was that monasticism – as it had been interpreted over a thousand years – had been far too committed to the established social order, and so in more recent times it had neglected its 'prophetic and iconoclastic function in the world', settling instead for mere survival as 'a dignified and established institution'.[135]

Merton found reason to be hopeful for the future of monasticism as he considered the Indian ashram of Dom Bede Griffiths, the Protestant community at Taizé, the Little Brothers, and the Brothers of the Virgin of the Poor. Merton wanted the ancient disciplines of monasticism without the deceits proffered by the Christendom model, but it was a telling combination of conservatism and radicalism – of looking back to the heart of a primitive monasticism and of looking out with searching questions to the world of his day – that he brought to the discussion.

Merton had no developed strategy to offer either to the church in general or to monasticism in particular. His observations – as with so many of his social criticisms – were too diffuse to be translated into public policy. But his achievement was to identify the crisis in which the church and monasticism were caught up. He warned against the seductive fantasies of looking back to an earlier age and of clinging, therefore, to a role and a task which were no longer relevant. He articulated and embodied a desert tradition, contemplative and prophetic, which may yet prove to be his most enduring legacy.

Merton asks that the desert tradition might be fully understood. His observation remains: 'When the windows of the monastery no longer open upon the vast horizons of the desert, the monastic community inevitably becomes immersed in vanity. All that is accidental, trivial, and accessory tends to assume a rank of high importance and to become the sole end of the monastic life.'[136] Merton comes down as a man who, standing firmly within the desert tradition of monasticism, speaks none the less to those who are lost in the far more barren deserts of contemporary life. Could it be that Merton's emphasis upon the necessity of the desert experience speaks to the church – and above all to a church in uncertain times – and not only to the monastery? Could it be that only a church that understands the desert tradition will know what it means to hold the faith in obscurity and in silence, living with its brokenness and its incompleteness, watching and waiting?

If the desert experience requires interior solitude and interior silence, if these things are also the seed-bed of contemplative prayer and contemplative living, it is in order that they might bear their distinctive fruit: a new awareness of the world's needs. Whatever is meant by a new perception of reality is to be found in the connection Merton makes between contemplative prayer and engagement with the world. He does not prescribe the form that it might take, but he points to the direction in which it is necessary to travel. If he affirms the importance of the contemplative dimension in human experience, if he pleads for a far greater contemplative orientation in the life of the church, it is in order that men and women might find new depths of awareness and meaning in their lives. The persistent and enduring crisis to which Merton returns is the 'struggle against alienation'.[137] Contemplative living is food for the journey, armour for the fight.

In any analysis of the dominant consciousness – either in world politics or in the religious life of humankind – Merton detected an identical fault line. His charge of arrogance against the great powers in relation to the rest of the world was more than matched by his condemnation of the sense of superiority that surrounded so much religious life and thought. What Merton sought by contrast was a recognition of the truth possessed by the stranger, an exploration of the common inheritance of faith, a sharing of experience and contemplative wisdom, and a discovery of an original unity.

The global perspective was all important; and in the arena of faith that required for Merton a new definition of the church's task, a wider ecumenism. He refused to operate within the particular and parochial boundaries that Catholicism so readily imposed. He claimed the universality implicit in Catholicism. He sought a far greater degree of inclusivity. He set his face against any theological syncretism, but declared himself 'rather uneasy about our dictating to all the "other religions" that we are the one authentic outfit that has the real goods'.[138] There was nothing in Merton's approach to the other world religions which required him to sit lightly to his Christian faith. His concern was only to draw fully upon his own tradition and go beyond it.

The starting point was a mystical tradition of faith which enabled Merton to see Christ in every person. 'I must learn that my fellow man, just as he is, whether he is my friend or my enemy, my brother or a stranger from the other side of the world … "is Christ".'[139] Like the prophets of the Old Testament who refused to let the children of Israel find their security in the land or the law or the temple, but only in God's saving acts in history, so Merton, mindful of the mystery of Christ, looked not for doctrinal orthodoxy or institutional allegiance but for 'a living theological experience of the presence of God in the world'.[140]

Merton's conviction that the churches were required to take full account of other communities of faith secures his place in the still largely undeveloped story of inter-faith activity. It is difficult to overestimate the importance of the wider ecumenism that he embraced. A later generation is more open to the insights which different traditions of faith can bring to an awareness of the God who transcends all names, all images. Merton's reflections may yet become of increasing importance as the East begins to exercise a dominant influence throughout the world. Many will see him as 'a man before his time – a kind of contemplative pioneer blazing the trail for a future generation of theologians and contemplatives involved in ecumenical and inter-faith dialogue. He affirms priorities, lays down guidelines and indicates the difficulties which are inevitably involved.'[141] If the religious awareness for which Merton pleaded possesses the importance that he attached to it, then his oft-repeated desire to explore the shared inheritance of faith and experience and illumination may yet represent the most compelling instance of a prophetic consciousness and a prophetic voice.

A theological humanism

Alienation takes many forms, but as Merton pursued his searching and passionate encounter with the world two dominant concerns were central to all that he had to say: the freedom and the integrity of the individual *and* the necessity of the religious dimension. The presenting problems might be the chaos and the confusion to be found in a time of crisis; the exploitation of the natural world; the subordination of women to men; the fantasies and the delusions that dominated the prevailing scene; the relation of the individual to institutions; the arrogance of the great powers; the appetite for war; the failure of the churches to realize the truth of the situation in which they found themselves. The persistent and enduring crisis was represented by experiences of fragmentation, of self-deception, of scapegoating, of disconnectedness. It was estrangement from anything that might be described as authentic living.

Merton understood the human predicament and the dynamics of the world at a time of radical transition. He observed with some disquiet 'the blank passivity and indifference of modern mass man.'[142] He pleaded for freedom, humanity and spontaneity in what seemed to him increasingly to be a 'world of massive conflict and collective unreason.'[143] But the responsibility for both the present and the future rested with humankind. He saw that the world was 'a complex of responsibilities and options made out of the loves, the hates, the fears, the joys, the hopes, the greed, the cruelty, the kindness, the faith, the trust, the suspicion of all.'[144] He knew the importance of social relationships and social obligations. Conscience implied a commitment 'to discover *all* the social implications of the Gospel.'[145] The global dimension was at the forefront of his mind, and living for God involved 'assuming full responsibility for our world, for our lives, for ourselves'.[146]

The sense of crisis, even of *kairos*, that Merton brought to his prophetic task compelled him to speak of the need for change, revolutionary change, in the secular world. In the place of programmes and policies, he pointed to the need for interior change. His appeal was that men and women might 'renounce [their] alienated and false selves'.[147] But the religious dimension would not be easily secured. Merton acknowledged the limitations of the words and the images which men and women have traditionally employed in their encounter with God. He had drawn upon his experience of contemplative prayer in talking of seeing and not-seeing, of knowing and not-knowing; but philosophers and theologians, writing from a different perspective, were more likely to speak of the *silence*, or the *absence*, or the *death* of God. The problem – as Merton understood it – was compounded in the West by what he called 'an inner split and self-alienation', which required people to concern themselves with 'only half of life: that which is exterior, objective, and quantitative'.[148] The casualty was any consciousness of God; and Merton, developing this particular train of thought, looked towards artists and poets and others concerned with the interior life for confirmation of his view that 'the reason why God has ceased to be present to man (therefore "dead") is that man has ceased to be present to himself, and that consequently the true significance of the statement "God is dead" is really that "MAN is dead"'.[149]

And yet, wrestling with a situation in which God is hidden and unknown, Merton persisted in offering a vision which had its roots in a theological humanism. He remained persuaded of the need to find 'an absolute and ultimate meaning in life',[150] and his sense of the universality of Christ compelled him to look for 'universal horizons'.[151] But the religious perspective that he sought did not represent any abdication of personal responsibility. 'For the world to be changed, man himself must begin to change it, he must take the initiative, he must step forth and make a new kind of history. The change begins within himself'.[152]

Merton called, then, for the freedom which enabled men and women 'to respond to life and to love beyond the limited requirements of the ego'.[153] It was an attitude of mind, a way of engaging with life, which Merton himself had come to represent and to embody: openness in faith, hope and love to the demands of the present and of an unknown future. His monastic vocation required him to see himself as an alien, a stranger; but his several vocations informed his prophetic consciousness and gave focus and depth to his prophetic voice. The contradictions in which he was caught up, the discontents with which he lived, might be seen in retrospect as his credentials to a world that struggles to come to terms with its persistent and enduring experience of alienation.

Merton had known throughout the long years at Gethsemani that there was a purpose – 'a particular goal, a fulfillment' – which was entirely personal to him.[154] It was implicit in the search for God, the encounter with God, to which he was entirely committed. It was a summons to life: 'We live in prophetic and eschatological times, and by and large everyone is asleep. We realize it dimly, like sleepers who have turned off the alarm clock without quite waking up.'[155]

It is scarcely surprising that from a variety of sources Merton's unique contribution has been so freely acknowledged. For some, he was 'a figure of reliable yet creative transition in a world of turmoil';[156] for some, he represented a type of discipleship which is compelling in a confused and uncertain age; for some, he was 'a prophetic voice for our times'.[157] One of his brothers at Gethsemani wrote that 'He continues to speak to us today in circumstances that, in many respects, are marked by the issues he identified half a century ago as crucial for our world.'[158] The fascination of the man remains. The voice continues to be heard.

Notes and Sources

The following abbreviations have been used to indicate the most frequent references in the Notes.

AJ	*The Asian Journal of Thomas Merton.* Edited from his Original Notebook by Naomi Burton Stone, Patrick Hart and James Laughlin. Sheldon Press 1974.
CGB	Merton, Thomas, *Conjectures of a Guilty Bystander.* Sheldon Press 1977.
CP	*The Collected Poems of Thomas Merton.* Sheldon Press 1978.
CPr	Merton, Thomas, *Contemplative Prayer.* Darton, Longman and Todd 1973.
CS	*Cistercian Studies.*
CWA	Merton, Thomas, *Contemplation in a World of Action.* George Allen & Unwin Ltd. 1971.
CWL	*Cold War Letters.* Orbis 2006.
DQ	Merton, Thomas, *Disputed Questions.* Harcourt, Brace & Co. 1988.
DS	Merton, Thomas, *Day of A Stranger.* Gibbs M. Smith 1981.
FV	Merton, Thomas, *Faith and Violence.* Notre Dame Press 1994.
GNV	*Gandhi on Non-Violence.* Edited by Thomas Merton. New Directions 1965.
IE	Merton, Thomas, *The Inner Experience.* Edited by William H. Shannon. SPCK 2003.
Ji	*The Journals of Thomas Merton.* Volume 1. *Run to the Mountain: The Story of a Vocation.* Edited by Patrick Hart. HarperSanFrancisco 1995.
Jii	*The Journals of Thomas Merton.* Volume 2. *Entering the Silence: Becoming a Monk and a Writer.* Edited by Jonathan Montaldo. HarperSanFrancisco 1996.
Jiii	*The Journals of Thomas Merton.* Volume 3. *A Search for Solitude: Pursuing the Monk's True Life.* Edited by Lawrence S. Cunningham. HarperSanFrancisco 1996.
Jiv	*The Journals of Thomas Merton.* Volume 4. *Turning Towards The World: The Pivotal Years.* Edited by Victor A. Kramer. HarperSanFrancisco 1996.
Jv	*The Journals of Thomas Merton.* Volume 5. *Dancing in the Waters of Life.* Edited by Robert E. Daggy. HarperSanFrancisco 1997.
Jvi	*The Journals of Thomas Merton.* Volume 6. *Learning to Love: Exploring Solitude and Freedom.* Edited by Christine M. Bochen. HarperSanFrancisco 1997.
Jvii	*The Journals of Thomas Merton.* Volume 7. *The Other Side of the Mountain: The End of the Journey.* Edited by Patrick Hart. HarperSanFrancisco 1998.
Li	*The Letters of Thomas Merton* (on Religious Experience and Social Concerns). Volume 1. *The Hidden Ground of Love.* Edited by William H. Shannon. Farrar, Straus, Giroux 1985.

Lii   *The Letters of Thomas Merton* (to New and Old Friends). Volume 2. *The Road to Joy.*
           Edited by Robert E. Daggy. Farrar, Straus, Giroux 1989

Liii   *The Letters of Thomas Merton* (on Religious Renewal and Spiritual Direction).
           Volume 3. *The School of Charity.* Edited by Patrick Hart. Farrar, Straus, Giroux 1990.

Liv   *The Letters of Thomas Merton* (to Writers). Volume 4. *The Courage for Truth.* Edited
           by Christine M. Bochen. Farrar, Straus, Giroux 1993.

Lv   *The Letters of Thomas Merton* (in Times of Crisis). Volume 5. *Witness To Freedom.*
           Edited by William H. Shannon. Farrar, Straus, Giroux 1994

LE   *The Literary Essays of Thomas Merton.* Edited by Patrick Hart. A New Directions
           Book 1981.

LL   Merton, Thomas, *Love and Living.* Edited by Naomi Burton Stone and Patrick Hart.
           A Harvest Book. Harcourt Inc. 1979.

LTM   *The Legacy of Thomas Merton.* Edited by Patrick Hart. Cistercian Publications 1986.

MA   *The Merton Annual.*

MAG   Merton, Thomas, *My Argument with the Gestapo.* Doubleday & Co. 1969.

MT   *Thomas Merton / Monk: A Monastic Tribute.* Edited by Patrick Hart. Cistercian
           Publications 1983.

MTM   *The Message of Thomas Merton.* Edited by Patrick Hart. Cistercian Publications 1981.

MZM   Merton, Thomas, *Mystics and Zen Masters.* Farrar, Straus, Giroux 1999.

NM   Merton, Thomas, *The New Man.* Burns & Oates 1962.

NMI   Merton, Thomas, *No Man Is An Island.* Burns & Oates 1993.

NSC   Merton, Thomas, *New Seeds of Contemplation.* Shambhala 2003.

NVA   Merton, Thomas, *The Nonviolent Alternative.* Farrar, Straus, Giroux 1980. The book
           (apart from the replacement of one article) was originally published under the title
           Thomas Merton On Peace.

OZ   Merton, Thomas, *Thomas Merton On Zen.* Sheldon Press, 1976.

PPCE   Merton, Thomas, *Peace in the Post-Christian Era.* Orbis Books 2004.

RMW   Merton, Thomas, *Reflections on My Work.* Edited by Robert E. Daggy. Collins Fount
           Paperbacks 1981.

RT   Merton, Thomas, *Redeeming the Time.* Burns & Oates 1966.

RU   Merton, Thomas, *Raids on the Unspeakable.* Burns & Oates 1993.

SC   Merton, Thomas, *Seeds of Contemplation.* Burns & Oates 1960.

SD   Merton, Thomas, *Seeds of Destruction.* Farrar, Straus, Giroux 1964.

SJ   Merton, Thomas, *The Sign of Jonas.* Hollis & Carter 1953.

SMTM   Mott, Michael, *The Seven Mountains of Thomas Merton.* Houghton Mifflin Company
           1984.

SprC   Merton, Thomas, *The Springs of Contemplation.* Farrar, Straus, Giroux 1992.

SSM   Merton, Thomas, *The Seven Storey Mountain.* SPCK 1993.

TM   Thomas Merton

TMC   Thomas Merton Center, Bellarmine University, Louisville, Kentucky.

TMR   *A Thomas Merton Reader.* Edited by Thomas P. McDonnell. Doubleday 1989.

WCT   Merton, Thomas, *The Way of Chuang Tzu.* Shambhala 2004.

ZBA   Merton, Thomas, *Zen and the Birds of Appetite.* New Directions 1968.

Notes

Chapter 1: The Fascination of the Man

1 TMR 1 (M. Scott Peck, *Introduction*).
2 CS (1969) iv 3 225 (Naomi Burton Stone, *I Shall Miss Thomas Merton*).
3 MT 122 (Thérèse Lentfoehr, *The Spiritual Writer*).
4 MAG 160–1
5 TMR 17 (An Author's Preface: *First and Last Thoughts*).
6 Seitz, Ron, *Song for Nobody: A Memory Vision of Thomas Merton*. Liguouri, Missouri: Triumph Books 1993, p. 123.
7 MT 265 (Flavian Burns, *Epilogue: A Homily*).
8 MT 39 (John Eudes Bamberger, *The Monk*).
9 LE 373 (*Message to Poets*).
10 Jv 67 (25 January 1964)
11 LTM 220 (Timothy Kelly, *Epilogue: A Memoir*).
12 Liii 385. TM to Sister J. M. (17 June 1968).
13 Jvi xxiii (Christine M. Bochen, *Introduction*).
14 Jiv 324 (26 May 1963).
15 Jv 267 (9 July 1965).
16 Merton was given the name Louis on his admission to Gethsemani, although his friends outside the monastery continued to know him as Tom, and in later years his brothers at Gethsemani would increasingly refer to him as Louie or Uncle Louie.
17 Liii 11. TM to Abbot James Fox (Spring 1949).
18 Forest, James, *Thomas Merton's Struggle with Peacemaking*, Erie: Benet Press 1983, p. 23.
19 Wilkes, Paul, Editor, *Merton By Those Who Knew Him Best*, New York: Harper & Row 1984, p. 105 (Flavian Burns).
20 Jii 84 (14 June 1947).
21 MT 46 (John Eudes Bamberger, *The Monk*).
22 References to the natural world are scattered throughout Merton's *Journals*. See with reference to this paragraph: Jiv 122 (30 May 1961); Jiv 279 (25 December 1962); Jv 26 (23 October 1963); Jv 100 (28 April 1964); Jvi 11 (24 January 1966); Jvi 238 (27 May 1967); Jvii 79 (9 April 1968); and also CGB 28.
23 Jv 313 (7 November 1965).
24 CGB 174.
25 Jii 423 (21 March 1950).
26 Jii 331 (27 June 1949).
27 CGB 287
28 CGB 174
29 Jiv 205 (27 February 1962).
30 Jv 162 (4 November 1964).
31 Jiv 274 (11 December 1962).
32 Jii 11 (Good Friday, 3 April 1942).
33 MT 94 (Jean Leclercq, *The Evolving Monk*).

34 Jv 212 (2 March 1965).

35 LE 345 (*Poetry and Contemplation*).

36 CWA 237.

37 DQ 197.

38 DQ 198.

39 Jiii 27 (29 December 1952).

40 CGB 204.

41 CS XIII (1978) 4 311 (Jean Leclercq, *Merton and the East*).

42 FV 213.

43 Lv 180. TM to Sister Anita Wasserman OCD (21 May 1953).

44 CWA 149.

45 Ibid.

46 RU 122.

47 LL 153.

48 CGB 136.

49 CGB 63.

50 Jiv 160 (9 September 1961).

51 Jvii 5 (25 October 1967).

52 Jvii 51 (8 February 1968).

53 CGB 313.

54 LL 202.

55 Jiv 265 (16 November 1962).

56 The *diaspora* refers historically to the dispersion of the Jews throughout Asia Minor following upon the Assyrian and Babylonian conquests of Jerusalem in 722 and 597 BC respectively. It has become a convenient way of referring to minority faith groups in unfamiliar and uncongenial situations.

57 Jvi 195 (7 February 1967).

58 CP 383 (*A Letter to Pablo Antonio Cuadra Concerning Giants* in *Emblems of a Season of Fury*, 1963).

59 AJ vii (*Preface* by Amiya Chakravarty).

60 CGB 266.

61 MT 125 (Charles Dumont, *The Contemplative*).

62 CGB 332.

63 TM *Commonweal* 1966. Cited by Woodcock, George, *Thomas Merton: Monk and Poet*, Edinburgh: Canongate 1978, p. 106.

64 Padovano, Anthony T., *The Human Journey. Thomas Merton: Symbol of a Century*, Doubleday & Co 1982, p. 170.

65 Wilkes, *op. cit.*, p. 26 (Robert Giroux).

66 Shannon, William H., *Silent Lamp: The Thomas Merton Story*, SCM Press 1993, p. 7.

67 Padovano, *op. cit.*, p. 168.

68 Inchausti, Robert, *Thomas Merton's American Prophecy*, State University of New York Press 1998, p. 105.

69 *Cross Currents* 27, Winter 1977–8 (Daniel Berrigan).

70 CS XIII (1978) 4 396 (Mark Gibbard, *The Friend I Never Met*).

71 Wilkes, *op. cit.*, p. 71 (Robert Lax).

72 Ibid., p.123 (John Eudes Bamberger).

73 NSC 49.

74 MA 15 (2002). (Interview by George Kilcourse with Bro. Paul Quenon OCSO).

75 AJ 334.

76 Jiv 101 (22 March 1961).

77 AJ 296 (September 1968, *Circular Letter to Friends*).

78 Atkinson, Morgan C. and Montaldo, Jonathan, Editors, *The Journey of Thomas Merton*, SPCK 2009, p. 84.

79 Jv 333 (*Some Personal Notes*, end of 1965).

80 CP 951 (A Translation of Pablo Antonio Cuadra's *Meditation Before An Ancient Poem*).

Chapter 2: The Trappist Monk

1 Jii 36 (14 January 1947).

2 Liii 280. TM to Dom Jean Leclercq (11 May 1965).

3 The land had been previously occupied by the Sisters of Loretto at the Foot of the Cross who had established a school named Gethsemani on the site.

4 Merton, Thomas, *Seasons of Celebration*, New York: Farrar, Straus and Giroux 1965, p. 208.

5 SSM 366.

6 Jii 32 (13 December 1946).

7 Ji 333 (7 April 1941).

8 Ji 416 (28 September 1941).

9 SSM 387.

10 Jv 172 (1 December 1964).

11 SSM 383.

12 Ji 347 (10 April 1941).

13 Ji 462 (29 November 1941).

14 New foundations were established in Georgia (1944), Utah (1947), South Carolina (1949), New York (1951), California (1955).

15 SSM.

16 Jv 79 (22 February 1964).

17 SSM 389.

18 SMTM 243.

19 Jii 217–8 (11 July 1948).

20 Jii 458 (13 June 1951).

21 CWA 228.

22 Jii 450 (3 March 1951).

23 Jiii 242 (28 December 1952).

24 MT 43 (John Eudes Bamberger, *The Monk*).

25 Jii 199 (11 April 1948).

26 SJ 8.

27   Jii 33 (24 December 1946).

28   Jii 34 (29 December 1946).

29   Jiii 202 (8 May 1958).

30   Jiii 364 (31 December 1959).

31   Jiii 359 (17 December 1959).

32   Jii 373 (25 November 1949).

33   Jii 381 (20 December 1949).

34   *Atlantic*, Vol. 191, No. 1 (1953), p. 72. (Aelred Graham, *Thomas Merton: A Modern Man in Reverse*).

35   LL 4.

36   MA 4 (1992), p. 203. (A. M. Allchin, *The Worship of the Whole Creation: Merton and the Eastern Fathers*).

37   Jvii 40 (13 January 1968).

38   Jii 228 (25 August 1948).

39   Jii 235 (3 October 1948).

40   Jiii 290 (11 June 1959).

41   MA 11 (1998), p. 163. (Interview with Chrysogonus Waddell OCSO).

42   Letter: Dom James Fox to Dom Jean Leclercq (13 June 1955). TMC.

43   Jvi 231 (8 May 1967).

44   Jvi 111 (7 August 1966).

45   Jvi 176 (30 December 1966).

46   Jvi 111 (7 August 1966).

47   MA 6 (1993). (Interview with John (Jack) H. Ford).

48   MT 246 (M. Emmanuel de Souza Silva, *The Friend of Latin America*).

49   MT 31 (Matthew Kelty, *The Man*).

50   Jiii 302 (5 July 1959); Jiii 293 (14 June 1959).

51   Jiii 325 (30 August 1959).

52   Jv 136 (16 August 1964).

53   Jvi 268 (22 July 1967).

54   CWA 228.

55   *New Blackfriars* v 47 (October 1965). (Thomas Merton, *The Council and the Religious Life*).

56   Jv 232 (18 April 1965).

57   Jvi 251 (15 June 1967).

58   Conversation with Bro. Patrick Hart OCSO at Gethsemani on 11 September 2011.

59   MA 3 (1990), p. 84. (Interview with Flavian Burns OCSO).

60   AJ 305 (Informal talk by TM at Calcutta, October 1968).

61   RT 113.

62   AJ 305 (Informal talk by TM at Calcutta, October 1968).

63   MT 183 (Tarcisius Conner, *Monk of Renewal*. Quoting from TM in *Renewal and Discipline*).

64   CGB 47.

65   CGB 153. 'Fourth' has now been re-named Mohammed Ali Blvd.

66   CGB 154.

67 RT 94.

68 Jiv 100 (16 March 1961).

69 CGB 246.

70 CGB 313.

71 RT 95–102.

72 Jiv 290 (17 January 1963).

73 RMW 74 (From Japanese edition of SSM 1963).

74 CWA 7.

75 CGB 204.

76 Jiv 99 (11 March 1961).

77 SD 10.

78 RU 6.

79 Jvi 358-9 (Some Personal Notes, January – March 1966).

80 MZM x

81 Lii 235–6. TM to Sister Thérèse Lentfoehr (30 May 1960).

82 Jiv 242 (2 September 1962).

83 Jiv 320 (20 May 1962).

84 CGB 258.

85 Jii 330 (27 June 1949).

86 Jv 276 (28 July 1965).

87 Li 63. TM to Abdul Aziz (2 January 1966).

88 Jv 211–2 (27 February 1965).

89 Jv 283 (21 August 1965).

90 CGB 18.

91 RU 16.

92 LL 22.

93 DQ 212.

94 DQ 174.

95 Jv 100–1 (28 April 1964).

96 Jv 101 (28 April 1964).

97 Jv 306 (18 October 1965).

98 Jvi 357 (Some Personal Notes, January – March 1966).

99 Jv 324 (16 December 1965).

100 Jvi 7 (15 January 1966).

101 Jv 326 (21 December 1965).

102 Jiii 176 (28 February 1958). See also Jiii 176 (4 March 1958); Jiii 182 (19 March 1958); Jiii 270 (19 March 1959).

103 Jiii 322–3 (30 August 1959); Jiii 326 (6 September 1959).

104 Jv 327 (25 December 1965).

105 Jiv 278 (22 December 1962).

106 Jv 281 (17 August 1965).

107 DQ 169.

108 Michael Mott, who was appointed by the Merton Legacy Trust as Merton's official biographer after the resignation of John Howard Griffin, chose to respect the anonymity

of the nurse by referring her to her as 'S' in SMTM. The editorial decision was subsequently taken in preparing Vol. 6 of Merton's Journals for publication to refer to her as 'M'. John Howard Griffin identified her as Margie Smith in his book *The Hermitage Years*, which was eventually published in 1993, and Griffin asserts in the Preface that the nurse had made no objection to the publication of her name. The decision has been taken here to follow the practice of the Journals and refer to her as 'M'.

109   Jvi 47 (28 April 1966).

110   Seitz, Ron, *Song for Nobody: A Memory Vision of Thomas Merton*, Ligouri, Missouri: Triumph Books 1993.

111   Jvi 50–1 (4 May 1966).

112   Jvi 61 (16 May 1966).

113   Jvi 62 (17 May 1966).

114   Jvi 44 (25 April 1966).

115   Jvi 154 (31 October 1966).

116   Jvi 45 (25 April 1966).

117   Jvi 68 (23 May 1966).

118   Jvi 99 (22 July 1966).

119   Jvi 108 (5 August 1966).

120   SMTM 450.

121   Jvi 156 (1 November 1966).

122   Jvi 338 (Midsummer Diary for 'M', 23 June 1966).

123   Jvi 342 (Midsummer Diary for 'M', 23 June 1966).

124   Jvi 129 (10 September 1966).

125   Jvi 218 (15 April 1967).

126   Jvi 265–6 (14 July 1967).

127   Jvi 235 (13 May 1967).

128   Jvi 213 (7 April 1967).

129   Jvii 54 (10 February 1968).

130   Jvii 49 (4 February 1968).

131   TMC. Mimeographed copy.

132   Jvii 41 (15 January 1968).

133   To Ohio with Dom James in 1952 when the possibility of a new foundation was under consideration; to Minnesota in 1956, together with Dom James and Fr. John Eudes Bamberger, for a psychological workshop; and to New York in 1964 for a meeting with Dr. Daisetz Suzuki, a Zen scholar to whom Merton was deeply indebted.

134   Jvii 153 (13 August 1968).

135   Jvii 166 (9 September 1968).

136   Ibid.

137   AJ 307.

138   Jvii 323–4 (4 December 1968); AJ 235–6.

139   Jvii 281 (17 November 1968).

140   Jvii 262 (7 November 19680; AJ 117.

141   Jvii 285 (19 November 1968); AJ 153–5.

142   Jvii 282 (17 November 1968).

143 SMTM 564.

144 SMTM 566–8.

145 Victor Hammer in July, Ad Reinhardt in August, and John Slate in September 1967.

146 Jvii 44 (21 January 1968).

147 Jvii 205 (15 October 1968); AJ 5.

148 Jvii 278 (16 November 1968); AJ 143.

149 SSM 422.

Chapter 3: The Writer

1 CGB 241.

2 *In the Dark Before the Dawn. New Selected Poems of Thomas Merton.* Edited by Lynn R. Szabo. Preface by Kathleen Norris. New York: A New Directions Book 2005, p. xxi.

3 TMR 17 (An Author's Preface: First and Last Thoughts).

4 Jii 400 (18 January 1950).

5 SJ 38 (16 April 1947).

6 *The Labyrinth*; *The Straits of Dover* (or *The Night Before the Battle*); *The Man in the Sycamore Tree*; and *The Journal of My Escape from the Nazis*.

7 SSM 231.

8 This novel was eventually published under the title *My Argument with the Gestapo* in 1969.

9 Ji 36 (1 October 1939).

10 SJ 85.

11 SJ 86.

12 Jii 315–6 (24 May 1949).

13 Jii 371 (21 September 1949).

14 Jii 381 (20 December 1949).

15 Jii 400 (18 January 1950).

16 Jii 70 (2 May 1947).

17 Jii 263 (8 January 1949).

18 Jii 306 (1 May 1949).

19 Jii 282 (15 February 1949).

20 Ji 133 (13 January 1940).

21 Jiv 138 (4 July 1961).

22 Jv 223 (3 April 1965).

23. Jii 480 (5 July 1952).

24 Jii 70 (2 May 1947).

25 Jii 154 (4 January 1948).

26 Jvi 234 (11 May 1967).

27 Ji 271 (4 December 1940).

28 Baker, James Thomas, *Thomas Merton Social Critic*, University Press of Kentucky 1971, p. 19.

29 Lii 209 (Editorial Note).

30 Jv 48 (22 December 1963).

31   Jii 394 (Footnote 50, Editorial Note).

32   MA 11 (1998) 166. (Interview with Chrysogonus Waddell OCSO).

33   Sheridan, Thomas, *Psyching Out Merton*, Book Review. *The Merton Seasonal* (Fall 2011), 26–33.

34   Lii vii (Preface).

35   Lii xii (Introduction).

36   SMTM 353.

37   *Six Letters: Boris Pasternak and Thomas Merton*. Edited by Naomi Burton Stone and Lydia Pasternak, King Library Press 1973.

38   *A Catch of Anti-Letters: Thomas Merton and Robert Lax*, Sheed, Andrews & McMead 1978; *When Prophecy Still Had a Voice: The Letters of Thomas Merton and Robert Lax*. Edited by Arthur W. Biddle, University Press of Kentucky 2001.

39   *Letters from Tom: A Selection by Wilbur H. Ferry*, Fort Hill Press 1983.

40   *Encounter: Thomas Merton and D. T. Suzuki*. Edited by Robert E. Daggy, Larkspur Press 1988.

41   *At Home in the World: The Letters of Thomas Merton and Rosemary Radford Ruether*. Edited by Mary Tardiff, Orbis Books 1995.

42   *Thomas Merton and James Laughlin: Selected Letters*. Edited by David D. Cooper, New York: Norton 1997.

43   *Striving Towards Being: The Letters of Thomas Merton and Czeslaw Milosz*. Edited by Robert Faggen, Farrar, Straus and Giroux 1997.

44   *Survival or Prophecy: An Exchange of Letters, Thomas Merton and Jean Leclercq*. Edited by Patrick Hart, New York: Farrar, Straus and Giroux 2002.

45   The first edition of the *Cold War Letters* (49 Letters) appeared in the spring of 1962, the second and complete edition (111 Letters) was printed in 1963. The Letters can be found in the five volumes of Merton's *Letters* (Li – v).

46   Liv 87–8. TM to Boris Pasternak (22 August 1958).

47   *At Home in the World*, p. xix.

48   *Striving Towards Being*, p. iv.

49   Liii 392. TM to Dom Jean Leclercq (23 July 1968).

50   Li 186–7. TM to Sister Emmanuel (16 January 1962).

51   Li 126. TM to Dona Luisa Coomaraswamy (13 January 1961).

52   Jvi 371 (A Postscript, April 1966).

53   Liii 384–5. TM to Sister J. M. (17 June 1968).

54   Wilkes, Paul, Editor, *Merton By Those Who Knew Him Best*, Harper & Row 1984, pp. 6–7.

55   Jvi 188–9 (29 January 1967).

56   Jvi 189 (29 January 1967).

57   Jii 217 (11 July 1948).

58   Jii 287 (6 March 1949).

59   Jii 458 (13 June 1951).

60   Letter: TM to James Laughlin (28 September 1952). *Thomas Merton and James Laughlin: Selected Letters*, p. 95.

61   Liv 76. TM to Czesław Miłosz (5 June 1961).

62   Jv 349 (Some Personal Notes, 4 December 1965).

63 Ibid.
64 *Motive* 27 (October 1967), pp. 32–3 (Thomas M. McDonnell, *An Interview with Thomas Merton*).
65 DQ viii–xi.
66 CGB 5.
67 RU 2–3.
68 RU 6.
69 RMW 97 (Preface to the Japanese edition of SC 1965).
70 RMW 99.
71 RMW 97.
72 MAG 6.
73 SSM 419.
74 LE 6 (*Blake and the New Theology*).
75 LE 186 (*The Plague of Albert Camus: A Commentary and Introduction*).
76 LE 28 (*A Footnote for Ulysses: Peace and Revolution*).
77 LE 39 (*The Pasternak Affair*).
78 Published initially as *Introductions East and West: The Foreign Prefaces of Thomas Merton* (1981), and then as *Reflections on My Work* (1981), and then as *"Honorable Reader"*, Edited by Robert E. Daggy (1989).
79 RMW 59 (Preface to the French edition of *Monastic Peace* 1960).
80 RMW 111–12 (Preface to the Korean edition of *Life and Holiness* 1965).
81 RMW 74–5 (Preface to the Japanese edition of *The Seven Storey Mountain*, 1963).
82 LE 168–77 (*William Melvin Kelley – The Legend of Tucker Caliban*).
83 LE 170–4.
84 Ibid.
85 Jiv 162 (19 September 1961).
86 Jiv 135 (29 June 1961).
87 Jvii 128 (7 June 1968).
88 Liii 219. TM to Father Hans Urs von Balthasar (3 July 1964).
89 LE 373 (*Message to Poets*).
90 LE 305 (*Rubén Darío*).
91 *Commonweal* XLIII 10 (23 June 1945). (Robert Lowell, *The Verses of Thomas Merton*).
92 *Saturday Review* 40 (6 July 1957). (Donald Hall, Review of *The Strange Islands*).
93 *Choice* 1. 1 (March 1964). (Review of *Emblems of a Season of Fury*).
94 New York *Times* (5 February 1978). (Richard Kostelanetz, Review of *The Collected Poems*).
95 *Leviathan* (April 1978). (Alan Prendergast, Review of *The Collected Poems*).
96 MA 7 (1994), p. 152. (Interview by George Kilcourse with Ron Seitz).
97 *Notre Dame English Journal* 14 (October 1978). (Elena Malits CSC, Review of *The Collected Poems*).
98 See for the purposes of comparison George Woodcock's distinction between the poetry of the choir and the poetry of the desert (*Thomas Merton, Monk and Poet*, Canongate 1978); and also George Kilcourse's distinction between the poetry of the choir, the poetry of the desert, the poetry of the forest and the poetry of paradise (*Ace of Freedoms: Thomas Merton's Christ*, University of Notre Dame Press 1993).

99   CP 90-2 (*A Letter to My Friends* from *A Man in the Divided Sea*, 1946).

100 CP 45-6 (*The Trappist Abbey: Matins* from *Thirty Poems*, 1944).

101 CP 108-9 (*After the Night Office – Gethsemani Abbey* from *A Man in the Divided Sea*, 1946).

102 CP 96 (*Trappists Working* from *A Man in the Divided Sea*, 1946).

103 CP 634-5 (*The Night of Destiny*, included in *Sensation Time at the Home*, 1968, Appendix I in CP).

104 These poems were included in Appendix III (*Humorous Verse*) of CP.

105 CP 35-6 (*For My Brother: Reported Missing in Action*, 1943, from *Thirty Poems*, 1944).

106 Merton, Thomas, *Eighteen Poems*, New York: New Directions 1985.

107 SJ 341-54, *Epilogue: Fire Watch* (4 July 1952).

108 CP 712-13, Appendix II. (*Fable for a War* from *Uncollected Poems*).

109 CP 130-1 (*La Salette*, from *A Man in the Divided Sea*, 1946).

110 Quoted by Cooper, David D., *Thomas Merton and James Laughlin: Selected Letters*, New York: Norton 1997.

111 CP 293-302.

112 Liv 172. TM to José Coronel Urtecho (15 March 1964).

113 Included in *Emblems of a Season Fury*, 1963.

114 CP 703-10. (Included in Appendix II, *Uncollected Poems*).

115 Included in *Emblems of a Season Fury*, 1963.

116 Ibid.

117 CP 455-593. *The Geography of Lograire* (Author's Note).

118 Woodcock, George, *op. cit.*, p. 140.

119 Lentfoehr, Thérèse, *Words and Silence: On the Poetry of Thomas Merton*, New Directions 1979, pp. 97-8.

120 Pearson, Paul M., *The Geography of Lograire: Thomas Merton's Final Prophetic Vision*, from *Thomas Merton: Poet, Monk, Prophet*, Papers Presented at the Second General Conference of the TM Society of Great Britain and Ireland, March 1998. Edited by Paul M. Pearson, Danny Sullivan and Ian Thomson, Three Peaks Press 1998, p. 89.

121 MA 1 (1998) 216. (David D. Cooper, *From Prophecy to Parody: Thomas Merton's Cables to the Ace*).

122 MT 98 (Jean Leclercq, *The Evolving Monk*).

123 Jii 365 (1 September 1949).

124 Jiv 255 (10 October 1962).

125 Jiv 318 (10 May 1963).

126 Liv 230. TM to Ludovico Silvo (27 April 1967).

127 CS (1969) IV 3 225 (Naomi Burton Stone, *I Shall Miss Thomas Merton*).

128 Quoted by Robert Inchausti in *The Journey of Thomas Merton*, Edited by Morgan C. Atkinson and Jonathan Montaldo, SPCK 2009.

129 Li 140. TM to Dorothy Day (23 August 1961).

130 Jiii 392 (21 May 1960).

131 Jv 216 (10 March 1965).

132 Jvii 129 (13 June 1968).

133 SMTM 242.

134 CP 243 (*Elias – Variations on a Theme* from *The Strange Islands*, 1957).

135 Shannon, William H., *Thomas Merton's Dark Path: The Inner Experience of a Contemplative*, New York: Farrar, Straus, Giroux 1981, p. 4.

136 Jvi 215 (8 April 1967).

137 SMTM 393: drawing upon a conversation with Dom Flavian Burns on 29 August 1980.

138 Jvi 297 (2 October 1967).

139 Jvi 296 (2 October 1967).

140 SMTM xxvi: drawing upon a conversation with Ron Seitz on 2 August 1980.

141 TMR 16 (An Author's Preface: *First and Last Thoughts*).

142 MT 27 (Matthew Kelty, *The Man*).

143 Jvi 297 (2 October 1967).

144 Ibid.

Chapter 4: The Contemplative

1 LE 340 (*Poetry and Contemplation: A Reappraisal*).

2 Liii 14. TM to Dom Humphrey Pawsey (21 June 1949).

3 Li 371. TM to Etta Gullick (9 June 1965).

4 NSC 3.

5 CS XIII (1978) 3 192 (Merton, Thomas, *Toward a Theology of Prayer*. Edited transcript of a taped talk given by Merton to Jesuit scholastics at St Mary's College, Darjeeling, India, on 25 November 1968).

6 CPr 25.

7 IE 147.

8 SJ 28.

9 Li 73. TM to Daniel J. Berrigan (10 March 1962).

10 CPr 40.

11 SSM 112.

12 SSM 111–13.

13 LL 13.

14 LE 385–453 (*Nature and Art in William Blake: An Essay in Interpretation*, 1939).

15 Jii 300 (6 June 1949).

16 Jii 392 (3 January 1950).

17 Liii 297. TM to Dame B (30 January 1966).

18 Li 502–3. TM to Rosemary Radford Ruether (9 March 1967).

19 Jii 382 (22 December 1949).

20 Merton, Thomas, *The Silent Life*. New York: Farrar, Straus and Cudahy 1957, p.54.

21 CP 122–6 (*St John Baptist* from *A Man in the Divided Sea*, 1946).

22 CP 199–202 (*The Quickening of St John the Baptist* from *The Tears of the Blind Lion*, 1949).

23 AJ 306.

24 CPr 25.

25 NSC 54.

26 CPr 86.

27 DQ 197.
28 DQ 178.
29 DQ 184.
30 LL 17.
31 DQ 189.
32 CPr 143.
33 Li 621. TM to John C. H. Wu (12 December 1961).
34 NSC 219.
35 IE 66.
36 SC 3 (Author's Note).
37 Jii 287 (6 March 1947).
38 Lii 233. TM to Sister Thérèse Lentfoehr (4 July 1959).
39 NSC 79.
40 NSC 41.
41 ZBA 53.
42 CPr 27–8.
43 CPr 53–4.
44 CPr 99, quoting John of the Cross, *Ascent to Mount Carmel* II iv 2.
45 CPr 111.
46 NMI 61.
47 Lv 329. TM to Katharine Champney (10 November 1966).
48 Li 63–4. TM to Abdul Aziz (2 January 1966).
49 NSC x.
50 Lv 328. TM to Katharine Champney (10 November 1966).
51 From Notes identified by Sister Thérèse Lentfoehr and taken at the retreat conducted by TM for the Superiors of contemplative nuns at Gethsemani in December 1967.
52 NMI 19
53 MT 80 (David Steindl-Rast, *Man of Prayer*, quoting TM).
54 NSC 188.
55 NMI 28.
56 LL 42.
57 John of the Cross, *The Ascent of Mount Carmel* I xiii 1.
58 DQ 184.
59 NSC 83.
60 LL 42.
61 NSC 247.
62 CP 452 (*Cables to the Ace*, 1968).
63 NSC 43.
64 NSC 211.
65 DQ 202.
66 NSC 134.
67 NMI 209.
68 CPr 116.
69 DQ 197.

70 NSC 273.

71 CPr 119.

72 SC 85.

73 SC 25.

74 RU 16.

75 Jii 476 (June 1951).

76 Abbé Monchanin, Ecrits Spirituels 126. Cited CPr 133.

77 TM: quoted by Shannon, William H., *Thomas Merton's Dark Path: The Inner Experience of a Contemplative*, New York: Farrar, Straus, Giroux 1981, p. 163.

78 RU 20.

79 SD 325.

80 CS XIX (1984) 2 150 (Thomas Merton, *The Inner Experience: Some Dangers in Contemplation (VI)*,

81 Li 156. TM to Dom Francis Decroix (21 August 1967).

82 IE 121.

83 Li 158. TM to Dom Francis Decroix (21 August 1967).

84 Li 359. TM to Etta Gullick (29 April 1963).

85 NSC 67.

86 Li 360. TM to Etta Gullick (29 April 1963).

87 Li 115. TM to Amiya Chakravarty (13 April 1967).

88 Merton, Thomas, *The Waters of Siloe*, New York: Doubleday Image Books 1962, pp. 262–3.

89 LL 22.

90 Li 482. TM to Pope John XXIII (10 November 1958).

91 CPr 84.

92 Li 158. TM to Dom Francis Decroix in response to the request from Pope Paul VI that there might be a message from contemplatives to the world (21 August 1967).

93 Ibid.

Chapter 5: The Social Critic

1 RT 119.

2 RT 69.

3 Li 273. TM to James Forest (17 January 1963).

4 Jii 451 (3 March 1951).

5 Jii 460 (13 June 1951).

6 Jv 294 (11 September 1965).

7 Liv 172. TM to José Coronel Urtecho (15 March 1964).

8 Liii 112. TM to Jaime Andrade (July 1958).

9 RMW 74 (Preface to the Japanese edition of SSM, 1963).

10 Li 640. TM to June J. Yungblut (20 January 1968).

11 Lv 26. TM to Josiah G. Chatham (December 1961). CWL 13.

12 CP 185 (*A Christmas Card* from *Figures for an Apocalypse*, 1947).

13 IE 29.

14   Lv 7. TM to Victor Hammer (May 1962). CWL 71.

15   FV 256.

16   CGB 222.

17   NSC 301.

18   Jiii 150 (29 November 1957).

19   Ji 223 (26 May 1940).

20   Jiii 341 (10 November 1959).

21   RU 44.

22   DQ 127.

23   DQ 128.

24   CGB 50-1.

25   Berdyaev, Nikolai, *Dream and Reality*. Cited by TM in RU 5.

26   Jiii 195 (20 April 1958).

27   Jiii 150 (27 December 1957).

28   DQ 99.

29   DQ x.

30   DQ 46.

31   DQ 47.

32   Jiv 297 (23 February 1963).

33   Jiv 340 (19 July 1963).

34   Jv 84 (3 March 1964).

35   FV 162.

36   Jvi 275 (11 April 1967).

37   Li 83. TM to Daniel J. Berrigan (30 June 1964).

38   Liv 237. TM to Cintio Vitier (1 August 1963).

39   RT 93.

40   RT 99, quoting from Karl Rahner, *Mission and Grace*, Steed & Ward 1963, Vol. 1, p. 20.

41   RMW 100 (Preface to the Japanese edition of SC, 1965).

42   Jiv 9 (6 June 1960).

43   Jiii 159 (23 January 1958).

44   DQ 194.

45   MT 32 (Matthew Kelty, *The Man*).

46   Jvi 160 (12 November 1966).

47   Jiii 194 (20 April 1958).

48   CP 389 (from *A Letter to Pablo Antonio Cuadra Concerning Giants* from *Emblems of a Season of Fury*, 1963).

49   CP 380 (from *A Letter to Pablo Antonio Cuadra Concerning Giants* from *Emblems of a Season of Fury*, 1963).

50   CGB 72.

51   CGB 259.

52   Li 185. TM to Sister M. Emmanuel (2 December 1960).

53   DQ 151.

54   Jiii 162 (31 January 1958).

55   DQ 10.

56 DQ ix.

57 Ibid.

58 CGB 114.

59 FV 131.

60 Liii 169. TM to Father Paul Bourne OCSO (1 May 1963).

61 CGB 33.

62 RMW 86 (Preface to the French edition of *The Black Revolution* 1963).

63 RMW 85 (Preface to the French edition of *The Black Revolution* 1963).

64 CGB 294.

65 Li 601. TM to Robert Lawrence Williams (1 May 1967).

66 FV 167.

67 Jiii 391 (18 May 1960).

68 RMW 87 (Preface to the French edition of *The Black Revolution* 1963).

69 Liv 165. TM to Alcen Amoroso Lima (November 1961). CWL 3.

70 Jiii 168 (15 February 1958).

71 FV 169.

72 CGB 39.

73 Jii 203 (4 May 1948).

74 Jiii 337 (25 October 1959).

75 CGB 216.

76 Lv 62. TM to Robert J. McCracken (August 1962). CWL 100.

77 *Catholic Worker* 28, October 1961. (Thomas Merton, *The Root of War*).

78 Lv 18. Editorial Footnote to CWL.

79 Lv 22. CWL Preface.

80 Lv 20. CWL Preface.

81 Jiv 318 (10 May 1963).

82 Jv 84 (3 March 1964).

83 Li 266–8. TM to James Forest (29 April 1962). CWL 69.

84 Li 218.TM to W. H. Ferry (8 June 1964).

85 Lii 117 (Midsummer 1968).

86 FV 20.

87 GNV 23.

88 CGB 81, quoting Gandhi.

89 Jiv 248 (18 September 1962).

90 FV 43.

91 Lii 93. TM to Professor Jean Hering (28 July 1964).

92 Jiv 211 (18 March 1962).

93 Li 286. TM to James Forest (11 November 1965).

94 Li 425. TM to John C. Heidbrink (4 November 1965).

95 Jv 341 (Some Personal Notes. End of 1965).

96 RMW 133 (Editorial Note, Preface to the Vietnamese edition of NMI, 1966).

97 Jv 250 (22 May 1965).

98 Jvi 41 (16 April 1966).

99 Ibid.

100   Jvi 142–3 (23 September 1966).
101   FV 109–10.
102   FV 7.
103   Liv 151. TM to Ernesto Cardenal (10 May 1965).
104   Jvi 187 (24 January 1967).
105   DQ 142.
106   Jiv 334 (7 July 1963).
107   CS XIII (1978) 4 384–9 (Louis J. Lekai, *Thomas Merton, the Historian?*).
108   NSC 118.
109   Liv 67. TM to Czesław Miłosz (6 May 1960).
110   Jvi 184 (10 January 1967).
111   NVA 221–2 (*Christian Action in World Crisis*).
112   Liv 79–80. Czesław Miłosz to TM (14 March 1962). Editorial Note.
113   Ibid.
114   Li 186–7. TM to Sister M. Emmanuel (16 January 1962).
115   RMW 51–2 (Preface to the Argentine edition of the complete works of TM, 1958).
116   CGB 216.

Chapter 6: The Ecumenist

1   CGB 141.
2   Li 52. TM to Abdul Aziz (4 April 1962).
3   RMW 98 (Preface to the Japanese edition of SC, 1965).
4   Lii 319. TM to Joseph Tjo Tchel-oung (28 April 1961).
5   RMW 102 (Preface to the Japanese edition of SC, 1965).
6   CGB 319.
7   Ibid.
8   CP 384–5 (*A Letter to Pablo Antonio Cuadra Concerning Giants* from *Emblems of a Season Fury*, 1963).
9   Jiv 49 (16 September 1960).
10   CGB 167.
11   Jiv 130 (21 June 1961).
12   Jiv 114 (1 May 1961).
13   Jiv 129 (21 June 1961).
14   MZM ix.
15   CGB 20.
16   Li 382. TM to Thich Nhat Hanh (29 June 1966).
17   ZBA 62.
18   CGB 20.
19   Li 317. TM to Erich Fromm (December 1961). CWL 5.
20   Li 433–4. TM to Cardinal Bea (14 July 1964).
21   Li 535. TM to Zalman Schachter (15 February 1962). CWL 37.
22   Li 434. TM to Abraham Heschel (9 September 1964).

23   Li 534. TM to Zalman Schachter (15 December 1961).

24   Woodcock, George, *Thomas Merton, Monk and Poet*, Canongate 1978, p. 152. Quoting TM.

25   Lii 281. TM to Ad Reinhardt (31 October 1963).

26   Lv 276. TM to Louis Massignon (18 March 1960).

27   Li 48. TM to Abdul Aziz (13 May 1961).

28   CP 748-9 (Appendix II, Uncollected Poems, *Readings from Ibn Abbad*).

29   Merton, Thomas, *Thoughts on the East*, Burns and Oates 1996, p. 55.

30   GNV 4.

31   GNV 5.

32   Merton, Thomas, *Thoughts on the East*, Burns and Oates 1996, p. 58.

33   AJ 349.

34   Jiv 92 (4 February 1961).

35   Jiv 93 (4 February 1961).

36   MZM 58.

37   WCT.

38   WCT 176-7 (*Tao*).

39   WCT 69 (*Man Is Born in Tao*).

40   Li 631. John C. H. Wu to TM (24 November 1965). Editorial Note.

41   WCT 99-102 (*Great and Small*).

42   Merton, Thomas, *Opening the Bible*, London: George Allen & Unwin 1972, p. 51.

43   Suzuki, D. T., *Introduction to Zen Buddhism*, London 1960, p. 38. Cited by TM in OZ 107.

44   OZ 11.

45   FV 106-8 (*Nhat Hanh Is My Brother*).

46   Li 561. TM to Daisetz T. Suzuki (12 March 1959).

47   OZ 52.

48   Li 629. John C. H. Wu to TM (2 August 1965). Editorial Note.

49   OZ 96.

50   OZ 97.

51   OZ 98.

52   Ibid.

53   OZ 114.

54   OZ 102.

55   OZ 126.

56   ZBA 81.

57   MZM x.

58   ZBA 84.

59   CP 383 (*A Letter to Pablo Antonio Cuadra Concerning Giants* from *Emblems of a Season of Fury*, 1963).

60   AJ 308.

61   CGB 141.

62   RMW 147 (Preface to the Japanese edition of NM, 1967).

63   CGB 87.

64   ZBA 32.

65   MT 101 (Jean Leclercq, *The Evolving Monk*).

66   MT 215 (TM quoted by Patrick Hart, *Ecumenical Monk*).

67   CS XIII (1978) 3 192 (TM, *Towards a Theology of Prayer*. Edited transcript of a taped talk given by Merten to Jesuit scholastics at St Mary's College, Darjeeling, India, on 25 November 1968).

68   AJ 106 (5 November 1968).

69   AJ 101 (4 November 1968).

70   AJ 113 (6 November 1968).

71   AJ 112 (6 November 1968).

72   AJ 113 (6 November 1968).

73   Jvii 266 (8 November 1968).

74   Dalai Lama, *Freedom in Exile, The Autobiography of the Dalai Lama*, A Cardinal Book 1991, p. 207.

75   AJ 95 (3 November 1968). Quotation from Sankaracharya, *The Crest-Jewel of Discrimination*.

76   AJ 95 (3 November 1968). Quotation from Tibetan poet Milarepa.

77   Jvii 246 (3 November 1968). From Merton's discussion with the Khempo of Namgyal, the Dalai Lama's private chaplain

78   Jvii 287 (19 November 1968). Quotation from Conze, *Buddhist Thought in India*.

79   AJ 81 (2 November 1968). Quotation from S. B. Dasgupta, *An Introduction to Tantric Buddhism*.

80   AJ 305–8. Appendix III. *Thomas Merton's View of Monasticism*. Informal talk delivered at Calcutta, October 1968.

81   Ibid.

82   AJ 309–17. Appendix IV. *Monastic Experience and East–West Dialogue*. Notes for a paper to have been delivered at Calcutta, October 1968.

83   Ibid.

84   Ibid.

85   Ibid.

86   Ibid.

87   AJ 326–43. Appendix VII. *Marxism and Monastic Perspectives*. Talk delivered at Bangkok on 10 December 1968.

88   Ibid.

89   Ibid.

90   Ibid.

91   Ibid.

92   Ibid.

Chapter 7: A Study in Divine Discontent

1   Jiii 137–8 (15 November 1957).

2   LTM 222 (Timothy Kelly, *Epilogue: A Memoir*).

3   Jii 81 (31 May 1947).

4   Jii 133 (13 November 1947).

5   Jii 47 (16 March 1947).

6   SSM 389.

7   SJ 74 (16 November 1947).

8   Jvi 276 (14 August 1967).

9   Jiii 325 (30 August 1959).

10 Jiii 181 (13 March 1958).

11 Jii 174 (29 February 1948).

12 Jv 136 (16 August 1964).

13 Jiii 378 (8 March 1960).

14 Jiii 225 (23 October 1958).

15 Jiv 221 (29 May 1962).

16 Li 501-2. TM to Rosemary Radford Ruether (14 February 1967).

17 Jiii 285 (25 May 1959).

18 Jvi 263 (13 July 1967).

19 DQ 179.

20 Jii 371 (21 September 1949).

21 Jiv 253 (2 October 1962).

22 Jiv 321 (20 May 1963).

23 Jiv 253 (2 October 1962).

24 Bro. Ramon SSF, *Soul Friends*, Marshall Pickering 1989, p. vi. Quoting Matthew Kelty OCSO in a letter from Gethsemani written the day after Merton's funeral.

25 Jiii 187 (30 March 1958).

26 Jvi 192 (4 February 1967).

27 See Cooper, David D., *Thomas Merton's Art of Denial*, University of Georgia Press 1989, p. 35.

28 Jiii 285 (28 May 1959).

29 Lv 131. TM to Naomi Burton Stone (3 March 1956).

30 Lv 135-6. TM to Naomi Burton Stone (17 May 1956).

31 Lv 138. TM to Naomi Burton Stone (4 June 1956).

32 Ibid.

33 The essay was published under the title *The Neurotic Personality in the Monastic Life* in MA 4 (1991), pp. 5-19.

34 Jiii 59-60 (29 July 1956).

35 Our knowledge of Merton's response to Zilboorg at this second meeting is based on interviews conducted by Michael Mott, Merton's biographer, with Abbot James Fox on 6 April 1980 and 11 July 1981. SSTM 611 (Footnote 364).

36 Jiii 59-60 (29 July 1956).

37 Lv 139. TM to Naomi Burton Stone (30 July 1956).

38 Jiii 60 (29 July 1956).

39 Liv 122. TM to Ernesto Cardenal (17 December 1959).

40 Li 135. TM to Jean Danielou (21 April 1960).

41 Mt. 10.34; Lk. 7.51.

42 Mt. 20.22; Mk. 10.38.

43 Lk. 14.41.

44   Mt. 21.12–13; Mk. 9.15–17; Lk. 19.45–6; Jn. 2.13–17.

45   CWA 144.

46   CWA 81.

47   LL 111.

48   Ibid.

49   LL 110–11.

50   SC 13.

51   LL 111.

52   Jiii 45 (17 July 1956).

53   Jii 487 (5 July 1952).

54   Liv 29. TM to Jacques Maritain (22 February 1960).

55   Ibid.

56   Li 52. TM to Abdul Aziz (4 April 1962).

57   Merton, Thomas, *The Ascent to Truth*. London: Hollis & Carter 1951, p. 131.

58   Benedicta Ward, Introduction to *Historia Monachorum in Aegypto*. Translated by Norman Russell, Mowbray 1980, p. 3.

59   Ji 339 (9 April 1941).

60   CP 263 (*The Tower of Babel*, from *The Strange Islands*, 1957).

61   Isa. 51.7.

62   Jii 389 (29 December 1949).

63   Jiii 236 (11 December 1958).

64   Jiv 342 (21 July 1963).

65   MT 83–4 (David Steindl-Rast, *Man of Prayer*, quoting TM).

66   Jii 80 (31 May 1947).

67   Jii 377 (9 December 1949).

68   Jv 232 (18 April 1965).

69   Jii 379 (15 December 1949).

70   CGB 18.

71   Li 361. TM to Etta Gullick (28 July 1963).

72   Jv 79 (22 February 1964).

73   Sister Kathleen Deignan CND: Cited by Morgan C. Atkinson and Jonathan Montaldo, *The Journey of Thomas Merton*, SPCK 2009, p. 1.

74   Li 156. TM to Dom Francis Decroix (21 August 1967).

75   CS XIX (1984) 2 149. Merton, Thomas, *The Inner Experience: Some Dangers in Contemplation*.

76   CGB 88.

77   Lv 255. TM to Robert Menchin (15 January 1966).

78   NSC 83.

79   NMI 2–3.

80   Brueggemann, Walter, *The Prophetic Imagination*, Fortress Press 1978, pp. 67–8.

81   SJ 9.

82   TMR 16 (An Author's Preface, *First and Last Thoughts*).

83   Jii 463 (29 November 1951).

84   Jiii 57 (29 July 1956).

85   Jiii 57–8 (29 July 1956).

86   SJ 354.

87   SSM 422.

88   Jii 236 (10 October 1948).

Chapter 8: A Prophetic Voice

1   MT 34–5 (Matthew Kelty, *The Man*).

2   Heschel, Abraham J., *The Prophets*, Harper & Row 1962, p. 12.

3   Brueggemann, Walter, *The Prophetic Imagination*, Fortress Press 1978, p. 13.

4   Ibid.

5   Ibid., p. 99.

6   Ibid., p. 22.

7   Heschel, *op. cit.*, p. 16.

8   Ibid., p. 22.

9   Ibid., p. 10.

10   Ibid., p. xix.

11   RU 2–3.

12   CWA 8.

13   Ibid.

14   Cunningham, Lawrence S., *Thomas Merton and the Monastic Vision*, Eerdmans 1999,
      p. 89.

15   Li vii (William H. Shannon, *Preface*).

16   Inchausti, Robert, *Thomas Merton's American Prophecy*, New York: State University of
      New York Press 1998, p. 1.

17   MA 19 (2006) 19 (John Eudes Bamberger, *Thomas Merton: Monk and Prophet of Peace.*
      The opening address at the International Thomas Merton Society General Meeting 2005).

18   LE 305 (Rubén Darío).

19   FV 68.

20   Wilkes, Paul, Editor, *Merton By Those Who Knew Him Best*, Harper & Row 1984, pp.
      156–7 (Bishop Jean Jadot).

21   Li 186–7. TM to Sister M. Emmanuel (16 January 1962).

22   Ibid.

23   LE 3 (*Blake and the New Theology*).

24   CGB 204.

25   FV 213.

26   SprC 157.

27   RU 2.

28   Brueggemann, *op. cit.*, p. 59.

29   Ibid., p. 22.

30   Ibid., p. 13.

31   Ronzani, Clare, *Towards An Integrated Spirituality: The Contemplative-Dimension in
      Thomas Merton's Spirituality*. Dissertation submitted for a Master's degree at Berkeley,

California. Ronzani uses Brueggemann's hypothesis and, in the light of Merton's writings, argues that for Merton *violence* is the dominant crisis in the contemporary world and that the alternative consciousness which Brueggemann judged to be necessary in any prophetic ministry is to be found in Merton's affirmation of *non-violence*.

32   NVA 221 (*Christian Action in World Crisis*).
33   RT 119.
34   IE 129.
35   FV 154.
36   Ibid., 153.
37   NVA 221–2 (*Christian Action in World Crisis*).
38   RMW 51–2 (Preface to the Argentine edition of *The Complete Works of Thomas Merton*).
39   CGB 63–4.
40   Lv 337–8. TM to Walter A. Weisskopf (4 April 1968).
41   RT 65.
42   AJ 333 (Appendix VII).
43   LL 79.
44   Ibid., 140.
45   NMI 56.
46   Jv 240 (*Day of a Stranger*, May 1965).
47   Lv 70. TM to Rachel Carson (12 January 1963).
48   Ibid.
49   Jiv 312 (11 April 1963).
50   Jv 227 (15 April 1965).
51   The words were used by Merton as a chapter heading in SC and NSC.
52   GNV 8.
53   Jv 260 (26 June 1965).
54   OZ 11.
55   Lv 71. TM to Rachel Carson (12 January 1963).
56   CWA 170.
57   TMR 395 (from *Bread in the Wilderness*).
58   Hart, Patrick, *Thomas Merton: First and Last Memories*, Bardstown: Necessity Press 1986.
59   Merton, Thomas, *Commentary on the Meditations of Guigo the Carthusian*. TM Tapes, No. 7, *Life and Truth*.
60   SC 9.
61   Merton, Thomas, *Day of a Stranger*, Salt Lake City: Gibbs M. Smith 1981, p. 51.
62   CS V (1970) 223. (Thomas Merton, *A Life Free From Care*. Merton's final talk as Novice Master, 20 August 1965.)
63   Liv 65. Czesław Miłosz to TM (28 February 1960). Editorial Note.
64   LL 120.
65   Jv 240 (*Day of a Stranger*, May 1965).
66   Merton, Thomas, *A Secular Journal*, London: Hollis & Carter 1959, p. 7.
67   CS XXVIII (1993) 1 104. Quoting from Thomas Merton, *St. Thomas: The Importance of Creation in God's View*. (3 April 1963). TMC Tape 95A.
68   CP 188 (*The Sowing of Meanings*, from *Figures for an Apocalypse*, 1947).

69   NMI 16. Merton draws here upon his interpretation of Rom. 8.19–21.
70   SprC 169.
71   Lv 4. TM to Victor Hammer (14 May 1959).
72   Ibid.
73   CP 367 (*Hagia Sophia* from *Emblems of a Season of Fury*, 1963).
74   LL 227.
75   CP 367 (*Hagia Sophia*).
76   Jvi 131 (10 September 1966).
77   Lv 111. TM to Miss Jeanne Beaumont (24 December 1965).
78   SprC 161–3.
79   Ibid.
80   Ibid.
81   LL 227.
82   SprC 163–70.
83   MA (2000) 127–43. (Interview by George A. Kilcourse with Sister Jane Marie Richardson SL).
84   SprC 175.
85   MA (2000) 127–43.
86   SprC 172–3.
87   Ibid., 199–200.
88   CGB 88.
89   FV 174.
90   Ibid.
91   RMW 96 (Preface to the Japanese edition of SC, 1965).
92   LTM 75 (Hilary Costello, *Pilgrim: Freedom Bound*).
93   RU 49–50.
94   SprC 136.
95   Ibid.
96   NVA 246 (*War and the Crisis of Language*).
97   LL 90.
98   FV 92–3.
99   Jvii 51 (8 February 1968).
100 Jiv 296 (10 February 1963)
101 FV 129.
102 FV 128.
103 CP 380 (*A Letter to Pablo Antonion Cuadra Concerning Giants* from *Emblems of a Season of Fury*, 1963).
104 FV 91–2.
105 Harford, James, *Merton and Friends: A Joint Biography of Thomas Merton, Robert Lax and Edward Rice*, Continuum 2006, pp. 125–6. Cites Thomas Merton, *Classic Chinese Thought*, *Jubilee* (January 1961), pp. 26–31.
106 CP 390 (*A Letter to Pablo Antonio Cuadra Concerning Giants* from *Emblems of a Season of Fury*, 1963.
107 NVA 67.

108 Merton, Thomas, *Thoughts on the East*, Burns & Oates 1996, p. 61.

109 FV 167.

110 Merton, Thomas, *Thoughts on the East*, Burns & Oates 1996, p. 61.

111 Jvii 47 (26 January 1968).

112 PPCE 6.

113 PPCE 5.

114 PPCE 19.

115 PPCE 65.

116 PPCE 72.

117 Lv 20 (CWL, Preface).

118 Merton, Thomas, *Note on Civil Disobedience and Non-Violent Revolution*. Submitted at the request of the National Commission on the Causes and Prevention of Violence, 1968. Mimeographed copy: Merton, Thomas, *Collected Essays*, Vol. 8 (Part 2), TMC.

119 Jv 341 (Some Personal Notes, End of 1965).

120 GNV 58 (Gandhi II – 56).

121 Jiv 115 (2 May 1961).

122 Lv 62. TM to Robert J. McCracken (August 1962).

123 NVA 106 (*The Machine Gun in the Fallout Shelter*).

124 FV ix–x.

125 PPCE 7.

126 NVA 105–6 (*The Machine Gun in the Fallout Shelter*).

127 FV x.

128 FV 142.

129 Lv 292. TM to Leslie Dewart (undated: between 10 May and 28 June 1963).

130 Lv 308. TM to Father David Kirk (5 January 1964).

131 FV 209.

132 Lv 249. TM to William Robert Miller (June 1962).

133 FV 196. (TM quoting from Vahanian, Gabriel *Wait Without Idols*, New York: George Braziller 1964).

134 RT 102.

135 Liii 342. TM to Colman McCarthy (15 August 1967).

136 DQ 175.

137 CGB 18.

138 Li 501. TM to Rosemary Radford Ruether (14 February 1967).

139 MTM 67 (E. Glenn Hinson, *Expansive Catholicism: Ecumenical Perceptions of Thomas Merton*).

140 OZ 98.

141 Bro. Ramon SSF, *Soul Friends: A Journey with Thomas Merton*, Marshall Pickering 1989, p. 201.

142 *Monastic Studies* 4, Advent 1960 (Thomas Merton, *Monastic Vocation and Modern Thought*).

143 FV 221.

144 *Commonweal* v 84 (3 June 1966). Thomas Merton, *Is the World a Problem?*

145 Jiv 9 (6 June 1961).

146 *Commonweal* v 84 (3 June 1966). Thomas Merton, *Is the World a Problem?*

147 Ibid.

148 Merton, Thomas, *Thoughts on the East*, Burns & Oates 1996, p.59.

149 LL 56.

150 Lv 198. TM to Sister Maria Blanca Olim (16 October 1967).

151 Lv 30. TM to John Ford SJ (January 1962). CWL 23.

152 DQ 65.

153 RT 56.

154 Lii 22. TM to Mark van Doren (30 March 1948).

155 Lv 249. TM to William Robert Miller (June 1962). CWL 81.

156 MTM 130 (George Kilcourse, *Pieces of the Mosaic – Earth: Thomas Merton and the Christ*).

157 MA 19 (2006) 19 (John Eudes Bamberger, *Thomas Merton: Monk and Prophet of Peace*. Opening Address, International Thomas Merton Society General Meeting, 2005.

158 Ibid.

Index of Names